THE 14 DAY STRESS CURE

*A New Approach For Dealing With Stress
That Can Change Your Life*

By Morton C. Orman, M.D.

BREAKTHRU PUBLISHING
Houston, Texas
713-522-7660
1991

FIRST EDITION

Cover design by: Robert Steven Pawlak

Library of Congress Cataloging-in-Publication Data

Orman, Morton C., 1948-
    The 14 day stress cure : a new approach for dealing with stress that can change your life / Morton C. Orman. — 1st ed.
        p.   cm.
    Includes bibliographical references and index.
    ISBN 0-942540-01-8 (hard : alk. paper) : $ — ISBN 0-942540-06-9 (soft : alk. paper) : $
    1. Stress (Psychology). 2. Stress (Psychology)—Prevention—Problems, exercises, etc. 3. Biolinguistics. I. Title II. Title: The fourteen day stress cure.
BF575.S750755   1991
155.9′042—dc20   91-73407
                                                            CIP

---

91 92 93 94 95   15 14 13 12 11 10 9 8 7 6 5 4 3 2 1

DEDICATION

To Tracie, with love.

We at Breakthru Publishing are pleased to bring you this outstanding work on the subject of human stress. As a result of editing and preparing this manuscript, our own lives were changed in many positive ways. We do have concerns, however, that some people might misinterpret Dr. Orman's message. We are concerned that some readers might discontinue exercise routines, abandon healthy eating habits, prematurely withdraw themselves from medications, or otherwise jeopardize their health or well-being. Neither we, nor Dr. Orman, intend for you to do these things. If any advice in this book conflicts with what your doctor or other health care provider has advised you to do, we urge you to discuss your opinions openly and honestly with those individuals. If you have a persistent physical or emotional problem, we also encourage you to contact your doctor. Also, we caution you about changing or discontinuing any treatment on your own, especially if you have a serious medical problem such as heart disease, high blood pressure, or diabetes; if you suffer from severe anxiety attacks, panic attacks, or major depression; or if you are currently under the care of a psychiatrist, psychologist, or other psychotherapist.

Robert Schwartz
President, Breakthru Publishing

The 14 Day Stress Cure is based upon the role of language in human stress. Because language is so central to Dr. Orman's ideas, we want you to know what he means by this term.

By "language" Dr. Orman means something very different from the collection of symbols, sounds, and grammar conventions that constitute a particular dialect or tongue, such as English, French, or Chinese. Human language encompasses many other complex activities such as speaking, listening, understanding, promising, and requesting. When Dr. Orman uses the term "language," therefore, he is talking about these general activities, which are similar for all human beings regardless of culture or tongue.

Human language also differs from other types of "languages" used by animals and computers. For example, dogs, cats, porpoises, and chimpanzees can all interact by uttering certain sounds. None of them can make a promise, however. As far as we know today, only human beings are capable of making or breaking promises. And all human beings make promises, whether they were raised in an English-speaking country, France, China, or the Amazon jungle.

This book is about winning against stress. It is not about how to exercise your stress away, relax it away, or otherwise manage the symptoms of stress and tension in your body. It is about a new way of understanding the causes of your stress and a new method for dealing with these causes that is much more natural, much more effective, and much more empowering than stress management.

As a physician, I have been helping people win against stress for more than a decade. During this time, I have developed a step-by-step approach for getting rid of stress that does not require drugs, relaxation exercises, or stress management techniques. Not only have I used this method successfully in my own life, but I have taught it to hundreds of patients in my medical practice. I have also lectured at medical schools, universities, and other institutions across the country and have conducted seminars and workshops for thousands of individuals, including doctors, lawyers, nurses, psychologists, business executives, and the public at large.

In all these endeavors, my message has been the same: that we keep suffering from stress not because life itself is so stressful, but because we *misunderstand* what stress really is, what causes it to occur, and what we can do about it. These misunderstandings are widespread among the general public. They are also shared by most stress experts as well. Thus, as you will learn from this book, much of what you have been told about stress, and much of what you currently believe about it, is not really true.

Once you free yourself from these myths and misconceptions, you will discover that you do have the power to end stress as a chronic, recurring problem in your life. You will be able to make negative moods and emotions such as anger, frustration, worry, guilt, and anxiety disappear naturally—without using drugs, relaxation exercises, or stress management techniques—anytime you choose. You will also be able to prevent or resolve relationship conflicts, reduce your stress at work, and eliminate many of the physical symptoms of stress in your body. And you will know how to successfully deal with other types of stress, including the stress associated with: 1) financial problems, 2) economic upheavals, 3) raising children, 4) public speaking, and 5) unexpected crises and changes.

My purpose in writing this book, therefore, is threefold:

1) To cure you of *five key myths* that are widely promoted by stress management experts but that actually reduce your ability to deal with stress successfully;

2) To teach you how to use a powerful, new coping method that has many advantages over stress management;

3) To show you that our present stress epidemic, in this country and around the world, is largely unnecessary and that it could be substantially reduced or even eliminated if the principles discussed in this book were more widely known.

Morton C. Orman, M.D.
Baltimore, Maryland

I would like to acknowledge the following people who either directly or indirectly contributed to this book:

Dr. James Lynch for his friendship, encouragement, and pioneering research regarding language and its effects upon the human cardiovascular system;

Dr. Joseph Mead, Jr. and **Dr. Jay Goodman** for teaching me how to enjoy the practice of medicine;

Dr. Marshall Franklin for inspiring me to become a physician.

Dr. Robert Shaw for showing me what it means to live with integrity, dignity, and purpose;

Dr. George Everly, Jr. for supporting me in my initial counselling efforts;

Dr. Alberta Flashman for being an excellent, compassionate psychotherapist;

Norman Cousins (deceased) for reviewing my earlier manuscripts and for encouraging me to publish this book;

Dr. Fernando Flores and **Dr. Humberto Maturana** for teaching me about the importance of language in human life;

Dr. Matthew Budd for his friendship and innovative work in the area of human stress;

Dr. John-Henry Pfifferling for his commitment to my well-being and to the well-being of other health care professionals;

Dr. Carmine Valente for providing me with opportunities to share my ideas with fellow physicians;

Bob Schwartz for having the courage and vision to publish this book;

Pat Boyd for taking good care of me and our patients, and for being an invaluable office manager, secretary, and friend;

My wife **Christina** for all her love, support, editing, proofreading, ideas, suggestions, and for her remarkable ability to inspire me whenever I got "stuck";

My daughter **Tracie** for granting me the time to work on this project;

My parents **Marge** and **Bob,** and my sister **Bonnie,** for providing me with a childhood in which I was free to pursue my talents and interests;

My **patients** for sharing both their problems and joys with me.

I would also like to thank Dr. Frank Reuter, my editor, as well as Dr. Charles Alpert, Dr. Jim Benjamin, Robert B. Brown, Bonnie Horvath, Dr. Donald Sessions, John Ware, Jan Steendam, and the countless other people who read, critiqued, commented upon, or otherwise contributed to this manuscript.

CONTENTS

INTRODUCTION

If you're like most people today, you probably experience some degree of stress in your life. Perhaps you have family problems at home or too many pressures and responsibilities at work. Maybe you feel tense, anxious, or irritable much of the time or can't seem to control your thoughts and emotions. Or perhaps you suffer from headaches, backaches, indigestion, insomnia, high blood pressure, heart disease, or some other physical problem that is either caused by, or aggravated by, acute or chronic stress.

Whatever your experience has been, you've probably tried to get rid of your stress without much long-term success. Perhaps you've already read a book on the subject, attended a seminar or lecture, or tried to use one or more of the following stress management strategies:

COMMON STRATEGIES FOR MANAGING STRESS

1) Learn to relax.
2) Exercise to relieve stress.
3) Avoid stressful situations.
4) Change your diet.
5) Take more frequent vacations.
6) Meditate daily.
7) Use biofeedback.
8) Get a massage.
9) Improve your time management skills.
10) Learn to be more assertive and/or more expressive of your feelings.

If you're like me, however, or like most of the people I see in my medical practice, you've probably discovered that managing stress is a losing proposition. No matter how much you try to relax, how many miles you run, how many vacations you take, or how many punching bags you personally demolish, stress just keeps on building in your life and there doesn't seem to be anything you can do to reverse this trend.

You Are Not The Problem

The reason why stress keeps happening in your life is not because you are unable to get rid of it. It is because *you and I live in a culture in which stress is largely misunderstood.* Many popular myths and misconceptions cloud our thinking and keep us from coping with our stress more successfully. These myths are not only prevalent in the general public, they are also shared by most stress experts as well.

Take the idea that stress is an inevitable, inescapable consequence of being alive, for example. While most educated people believe in this idea, it is not really true. As Richard Ecker points out in his 1985 book *The Stress Myth:*

> We like to believe that stress is inevitable—that life is so much more complex these days, that we're being dragged along by a runaway world which offers us less and less that we can depend on. But this belief is nothing but a myth, a myth that is at the core of the stress problem ... This myth ... has done more to perpetuate unwanted stress in our society than any other single factor. Ironically, the main proponents of this myth are the very ones who claim to be teaching people how to deal with stress. (p. 10)

This myth of inevitability is only one of our popular misconceptions. It stems from five other deep-seated myths that comprise what I call the "stress management mentality" of our time. To see that you too have been influenced by these five myths, check off your answers to the following simple test:

A TEST OF YOUR PRESENT BELIEFS ABOUT STRESS

1. Stress is something that actually exists. □True □False

2. Some degree of stress is good or healthy for you. □True □False

3. Stress is primarily caused by external events, situations, and demands in your life. □True □False

4. Your mind plays a role in much of the stress you experience. □True □False

5. The best way to deal with stress is to learn how to manage or avoid it. □True □False

While most people assume all five of these statements—or at least four of the five—are true, this book will show you that each is actually false. Specifically, this book will show you that: a) stress does not exist; b) there is no such thing as "good" or "healthy" stress; c) stress is *not* primarily caused by external situations and events you encounter; d) your mind does *not* play a role in most of the stress you experience; and e) there is a much better way to deal with stress than learning how to manage or avoid it.

Three Coping Options

The best way to understand how this book differs from other books on this subject is to recognize that we have only three basic options for coping with stress (other than simply ignoring or denying our problems):

A) The Band-Aid Approach
B) The Stress Management Approach
C) The Ultimate Approach

The Band-Aid Approach

We make use of the band-aid approach when we turn to alcohol, drugs (prescription or recreational), cigarettes, food, sex, or anything else to temporarily relieve the symptoms of our stress. In the short-run, these coping strategies work very well. Since they quickly relieve much of the physical or emotional pain we experience, we can easily overlook their harmful effects. In addition, the more we depend upon such "quick-fix" agents, the less likely we are to address the true causes of our suffering.

The Stress Management Approach

Our second option is to rely upon a group of strategies and techniques collectively known as "stress management" (see page xi). While these strategies have advantages over alcohol, cigarettes, drugs, and other chemical coping solutions, they still focus mainly on the *symptoms* of our difficulties. With few exceptions, they don't help us recognize or deal with the underlying causes of our stress.

The Ultimate Approach

The third coping option—which I consider the "ultimate" approach—is to make stress disappear naturally—i.e. without using drugs, relaxation exercises, or stress management techniques—by recognizing and dealing with its *underlying causes*. This approach also reduces the symptoms of our stress, but it does so indirectly—by addressing their causes—rather than by directly changing or manipulating the state of our bodies.

The Three Basic Options For Coping With Stress

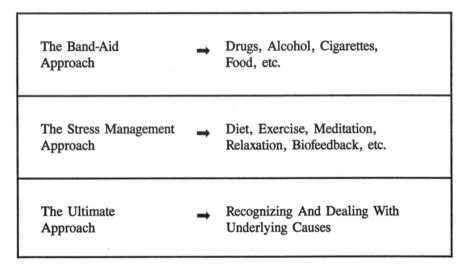

The Band-Aid Approach	→	Drugs, Alcohol, Cigarettes, Food, etc.
The Stress Management Approach	→	Diet, Exercise, Meditation, Relaxation, Biofeedback, etc.
The Ultimate Approach	→	Recognizing And Dealing With Underlying Causes

The problem with choosing the third—and best—approach is that most of us have not been trained to use it. We have not been taught to identify the real causes of our stress—many of which are hidden from our view—nor have we been trained to deal with these causes once they are identified. In my experience, once people learn to do these two things—identify the hidden causes of their stress and deal with these causes successfully—they can reduce or eliminate most of the stress they normally experience.

In addition, once you learn to master this ultimate approach, you will have a life-long coping method that not only makes your stress go away, but that also enables you to:

• improve your health;

• enhance the quality of your interpersonal relationships;

• increase your productivity;

• raise your confidence and self-esteem;

• become more successful in other areas of your life.

This is what I call "winning" against stress. When you know how to use the coping method outlined in this book, you not only "win" by getting rid of your stress, but you also "win" by improving your mastery and competence in life as well.

My Own Victory Over Stress

How do I know this approach really works? I know it because I use it myself and because I have trained many others to use it as well. For most of my life, however, I struggled unsuccessfully to cope with my stress. As a teenager, I felt nervous, anxious, and insecure much of the time. These feelings intensified as I went through college, medical school, residency training, and my first few years in private practice. In addition, the older I became, the more angry and impatient I felt. Speaking to a group made me especially anxious, and whenever I made a mistake in any endeavor, I would easily become irritated and frustrated with myself.

The quality of my interpersonal relationships was nothing to write home about either. While I had a few close friends, mostly from high school days, I felt uncomfortable and insecure around everyone else. I was abrasive, insensitive, and highly competitive toward others. I always wanted to be right, even in minor disagreements, and I only felt satisfied when I got my own way.

As you might have guessed, I had little success with women. The few long-term relationships I did manage to establish always ended as failures. My relationships with my mother, father, sister, and other family members weren't much better.

Despite my lack of success, I continued to search for ways to get rid of my stress. I tried positive thinking, taking more time to relax, exercising, changing my diet, and a host of other stress management techniques. Some of these helped temporarily, but my problems always came back. I also tried psychotherapy. While I found these sessions very rewarding and enriching, I still didn't learn how to control my emotions or improve the quality of my close personal relationships.

It wasn't until the late 1970s—a few years after I started my private practice—that I had any idea I could win against stress. Around that time, I began to explore a variety of human potential courses and workshops. While none of these cured me of stress immediately, they did help me realize that much of what I had been taught about stress and about human beings, both in college and medical school, wasn't completely true.

As a result of these eye-opening experiences, I became interested in the work of several contemporary scholars and psychotherapists such as Gregory Bateson, John Searle, Robert Shaw, Fernando Flores, Humberto Maturana, among others. Each of these people rejected the traditional understanding of human problems and human stress. Each also developed new insights and coping strategies that were useful to many individuals.

As I immersed myself in the ideas of these thinkers, I began to gain a new understanding of myself as a human being. I also noticed that my life started to change for the better. I became much less annoyed and frustrated with myself; I was less impatient and intolerant of others; I was much better able to deal with my negative thoughts and emotions; and the quality of my relationships improved as well.

I also became more aware of what was really going on with my patients who were suffering from stress. As my understanding of their personal problems improved, so did my ability to help them cope with their difficulties. Soon, I began to offer seminars and workshops to share what I had learned with others. Many of the people who attended these classes began to have similar beneficial improvements.

Today, despite having many more pressures and responsibilities than in the past, I have very little stress and tension in my life. I rarely get angry, frustrated, or anxious anymore, and even when I do, I know how to make these feelings rapidly disappear whenever I want. I have a wonderful wife, Christina (we married in 1984), and a daughter Tracie, who was born in 1987. Whereas I previously had trouble dealing with unexpected crises and changes, I can now deal with almost any problem or difficulty with ease, comfort, and a sense of confidence that was never available to me before. While I still experience some stress from time to time, I have a step-by-step method for eliminating it that works most of the time. In short, I have discovered what it takes to win against stress, and the knowledge I have gained has changed my life dramatically.

You Too Can Become A Winner

Despite what you currently think or what you may have been told, you too can learn to win against stress. You can learn how to make negative moods and emotions—such as anger, frustration, worry, guilt, and anxiety—totally vanish whenever you want. You can also learn to prevent or resolve relationship conflicts, reduce your stress at work, eliminate many of the physical symptoms of stress in your body, and relieve almost any other type of stress you encounter.

And believe it or not, you can discover what it takes to do this *in just fourteen days*! I know this sounds impossible, but it really can happen. While it may take much longer to master all of the strategies and tools presented in this book, *your understanding of human stress*—what it is, what causes it to occur, and what you can do about it—*can definitely change in just two weeks*. While no book is likely to cure you of stress right away, this book will introduce you to a whole new way of thinking about your stress and a step-by-step approach for dealing with it that is much more natural, effective, and empowering than stress management or any other method.

This book will also introduce you to a new way of understanding yourself as a human being. It will provide you with a new way of comprehending your thoughts, feelings, moods, and emotions that is very different from currently accepted mind-body theories. This new viewpoint—called Biolinguistics—is already beginning to change our understanding not only of stress, but of many human problems such as obesity, drug addiction, relationship conflicts, among others.

Biolinguistics focuses on the central role of language in human stress. It argues that most of our mind-body theories are outdated and incorrect and that human language is a biological (i.e. a body-mediated) phenomenon, not a "mental" or "intellectual" function. As you will learn in this book, this new understanding has important implications for helping us recognize and deal with the internal causes of our suffering.

While a growing number of scholars, scientists, psychotherapists, and other health professionals have recently embraced this Biolinguistic perspective, most stress experts today are completely unaware of its existence. Thus, another of my purposes for writing this book is to make these new insights available to professionals as well.

How This Book Is Organized

This book is organized into fourteen chapters, each of which can be read and assimilated in a day:

The first three chapters will introduce you to Biolinguistics and to other recent advances in our understanding of human stress.

Chapter 4 will inform you about the step-by-step approach for coping with stress that I currently use in my medical practice.

Chapters 5-8 will explain each step of this method in more detail.

Chapters 9-13 will then show you how this very same approach can be used to deal with any type of stress you experience.

Chapter 14 will show you how to overcome some of the common obstacles that might hinder you from using this method successfully in your life.

Each chapter concludes with a few simple exercises. These exercises are just as important as reading the text, as they can significantly improve your understanding of the material.

In addition, I have also included four helpful appendices:

Appendix A lists the hidden causes of stress discussed throughout the book;

Appendix B explains the rationale behind "Flipping To The Opposite Reality," an important stress-relieving strategy which I introduce in Chapter 6;

Appendix C reviews some of the arguments both for and against the mind-body viewpoint;

Appendix D provides you with one of the most valuable features of this book—information for creating your own personal index cards for six negative moods and emotions (anger, frustration, worry, guilt, anxiety, and sadness). These index cards, which are explained in the text, have been extremely helpful for virtually all of my patients.

The Suggestions For Further Reading section contains a list of carefully selected books that might also be of interest to you. For each selection, I have included my own personal comments and a brief synopsis.

How To Get The Most From This Book

Here are some tips for getting the maximum benefit from reading this book:

1) Read one chapter a day for the next fourteen days. This will give you ample time to think about each chapter and ponder its implications. If it takes you more than one day to complete any chapter, that's fine too. Of course, you could also read several chapters a day, as many people like to do, but I think you will get more value from the text if you resist this normal temptation.

2) Do all the exercises at the end of each chapter—they are not very difficult.

3) Don't be afraid to write in this book. Think of it as your own personal diary or workbook which is yours and yours alone.

4) As you move along in the book, don't expect to benefit right away. Sometimes you won't fully appreciate the value of a particular chapter or discussion until much later in the book. Also, some of the strategies and tools you will learn about may take you more than two weeks to fully understand and master.

5) Don't worry if you occasionally feel angry, anxious, confused, or depressed while reading this book. Challenging your established theories and beliefs can be upsetting. No matter how the text makes you feel, you can still profit from exposing yourself to the ideas it contains.

6) Don't be concerned if you disagree with some of the assertions I make. It took me a long time to get comfortable with some of them myself and to understand both their strengths and limitations. Even if you don't agree with all of my ideas, such as my views about language or my comments about the human mind, you can still benefit greatly from many of the other insights, strategies, and tools I discuss.

7) Even though this book is titled *The 14 Day Stress Cure*, it is not a "quick-fix" remedy for the problem of human stress. It is merely the beginning of a long-term process of growth and understanding that hopefully will continue to unfold for the rest of your life. While this book provides you with a "road map" for better understanding and dealing with your stress, much hard work and dedication will be required of you to apply this road map successfully. The amount of time, practice, and energy you might need to invest, especially in the beginning, can be considerable. But the rewards you will obtain are well worth the effort.

8) Don't be too hard on yourself if you fail to apply the method described in this book successfully. While the method has been well-tested, and while it works consistently, it may take a while before you become adept at using it.

Good luck on your journey. If you follow the suggestions I offer in this book, you will not only find out how to deal with stress more successfully, but you will also learn how to improve your life in other ways as well.

DAY 1

STRESS IS JUST A WORD

Pick up any book on the subject of stress and you will usually find a brief, authoritative-sounding definition within the first several pages. Each author begins as if:

1) stress is something that actually exists;

2) some degree of stress is "good" or "healthy" for you;

3) the best way to deal with stress is to manage or avoid it.

These assumptions are part of the "stress management mentality" of our times. While they are generally accepted by most educated people, they are not really true. This chapter will show you that: a) stress is not a "thing" that exists; b) there is no such thing as "good" or "healthy" stress; and c) there is a much better way to deal with stress than learning how to manage or avoid it. In order to become a winner against stress, you must start by understanding these three points.

What Is Stress—Really?

Many experts endorse the original definition proposed by Hans Selye in 1926: STRESS IS THE NON-SPECIFIC RESPONSE OF THE BODY TO ANY DEMAND PLACED UPON IT.

Selye was an Austrian-born, Canadian physician who conducted hundreds of laboratory studies on animals and humans during the 1920's and 1930's. He was the first person to document the chemical and hormonal changes that occur with stress. He was also the first to introduce the term to the scientific community.

Selye believed that stress results whenever we are faced with external changes or demands. Such demands include variations in environmental temperature, overcrowding, painful stimuli, and loud noises. In fact, Selye believed most of life was "stressful." In the preface to his 1956 book *The Stress Of Life* he commented:

> No one can live without experiencing some degree of stress all the time. You may think that only serious disease or intensive physical or mental injury can cause stress. This is false. Crossing a busy intersection, exposure to a draft, or even sheer joy are enough to activate the body's stress-mechanism to some extent. Stress is not even necessarily bad for you; it is also the spice of life, for any emotion, any activity causes stress. (p. vii)

Selye conceived of external demands as *stressors* and the internal body changes they produced as the *stress response*. He also reasoned that the stress response occurs whether the demands we experience are positive or negative. In other words, if you inherit a large sum of money or lose a large sum of money, your body would respond in exactly the same way. According to Selye, what matters most is how well you *adapt* to each new demand. He coined the term "eustress" (pronounced u-stress) to stand for good or healthy stress— to times when the adaptation process resolved itself quickly—and he chose the term "distress" to stand for bad or unhealthy stress— to times when the adaptation response was excessive or prolonged. Thus, Selye not only gave us the "external demand model" of human stress, but he also gave us the idea that two types of stress occur for human beings: 1) a "good" or "healthy" type, and 2) a "bad" or "unhealthy" type.

Although Selye's ideas were widely accepted, subsequent researchers proposed other definitions. Some theorists noted similarities between the body's stress response and the "fight or flight" response, a well-known survival mechanism present in most animal species. These researchers viewed stress as AN EXCESSIVE OR INAPPROPRIATE ACTIVATION OF THE BODY'S "FIGHT OR FLIGHT" RESPONSE, which is induced by threats of danger in our environment.

In the 1960's and 1970's, other researchers began to focus upon cognitive and behavioral causes. Mental processes, such as our *interpretations* of events (e.g. good/bad; positive/negative), our *appraisals* of situations (e.g. threat/no threat; danger/no danger) and our *judgements* about our ability to cope with our problems successfully, were believed to activate the body's stress response. Memories of past experiences and habitual behavior patterns were also found to be important. Thus, stress became viewed as a mind-body, "psychosomatic," or psycho-physiologic phenomenon. This mind-body viewpoint is clearly expressed in the following definition which is endorsed by many experts today: STRESS IS A PSYCHO-PHYSIOLOGIC AROUSAL RESPONSE OCCURRING IN THE BODY AS A RESULT OF A STIMULUS WHICH BECOMES A "STRESSOR" BY VIRTUE OF THE COGNITIVE INTERPRE-TATION OF THE INDIVIDUAL.*

Meanwhile, while scientists argued about what stress really was, members of the general public began to use the term in a variety of ways. Some people defined stress as having too many pressures, responsibilities, or demands in their lives. Some used the term to refer to internal states, such as feeling tense, nervous, tired, or exhausted. Others considered stress to be the inability to concentrate or focus mentally. Still others used the term to refer to any negative mood or emotion, such as anger, frustration, guilt, or anxiety, or to a host of stress-related physical problems, such as headaches, muscle tension, sleep disturbances, and high blood pressure.†

Humorous definitions also emerged. One of these—STRESS IS CREATED WHEN ONE'S MIND OVERRIDES THE BODY'S BASIC DESIRE TO CHOKE THE LIVING DAYLIGHTS OUT OF SOME JERK WHO DESPERATELY DESERVES IT!—frequently appears on posters, T-shirts, coffee mugs, and other novelty items.

Thus, as we enter the 1990's, we are faced with a multitude of definitions of stress, both popular and scientific. Unfortunately, all of these definitions ignore one major fact. This fact is emphasized in the definition I use and also encourage my patients to adopt:

---

* Everly, G.S., and Rosenfeld, R., *The Nature And Treatment Of The Stress Response*, pp. 4-5.
† There are actually no "negative emotions," only emotions people consider to be negative. All emotions can have both positive and negative consequences. Fear, for example, can be devastating, while at other times it can save your life. Anger can be destructive, both individually and socially, while at other times it can be constructive for you and for others.

Dr. Orman's Definition

STRESS IS JUST A WORD!

While the same could be said about any term in the English language (or any other language), there are several important advantages to thinking of stress in this way. One advantage is that this definition will remind you that *stress does not exist*. It will also remind you that it is not really possible to cope or deal with your stress *directly*.

These two points are intimately connected. The reason neither you, nor I, nor anyone else can cope with stress directly is because STRESS DOESN'T TRULY EXIST IN THE WORLD. It is not some "thing" that occurs in space or time or that "afflicts" us like a disease. It is merely a word that we use—an abstract linguistic device—that stands for hundreds of specific problems and difficulties which do exist and which trouble us from time to time.

Stress = Problems In Our Lives

Why do I say that stress is just a word? I do so because that's what it is—an abstract concept that has no real existence outside of human language. Selye himself admitted this point. In *The Stress Of Life* (1956), he acknowledged that stress is an abstraction, but that it is necessary to have some operational definition in order to study it scientifically:

> If we are to use this concept in a strictly scientific manner, it is important to keep in mind that stress is an abstraction; it has no independent existence. (p. 43.)

Unlike Selye, however, most of us confuse the abstraction (stress) with the reality (problems), and this leads to a great deal of confusion and misunderstanding.

Stress = Problems Inside And Outside Our Body

Whenever I conduct a seminar or workshop on this subject, I start by asking participants to name some of the problems they are having whenever they say they are suffering from "stress." Within minutes, each group generates a list that fills an entire blackboard. Here are some of the items almost every group includes:

Figure 1-1

WHAT DOES THE WORD "STRESS" MEAN TO YOU?

Feeling nervous	Too much work	Upset stomach
Feeling anxious	Too many responsibilities	Tension headaches
Tense muscles	Too little time	Noisy neighbors
Rapid heart beat	Feeling hopeless	Traffic jams
Family problems	Feeling bored	Inconsiderate people
Money problems	Feeling trapped	Feeling angry

As you can see, each of these problems is highly specific. Despite this, each is generally referred to by the same general term: "stress." Also, all of the problems listed above can be divided into two major sub-groups:

1) problems that occur *outside* our bodies (such as traffic jams, family problems, financial problems, and noisy neighbors);

2) problems that occur *inside* our bodies (feeling nervous, feeling angry, tense muscles, and upset stomach).

Thus, *"stress" is a word that stands for problems and conflicts that occur either outside or inside our bodies*. Whenever I use the word "stress" in this book—whether or not it appears in quotations—substitute the word '*problems*" instead.

► NOTE: Problems that occur outside our bodies clearly affect what goes on inside and vice versa. Most types of stress, however, can usually be divided into internal and external components.

A larger list of problems included under the general heading of "stress" is shown in Figure 1-2. Take a few moments to review this list. Check off any problems that might be bothering you right now. (If you are concerned that someone else might look at your list, write down your responses on a separate sheet of paper.)

Figure 1-2

Things That Happen OUTSIDE Your Body	"STRESS"	Things That Happen INSIDE Your Body

SITUATIONS/EVENTS
- ☐ Relationship conflicts
- ☐ Job changes
- ☐ Stock market fluctuations
- ☐ Illness in a loved one
- ☐ Divorce or separation
- ☐ Being sued
- ☐ Losing a job
- ☐ Going to the doctor/dentist
- ☐ Failures/mistakes
- ☐ Retirement
- ☐ Overcrowding
- ☐ Disasters
- ☐ Death of a loved one

DEMANDS
- ☐ Deadlines
- ☐ Competition
- ☐ Tests/Examinations
- ☐ Time pressures
- ☐ Family/children problems
- ☐ Financial pressures
- ☐ Too many responsibilities
- ☐ Public speaking
- ☐ Public performances
- ☐ Caring for others
- ☐ Dieting
- ☐ Quitting smoking

OTHER EXTERNAL PROBLEMS
- ☐ Inconsiderate neighbors
- ☐ Unappreciative boss
- ☐ Traffic jams
- ☐ Construction problems
- ☐ Economic recessions
- ☐ Business problems
- ☐ Employee problems
- ☐ Travel problems
- ☐ Car problems
- ☐ House problems

THOUGHTS
- ☐ Trouble concentrating
- ☐ Compulsive ruminating
- ☐ Being overly critical
- ☐ Thinking negatively
- ☐ Awfulizing
- ☐ Catastrophizing

FEELINGS
- ☐ Feeling tired
- ☐ Feeling trapped
- ☐ Feeling irritable
- ☐ Feeling tense or nervous
- ☐ Diminished libido

MOODS/EMOTIONS
- ☐ Acute anxiety(Fears/phobias)
- ☐ Chronic anxiety
- ☐ Anger
- ☐ Sadness
- ☐ Frustration
- ☐ Worry
- ☐ Guilt
- ☐ Impatience
- ☐ Depression
- ☐ Resentment
- ☐ Hostility
- ☐ Hopelessness
- ☐ Powerlessness
- ☐ Resignation
- ☐ Despair
- ☐ Boredom
- ☐ Apathy

OTHER BODY RESPONSES
- ☐ Muscle aches/tension
- ☐ Teeth grinding
- ☐ Jaw clenching
- ☐ Cold hands/cold feet
- ☐ Rapid heart beat

Things That Happen OUTSIDE Your Body	"STRESS"	Things That Happen INSIDE Your Body

☐ Crime	☐ Headaches
☐ Vandalism	☐ Neck pains
☐ Harassment	☐ Back pains
☐ Prejudice/discrimination	☐ Upset stomach
☐ Lack of resources	☐ Diarrhea
☐ Lack of opportunities	☐ High blood pressure
☐ Lack of education/training	☐ Skin rashes
☐ Bureaucratic hassles	☐ Increased appetite
☐ Social unrest	☐ Decreased appetite
☐ Unexpected crises/changes	☐ Sleeping problems
☐ Corporate takeovers	☐ Sexual problems

Again, while all of these problems are highly specific, they are commonly referred to by the very same word—"stress." This is why there is so much confusion about stress today. When people use this word in everyday speech, they can be referring to any one of the problems in Figure 1-2. They can also be referring to either external or internal problems or even to unwanted consequences of these problems, such as illness, burnout, interpersonal conflicts, and the like. Thus, as Dr. Paul Rosch, M.D., founder and President of the American Institute of Stress, points out: "Stress, in addition to being itself, can also be the cause of itself and the result of itself."*

Human Beings Never Suffer From "Stress"

Since "stress" is a word that stands for problems and conflicts in our lives, it is these specific problems—not the abstract concept called "stress"—that we truly want relief from. Thus, whenever we say we are "suffering from stress," we are really suffering from problems or conflicts that are painful or troubling to us.

▶ NOTE: Even though stress does not exist, I will continue to use the term throughout this book. I have elected to do this for two reasons. First, the term is not going to go away, no matter how much

---

* Dr. Rosch attributes this quotation to a British observer, who commented more than 40 years ago about the tremendous amount of confusion the term "stress" has generated. Everly, G.S., *A Clinical Guide To Treatment Of The Human Stress Response*, p. 6.

confusion and misunderstanding it produces. Second, you need to begin training yourself to listen to it in a different way. Thus, sometimes I enclose this word in quotations ("stress"), while other times I intentionally leave the quotations out (stress) so that you have to remember to supply them yourself.

I am continually amazed at how often we fail to appreciate that stress is just a word. For example, people will come to me with complaints such as: "I'm having trouble coping with stress," or "I've got too much stress in my life right now," or "is there anything you can do to help me get rid of my stress?" As I listen to them speak, I know these people are struggling with many serious problems in their lives. But the specific nature of these problems is often hidden—both from me and from them— as long as they think they are suffering from "stress."

The following example illustrates this point. Paul, a 36-year-old management executive, was referred to me for treatment. A portion of our initial conversation is reproduced below:

Paul: I've been under a great deal of stress lately.

Dr.O: Can you tell me what you mean by "being under stress?"

Paul: Well, I've recently been transferred to a new department and my boss is riding me pretty hard. I've got many new responsibilities and not enough time to learn how to handle them all.

Dr.O: Is there anything else going on that makes you say you are under stress?

Paul: Yes. I'm not sleeping very well and I've become overly preoccupied with my performance at work. I felt confident and secure in my old position, but now I don't have any self-confidence at all. I'm worried that if I don't increase my productivity, I'm going to get fired.

Dr.O: Anything else?

Paul: No, that's it. Oh, yes, there's one more thing. I've been so concerned about work lately that my sex drive has diminished, and my wife is beginning to pressure me.

From this brief exchange, you can see how Paul contributed to his own lack of success by failing to recognize that stress is just a word. In truth, he had seven specific problems that were troubling him: 1) a relationship conflict with his new boss; 2) adjusting to new job responsibilities; 3) poor sleep; 4) loss of self-confidence; 5) fear of being fired; 6) reduced sexual desire; 7) increasing pressure from his wife.

Instead of treating him with medication, relaxation exercises, or other stress management techniques, my first goal was to help Paul forget about dealing with "stress" per se and focus instead upon the specific problems he was facing. Once he did this, we were able to examine and solve each of these problems successfully.

▶ NOTE: Each specific problem or conflict we experience has specific underlying causes. Knowing how to "win" against stress means knowing how to identify and deal with these causes effectively.

All Other Definitions Of Stress Are Incomplete Or Misleading

Failing to recognize that stress is just a word can also cause you to underestimate the amount of stress (i.e. problems) you have. If you operate from a definition that is too narrowly focused—i.e. which includes certain problems but leaves out many others—you will only consider yourself to have "stress" if you meet your specific criteria. Other problems could exist in your life that don't fit your definition, and because they don't, you may not take these problems seriously even though they could be harmful to you.

I see this quite often in my medical practice. People will come in to see me because of a stomach ulcer, high blood pressure, migraine headaches, or some other "medical" condition. When I ask if they have any "stress" in their life, they frequently respond "No, not at all." On further questioning, however, I find that many of these people have serious family, relationship, or work-related problems that are not included in their personal definition of "stress." They often have a loved one or family member who is not doing well, or they are about to be fired from their job, or they are feeling angry, frustrated, worried, or depressed.

EXAMPLE: One young man came to me because he was having either a cold, sinus infection, or lung infection three out of every four weeks for several months in succession. After a thorough medical evaluation revealed no major problems, he vehemently denied having any type of stress in his life. This was because he defined stress as "having more work to do than a person can handle." Since he didn't have this particular problem, he concluded he didn't have any "stress." On further questioning, however, I found out that: a) he was the owner of a small retail business which had not been doing well for more than a year; b) his two key employees were his wife and his sister; c) he was not very happy with their performance at work, but he was reluctant to express his displeasure; and d) he and his wife were having serious conflicts about how they should raise their children.

Needless to say, while this man did not think he had stress according to his narrow definition of the term, he did have *problems* that could have contributed to his physical difficulties. As we tackled each of his problems successfully, and as he learned to improve his relationships with his wife and sister, his colds, sinus infections, and lung infections became much less frequent.*

Since all other definitions except:

STRESS = PROBLEMS

---

will in some ways be exclusive, they are all either incomplete or misleading. Thus, instead of saying "I've got stress," you should say to yourself "I'VE GOT PROBLEMS IN MY LIFE THAT ARE PAINFUL OR TROUBLING TO ME."

There Is No Such Thing As "Good" Or "Healthy" Stress

Another reason we fail to address certain problems in our lives is because we have been taught to believe that some degree of stress is "good" or "healthy" for us. This confusion also results from failing to appreciate that stress is just a word.

Do you really believe it is good to have unwanted problems in your life? Are you usually delighted to feel frustrated, angry, irritable, or depressed? Do you consider yourself fortunate because you have relationship conflicts, or because you're business is failing, or because you're having trouble meeting your deadlines?

There are many times, of course, when we intentionally seek out situations that make us feel fearful, exhilarated, or otherwise aroused.

---

* While this does not prove a cause-effect relationship between "stress" (i.e. problems in his life) and his physical symptoms, I have seen so many similar cases that I find it hard to reject this hypothesis.

Getting passionately excited about your favorite sports team, getting physically or emotionally "psyched up" for your own athletic performances, or experiencing the emotional ups and downs of a powerful movie or play are just a few examples. But these are all instances of *desired* problems.* They are not at all similar to the *unwanted* problems, conflicts, and other types of "stress" we would prefer to do without.

And while we can label happy moments, joyous moments, and other positive aspects of life "good stress" if we want, they have nothing to do with stress at all—at least in the sense in which most people use the term. For instance, no one has ever walked into my office and said, "Doc, I've got too much happiness and excitement in my life. Is there anything you can do to help me get rid of these?"

The notion that stress can sometimes be healthy for us is also largely a myth. While being active, challenged, and stimulated in our daily endeavors may indeed be good and healthy for us, these things also have little to do with "stress." Anyone who believes that a certain amount of anger, frustration, anxiety, guilt, or other problems improves their health and well-being is ignoring the fact that these emotions can lead to illness, depression, and sometimes even death in human beings. And while some negative emotions or other types of problems can at times be useful to us, this doesn't mean they are "good" or "healthy," nor does it mean that we necessarily *need* to experience them.

Thus, while you might think I have been harping on a trivial semantic point, there are very real dangers in believing that some types of "stress" are good or healthy for you. Such beliefs can lead you to endure a great number of unhealthy problems in your life, many of which you could learn to prevent or eliminate.

How Do You Benefit From Remembering "Stress Is Just A Word"?

In summary, there are several ways you benefit from remembering stress is just a word. First, it will help you better understand what stress is and what stress is not. Second, it will make you cautious about assuming you know what other people mean when

---

* Just because a problem or feeling is desired does not mean it is necessarily "good" or "healthy" for you.

they use this term in everyday speech. Third, it may make you skeptical about programs and treatment approaches that encourage you to deal with your "stress" directly. And fourth, it will force you to become more specific about the individual problems and conflicts that are troubling you. Once you do this, you will then be in position to recognize and deal with their underlying causes.

Thus, by consciously reminding yourself that stress is just a word, you will be taking the first important step toward learning how to win against it.

DAY 1: EXERCISES

1. *List three major problems that are bothering you right now.*

A _____

B _____

C _____

2. *Is each problem listed above located outside your body, inside your body, or both? (If your response is "both," see if you can separate the problem into internal and external components.)*

A ☐ OUTSIDE ☐ INSIDE ☐ BOTH

B ☐ OUTSIDE ☐ INSIDE ☐ BOTH

C ☐ OUTSIDE ☐ INSIDE ☐ BOTH

3. *Ask at least three different people what the word "stress" means to them. Write down the answers you receive.*

A _____

B _____

C _____

4. *What definition of stress were you using, either consciously or unconsciously, before you read this chapter?*

_____

_____

5. *List three types of problems your previous definition excludes.*

A _____

B _____

C _____

DAY 2

INTERNAL VS. EXTERNAL CAUSES

Blindness And Certainty: A Parable

In ancient times, there lived a wise man named Asan. As legend goes, Asan was one of the happiest and most successful men in all the land. He was also very generous with his wisdom, and people would travel from far and wide to seek his advice about their personal affairs.

Most of Asan's visitors returned home feeling hopeful and inspired. In no time at all, they became happier and more successful than they ever dreamed possible. Some of his visitors, however, went home unsatisfied and depressed. Their lives did not change, even though Asan had given them the very same advice that he gave to everyone who sought his expert counsel.

One morning, as Asan was relaxing by a river near his home, a young man approached and asked to speak with him.

Man: *I beg of you sir, please grant me a moment of your time, as I have traveled many miles to talk with you. I have heard you are wise about matters of personal happiness and that you have helped many people achieve this state.*

Asan: *Please proceed. I will gladly offer you my assistance.*

Man: *Can you to tell me, then, why do I suffer so greatly? I have plenty of money, but I do not feel good inside. I have a wonderful wife and family, but we argue all the time and I don't feel loved or appreciated. I have many*

*strong slaves and a prosperous business, but I do not feel
like arising in the morning. I am in good health, I have
no aches or pains, but I do not feel happy and I don't
understand why.*

Asan: *The answer is this—you are unhappy because you don't
see life correctly.*

Man: *But this can't be so, for I do see life correctly. I see you
standing before me. I see the trees. I see the river. I see
people playing in the river. I see birds in the sky.*

Asan: *Yes, but you only see what is easily seen. You do not see
what is important to be seen.*

Man: *But I see what most other people see. Doesn't this prove I
am seeing life correctly?*

Asan: *No. It only proves that you see what most other people
see. To be happy, you must first understand that you don't
really see.*

Man: *But I assure you, sir, I do see life correctly. Is that not a
tree over there? Does not the river run? Are there not
birds in the sky this very moment?*

Asan: *Ah, now I can answer your original question more completely. You suffer first because you do not see. You suffer
second because you do not see that you do not see. And
you suffer third because you are certain that what you do
see is the truth about life.*

Man: *But I still don't understand.*

Asan: *This only means you don't want to understand. Suffering
is the price you have to pay for holding on to your certainty. Therefore, it must be more important to you to be
right than to be happy.*

Man: *But I disagree. I do not want to be right. I would much
rather be happy and free of my suffering.*

Asan: *I see.*

Man: *Will you help me then?*

Asan: *I am sorry, but I cannot help a man as certain as you.
Perhaps another time, after you've suffered a little more,
you will remember the secrets I have offered you today.
Until then, I suggest you continue to enjoy the trees,
enjoy the birds, and play in the river with other people
who see things as you do.*

Obvious vs. Non-Obvious Causes

Like the man in the parable, we often misunderstand the true causes of our "stress." We usually see what is easily seen, but we fail to see what is important to be seen. Consider these examples:

John (a 35-year-old sales executive): I have a terrible time coping with traffic jams. I've got a busy schedule, and I really get steamed when some jerk doesn't keep his eye on the road and causes me to miss an important meeting. Sure, I know what's causing my stress to occur, but most of the time, it's beyond my control.

Sally (a 28-year old housewife, mother of two, and part-time legal secretary): Sometimes the pressures and demands in my life are too much for me to bear. My husband wants me to do things for him, my kids need to be transported all over kingdom come, and my boss is constantly asking me to work overtime. Then there's the house-cleaning, the laundry, the shopping, spending time with my friends, and my own needs for peace and quiet. Do I know what's causing my stress to occur? I think it's pretty obvious, don't you?

Steve (a 23-year-old medical student): I'm doing O.K. in school, but sometimes I get so nervous I think something serious might be wrong with me. Whenever I'm called on to speak in class, my whole body starts shaking. My heart begins to pound, I feel short of breath, and I have trouble concentrating on what I want to say. I know I'm probably suffering from anxiety attacks, but I just wanted to make sure I don't have heart disease or an overactive thyroid gland or anything like that.

Mary (a 45-year-old, divorced business owner): I just can't relax any more. My business used to be fun, but now my employees are driving me crazy. They make me mad as hell, and every time I blow up at them it only makes matters worse. The more I try to correct them, the more frustrated and angry I become. Sure, I know what's causing my stress to occur—my employees. I just don't see how I can do much about it.

John, Sally, Steve, and Mary do not really understand what is causing their stress to occur. Each believes that external factors—things
that happen to them in life—are primarily responsible for the stress
they experience. While millions of people share this belief, it is not
really true. Events, situations, and other external pressures are rarely the *primary cause* of any "stress" we experience.

Internal Vs. External Causes

Consider the list of external causes below. Which of these causes
do you believe are responsible for "stress" in your life? (Check all
that apply.)

☐ Traffic jams
☐ A busy schedule
☐ Too many responsibilities
☐ Public speaking
☐ Your boss
☐ Your employees
☐ Co-workers
☐ Your spouse
☐ Your children
☐ Financial pressures
☐ Your job
☐ Other family members
☐ Deadlines
☐ Caring for others
☐ Unexpected crises and changes

While external factors such as these do play a role, *internal causes*
are also involved. These internal causes are usually hidden from your
view—i.e. they are not usually obvious to you. Traffic jams, for example, don't cause you to feel "stressed" unless you judge or interpret
your predicament in certain ways. Speaking to a group only makes
you nervous if you are trying to please every listener, if you are trying to be too perfect, if you are afraid of appearing foolish, or if
you are pretending to be more knowledgeable than you really are.
Other people's behavior only causes you to suffer if you don't know
how to deal with their behavior effectively. And having too many
external pressures, demands, and responsibilities is only a problem
if you don't know how to extricate yourself from such situations.

Take the problem of depression, for instance. Feelings of depression often occur after negative external events. But depressed individuals are also plagued by negative internal thoughts and beliefs. These can include:

-"I'm not good enough."
-"I'm never going to amount to anything."
-"Nobody really cares about me."
-"Things are never going to get any better."
-"I have no future."
-"Maybe it would be better if I were dead."

In addition, depressed people tend to act in ways that reinforce their negative viewpoints. They fail to confront their problems optimistically, and they spend much of their time feeling sorry for themselves, judging both past events and their future possibilities in an unfavorable light.

Depression, therefore, is not just caused by external situations and events. It is also caused by non-obvious factors that occur within the depressed individual.*

The Importance Of Language In Human Stress

One reason we believe that external situations and events cause our stress to occur is because Selye's early experiments were based upon animals. When he subjected these animals to external "stressors," measurable stress responses always occurred in their bodies.

But human stress differs from stress in animals and non-living materials.† It differs because we *live our lives in language.* Everything we think, do, feel, and perceive is strongly influenced by linguistic factors.

While some animals, such as porpoises, whales, and chimpanzees, can engage in rudimentary forms of "linguistic" interaction, we are the only species—as far as we know today—that can engage in

---

* These internal causes can also include biochemical imbalances and other physical problems.
† Selye borrowed the term "stress" from the fields of physics and engineering, where scientists had long been testing structural materials for signs of "stress" and "strain."

higher-level forms of language. This is what distinguishes our type of language from all other forms of animal communication:

> (Human) language is—in addition to being more complicated—immeasurably more flexible than the animal cries from which it was developed, so flexible indeed that it can be used not only to report the tremendous variety of things that go on in the human nervous system but also to *report those reports.* That is, when an animal yelps, he may cause a second animal to yelp in imitation or alarm; the second yelp, however is not *about* the first yelp. But when a man says, "I see a river," a second man can say, "He says he sees a river"—which is a statement about a statement... *(Human) language, in short, can be about language.* This is a fundamental way in which human noise-making systems differ from the cries of animals. (S.I. Hayakawa, *Language In Thought And Action,* p. 9.)

In addition, our form of language enables us to do many things that animals can't do. These include:

• Judging, evaluating, and interpreting what happens to us;
• Imagining future possibilities;
• Contemplating our own death;
• Asking questions about the world in which we live;
• Engaging in complex linguistic acts (speech acts) such as making promises, declarations, and assertions of "fact."

All of these capacities arise from our unique form of language. This was recognized thousands of years ago by early Greek philosophers. Their insights were forgotten, however, as a result of later Greek thinkers such as Socrates, Plato, and Aristotle who focused upon our rational and intellectual abilities as if these existed apart from our linguistic capabilities.*

Human "Perception" and "Understanding" Depend Upon Language

Ludwig Wittgenstein was one of the first modern philosophers to rediscover the central role of language in human life. Wittgenstein developed his ideas about language in Cambridge, England, during the early 1900s. According to historian William Barrett, Wittgenstein recognized that language is much more than a tool human beings use to

---

* Even those human qualities we refer to as "spiritual" actually arise from our linguistic capabilities.

communicate about their thoughts, feelings, and observations. Wittgenstein correctly understood that *language is a fundamental part of the human condition*—a capacity which must be present for us to think or become aware of our world in the first place. According to Wittgenstein, our perceptions, inner experiences, and other forms of awareness come into being only *through* and *within* language:

> ...our world—the concrete world in which we live—does not come to us as something independent of language; we do not construct a language independently and then add it on to experience. Our world transpires within language. (Barrett, 1979, p. 84).

Wittgenstein, as well as others before him, realized that our personal observations and experiences are not primarily determined by what happens to us in life—they are primarily determined by the socio-linguistic discourses in which we live.*

Suppose, for example, you were living on the coast of Spain in the year 1491. If you saw a boat disappear beyond the horizon, this event would probably trigger tremendous grief, sadness, or other strong emotions in your body. These feelings would occur not just because you witnessed the boat's disappearance with your eyes, but because you also "perceived" and "understood" it in terms of the linguistic distinctions (e.g. horizon = end of the earth) and discourses ("everyone knows the world is flat and you will die if you go over the edge") which were part of your socio-linguistic conditioning. Today, we see boats disappear beyond the horizon all the time, but nothing much happens inside us. This is because the social discourses in which we were born and raised have changed dramatically since the fifteenth and sixteenth centuries.†

* I use the term "socio-linguistic" to refer to the social and cultural—as opposed to individual—aspects of human language. (These social aspects are discussed in Chapter 3.) The term "discourse" refers to a cohesive set of conversations, assumptions, and beliefs about a particular topic or subject.
† This idea was expanded upon in the 1930s by linguistic anthropologists Benjamin Lee Whorf and Edward Sapir, co-authors of the Sapir-Whorf hypothesis, which states that our perceptions of reality are largely determined by the linguistic habits and customs of our native culture. *Language, Thought, And Reality:* Selected Writings of Benjamin Lee Whorf. John. B. Carroll, editor. M.I.T. Press, Cambridge, Massachusetts, 1956.)

In addition, many of our actions and habitual behavior patterns are also influenced by language-mediated factors. How we "perceive" and "understand" ourselves and the world we live in has much to do with the way we behave. Our "perceptions" and "understandings," in turn, are strongly influenced by what our parents and other individuals said to us when we were young, how our parents trained us to think and behave, and how they thought, perceived, and behaved themselves.

Thus, while external situations, events, and demands do contribute to the development of human stress, *internal linguistic factors also play a role.* It is these internal, non-obvious causes—not the external events or circumstances in our lives—that produce most of the stress we normally experience.

Conversations And Action Patterns: The Primary Causes Of Stress In Human Beings

What are these internal, non-obvious factors that cause most of our stress to occur? Over the years, many people have tried to answer this question:

- Freud believed, for example, that unconscious "drives" and "defense mechanisms" cause most of our problems to occur.

- Jung, on the other hand, believed that our lives are controlled by other non-obvious factors—which he called "archtypes"—that pass from generation to generation in what he called the "collective unconscious" of mankind.

- Cognitive therapists such as Aaron Beck and Albert Ellis argue that our problems are largely caused by irrational thoughts and beliefs.*

- Behavioral theorists, in contrast, downplay the role of thoughts and beliefs. They insist that most of our problems result from faulty behaviors, which can be changed or controlled regardless of mental or cognitive factors.

* Cognitive Therapy is a form of psychotherapy based upon the theory that human behavior and human emotions are primarily determined by our thoughts—i.e. by our cognitions.

Other theorists have proposed additional causes for human "stress." These include:

• Personality types that make people either stress-prone or stress-resistant.

• Lifestyle factors such as exercise, diet, smoking, and overwork.

• Individual coping styles.

• Adequacy of social networks.

• Quality of social support.

The problem with all such theories—including Selye's external demand model—is that they all ignore the central role of language in human life. In the final analysis, all of the causes of human stress proposed to date arise from two—and only two—types of internal factors—*conversations* and *action patterns*—which are usually not obvious to us unless we know how to look for them.

THE MAJOR PURPOSE OF THIS BOOK IS TO SHOW YOU HOW TO IDENTIFY AND DEAL WITH THESE INTERNAL CONVERSATIONS AND ACTION PATTERNS SUCCESSFULLY.*

Traffic Jams

The internal conversations and action patterns that contribute to our "stress" are not complex, nor are they mysterious. Many of them are common to most human beings, while others predominate in certain cultures, communities, or geographical regions.

Take the problem of traffic jams, for example. People who know how to win against stress rarely view the traffic jam itself as the primary source of any stress they experience. Instead, they look within themselves for specific conversations and action patterns that usually become triggered by such situations.

---

* I do not mean to imply that stress is caused *only* by internal factors. External factors, social factors, cultural factors, and situational factors also play a role. It is very useful, however, to focus on our internal causes, since these are the causes we don't normally "see" and because they are also the ones we can do the most about.

Consider the list below. Do any of these conversations become triggered in you when you get stuck in a traffic jam? (Check all that apply.)

Conversations:

☐ "This shouldn't be happening."
☐ "Something terrible will occur if I don't reach my destination."
☐ "People will think badly of me if I don't arrive on time."
☐ "I should always be able to get where I want, whenever I want."
☐ "Whoever caused this mess to occur must have been an imbecile."
☐ "Somebody should have warned me about this tie up."
☐ "Sitting in traffic jams is a stupid waste of my time."

Sometimes, these conversations will be obvious to us, but most of the time they will not. In addition, our obvious conversations often arise from *a deeper level of unconscious thoughts and beliefs* which we usually take for granted. Some of these deeper conversations include:

Good/Bad	= The tendency to view things or events as either "good" or "bad."

  ex. "A traffic jam is something bad."
  ex. "Being a courteous, attentive driver is something good."

Right/Wrong	= The tendency to judge your own or others' behavior as either "right" or "wrong."

  ex. "Whoever caused this mess to occur must have been an imbecile." (They must have done something "wrong.")
  ex. "Someone should have warned me of this tie up." (It would have been the "right" thing to do.)

| Cause/Effect | = | Explaining why something happened or should happen in life by dividing events into separate "causes" and "effects." |

    ex. "Something terrible will happen (effect) if I don't reach my destination (cause)."

    ex. "People will think badly of me (effect) if I don't arrive on time (cause)."

| Credit/Blame | = | Explaining why something happened or should happen in life by first judging what happened as either "good," "bad," "right," or "wrong" and then assuming that someone or something "caused" it to occur. |

    ex. "What idiot caused this mess to occur (blame)?"

    ex. "If someone had warned me about this tie up, he or she would have been doing a good job (credit)."

Without the presence of hidden conversations such as GOOD/BAD, RIGHT/WRONG, CAUSE/EFFECT, and CREDIT/BLAME in the background of our thinking, *we would find it hard to experience much stress at all.* We would also be unable to think the thoughts that usually occur in such situations.

Harold Kushner points this out in his book *When Bad Things Happen To Good People*:

> Human beings live in a world of good and bad, and that makes our lives painful and complicated. Animals don't; their lives are much simpler, without all the moral problems and moral decisions we humans have to face. Categories such as 'good' and 'bad' don't really exist for animals. They can be helpful or messy, obedient or disobedient, but they cannot be good or bad. (p.75)

In addition, internal action patterns—including patterns of not taking action—also contribute to our "stress."* Consider the problem of traffic jams again. Notice how the following actions or lack of actions can contribute to the stress you experience in such situations:

☐ You allowed enough time to get to your destination, but only if everything went smoothly and without interruption.
☐ You blamed yourself for not deciding to go by another route.
☐ You blamed someone else for causing you to be inconvenienced.
☐ You sat in the traffic jam moaning, groaning, and "fussing" about your plight.
☐ You didn't find something valuable to do while you were waiting.
☐ You reacted much more violently or intensely than the situation called for.

These are specific examples of more general stress-producing action patterns such as:

- FAILING TO ANTICIPATE BREAKDOWNS AND DELAYS
- BLAMING YOURSELF OR OTHERS
- MOANING, GROANING, AND COMPLAINING
- FAILING TO DEAL WITH PROBLEMS CREATIVELY
- TAKING THINGS TOO SERIOUSLY

► NOTE: The next time you get stuck in a traffic jam, see if you can identify some of the internal conversations and action patterns noted above. Remember, they won't always be obvious to you, so you may need to dig deep to find them. Just by simply noticing their presence, you can often eliminate much of the stress you experience in such situations.

In much the same way, all types of stress in human beings result from internal conversations and action patterns that we don't normally see.

---

* For instance, failing to make a request, failing to attend to certain tasks, or failing to ask for help can cause stress to occur.

Figure 2-3

Internal Causes Of Stress In Human Beings

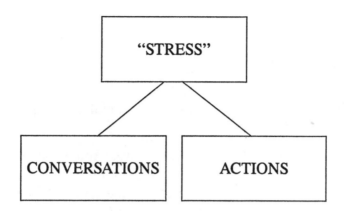

Non-Obvious Causes
(Within Us)*

Even when a traffic jam does cause you to miss an important meeting or suffer a negative consequence, *it is still largely the hidden conversations and action patterns within you that determine how much stress you experience.*

EXAMPLE: Years ago a traffic jam caused me to miss my plane for an important medical conference that I had been looking forward to for several months. While I could have been greatly "stressed" by what happened, I wasn't. This was because I knew what types of conversations and action patterns were going to become triggered within me, and because I also knew how to deal with them effectively.

---

* I use this type of diagram many times throughout this book. I also use the words "patterns" and "tendencies" when referring to both conversations and actions. "Patterns" are habitual ways of thinking or behaving that we have repeated many times in the past. "Tendencies" are urges or impulses to think or behave in certain ways, whether or not these urges are ever carried out. I also use terms such as "action patterns" and "behavior patterns" or "action tendencies" and "behavior tendencies" interchangeably (each of these terms includes the absence of actions as well).

The Hidden Causes Of Fear In Human Beings

Consider the emotion of fear as another example. Suppose you are home alone one evening and you are startled by the sound of a window in your house being broken. What was the cause of your alarm reaction?:

☐ A. The noise you heard
☐ B. The presence of an intruder
☐ C. The fact you were alone
☐ D. The time of day this occurred
☐ E. Not having a gun or weapon to defend yourself
☐ F. None of the above

The correct answer is "none of the above." You do not experience fear as a direct result of the noise itself—some people hearing the same noise, for instance, might not become afraid. You also don't become afraid because of the presence of an intruder, since you don't really know if one exists. The other three answers are equally insufficient.

The truth about fear is that we only feel afraid when:

SPECIFIC FEAR-PRODUCING CONVERSATIONS AND ACTION PATTERNS BECOME TRIGGERED WITHIN US.

Here, for example, are the specific conversations that produce fear in human beings:

CONVERSATIONS THAT PRODUCE FEAR IN HUMAN BEINGS:

1) Something bad might happen.
2) Someone or something (including myself) may be hurt or harmed.
3) I don't have the power (control) to keep #1 or #2 from happening.
4) I should never feel afraid, since fear is a sign of weakness.*

---

* Even though this conversation may not appear to be involved, it is always present in the background of our awareness whenever we are afraid. It is similar to other socially-determined background conversations, such as "men shouldn't cry," "people should be considerate of others," and "we should not lie, cheat, or steal."

The first three of these conversations must be present—whether we are aware of them or not—in order for us to feel afraid. If you look at your own experience, you will see that this is ALWAYS THE CASE.

In addition, fear-producing or fear-maintaining action patterns also become triggered within us:

ACTION PATTERNS THAT PRODUCE OR MAINTAIN FEAR IN HUMAN BEINGS:

A) Remaining immobile ("freezing") in response to a fear-producing agent (this sometimes keeps the agent from attacking us);

B) Fleeing or avoiding the situation (while this removes us from immediate danger, it reinforces conversations #1 and #2 and keeps us from developing a sense of mastery and control over similar situations in the future);

C) Trying to appear unafraid (this tactic uses a certain amount of coping energy, which could otherwise be used to deal with our situation);

D) Not taking action to deal with the situation effectively (this reinforces each fear-producing conversation above).

▶ NOTE: Most of our stress-producing conversations and action patterns are not part of our conscious awareness or "self-talk." They are not conversations we say to ourselves, nor are they behavior patterns we consciously adopt. In other words, when we are afraid, we don't consciously say to ourselves "something bad is going to happen." We also don't consciously decide to "freeze" when we see something that scares us. These hidden patterns exist in the background of our awareness. They become triggered automatically, like "knee-jerk" reflexes, and, as we will see in later discussions, they are equally difficult to change or control.

Other Stress-Producing Conversations And Action Patterns

Besides the patterns we have already discussed, there are many other conversations and action patterns that contribute to our stress. Some of these include:

CONVERSATIONS:

Unrealistic
Expectations = The tendency to assume things about one-self, about other people, or about what is possible in life which are not consistent with reality.

   ex. "I can abuse and neglect my body and not pay any price for this."

   ex. "If you treat people well, they will always behave the same towards you."

Negative
Thinking = The tendency to view things in life "nega-tively" instead of "positively" when both choices are equally available.

   ex. "The glass is half empty."

   ex. "Something bad is probably going to happen."

Perfectionism = "Perfectionism" is a short-hand designation for a number of related conversations:*

-"I should always do things right."
-"I should never make mistakes."
-"Other people should always do things right and never make mistakes."
-"I should always be certain before I act."

---

* Many of these conversations are also examples of unrealistic expectations.

Control

=   Similarly, the conversation called "control" consists of numerous conversations, such as:

-"I should be able to change/control my mind."
-"I should be able to change/control my feelings."
-"I should be able to change/control my body."
-"I should be able to change/control my behavior."
-"I should be able to change/control other people."
-"I should be able to change/control external situations and events."

ACTION PATTERNS:

Failing To Make Requests Or Demands Of Others

=   It is difficult for human beings to be healthy, happy, and successful in life without making requests or demands of others. Unfortunately, many people are reluctant to make such requests, and they frequently suffer stress as a consequence.

Failing To Decline Requests From Others

=   People who find it difficult to decline requests or demands from others also suffer as a result of this behavior pattern. The ability to say "no" to others' requests and not feel guilty is often needed to prevent certain types of stress from occuring.

| Failing To Clarify Agreements And Expectations | = | When we make unconscious assumptions about the promises others have made to us or about any expectations we have of ourselves or others, we set ourselves up for failure and disappointment. On the other hand, when we openly clarify and discuss our agreements and expectations, many of these problems can be averted. |

▶ NOTE: For a more complete list of stress-producing conversations and action patterns see Appendix A.

It is important to note that all of our stress-producing conversations and action patterns also have positive benefits as well. For example, the conversations PERFECTIONISM and CONTROL are very useful in certain occupations (e.g. brain surgery, air traffic control). CAUSE/EFFECT theories are essential for science and engineering. And other stress-producing conversations such as "I've got to do it myself," "Don't take risks," and "Don't make mistakes" can often keep us from getting into trouble.

It is also important to notice that conversations and action patterns frequently work in concert with each other.* For example, the following conversations and action patterns are closely related:

Conversation	Action Pattern
"I should never make a mistake."	Being overly cautious
"I want everyone to like me."	Trying to please others
"I should always be in control of my thoughts and emotions."	Trying to control your thoughts and emotions.

Where Do Our Internal Conversations And Action Patterns Come From?

Most of our internal conversations and action patterns can be traced to our past. Conversations such as "Don't take risks," "Don't make mistakes," and "I should always be in control of my thoughts

---

* In truth, conversations and action patterns are not really separable. As artificial distinctions, however, these concepts are very useful.

and feelings" are frequently given to us by our parents.* Ingrained behavior patterns such as NEEDING TO BE RIGHT, TRYING TO CHANGE OTHERS, and MOANING, GROANING, AND COMPLAINING also can become established from the influence of key individuals in our lives.

Our stress-producing conversations and action patterns can also result from:
a) faulty decisions or conclusions we formed when we were young;
b) parental abuse;
c) parental neglect or absence;
d) other negative childhood experiences.

For example, some people suffer from unconscious guilt over "injuries" they believe they caused other people. Children of divorced parents, for instance, may incorrectly assume that they were somehow responsible for their parents' unhappiness. As adults, these children may avoid getting married or sabotage their intimate relationships because of unconscious fears that they will harm whomever they love. Also, when children are repeatedly told that they are bad, rotten, or unlovable, they will often develop unconscious patterns of thinking and behaving that confirm these linguistic "realities."

In an excellent book titled *Imaginary Crimes: Why We Punish Ourselves And How To Stop*, Lewis Engle, Ph.D. and Tom Ferguson, M.D., describe over 60 negative messages parents often tell their children.† Messages such as "I'm sorry you were ever born," "You're going to turn out just like your father," or "You're never going to amount to very much," can have a lasting effect upon a person's self-image and self-esteem. They can also produce other unconscious conversations and action patterns that contribute to stress, tension, and suffering throughout an individual's life.

More To Come About The Hidden Causes Of Your Stress

Throughout this book, I will provide you with additional tools and suggestions for identifying the internal causes of your stress. For now, it is only important to remember that whenever you experience any type of stress in your life, *hidden conversations and action patterns within you* are always involved.

---

* Other social factors, such as cultural and peer influences, also play a role. In addition, our parents' internal conversations and action patterns were largely given to them by their parents, who got them from their parents, and so on.
† This book is listed in the Suggested For Further Reading Section.

DAY 2: EXERCISES

1. *Reread the Blindness and Certainty parable at the beginning of this chapter. After completing this task, indicate whether your understanding of this parable has changed since your initial reading?*

☐ YES ☐ NO ☐ PERHAPS

2. *For the rest of today, keep track of the number of times you use, or hear someone else use, the following words (or similar expressions):*

	NUMBER OF TIMES I USED THESE WORDS OR CONCEPTS TODAY	NUMBER OF TIMES OTHER PEOPLE USED THESE WORDS OR CONCEPTS TODAY
A. *"Good"*	_____	_____
B. *"Bad"*	_____	_____
C. *"Right"*	_____	_____
D. *"Wrong"*	_____	_____

3. *Recall the last time you felt afraid. Write down whatever you remember about this incident.*

_____

_____

_____

A. *Now, turn to page 28 and confirm for yourself that the first three fear-producing conversations were triggered within you.*

☐ Check here when you have done this.

B. *Turn to page 29 and also confirm for yourself that one or more of the fear-producing action patterns also became triggered within you.*

☐ Check here when you have done this.

DAY 3

BIOLINGUISTICS: A NEW UNDERSTANDING OF HUMAN BEINGS

The idea that internal conversations and action patterns contribute to our stress is not new. What is new is the realization that these hidden causes *exist in our bodies*, not our minds. Our failure to understand this point leads to a great deal of confusion and suffering.

EXAMPLE: Richard was a real-estate broker who frequently suffered from "stress." He maintained a very busy schedule, dealing mostly with high-powered executives and entrepreneurs who frequently changed their plans at the very last moment. His income was dependent upon these people, many of whom failed to keep their promises.

With the help of counseling, Richard began to understand that much of his "stress" came from conversations and action patterns within him, not from the behavior of others or from the nature of his occupation. These internal causes included conversations such as RIGHT/WRONG, NEGATIVE THINKING, PERFECTIONISM and CONTROL and action patterns such as FAILING TO ASSESS THE COMMITMENT OF OTHERS, FAILING TO ANTICIPATE UNEXPECTED BREAKDOWNS AND DELAYS, and FAILING TO DECLINE REQUESTS AND DEMANDS FROM OTHERS.

As he began to recognize how these internal conversations and action patterns contributed to his stress, Richard's first response was to try to change or eliminate his internal patterns. When he failed to do this, he felt even worse! He became frustrated, depressed, and thoroughly demoralized. He also believed that since he was unable to control his own "mental" processes, he was psychologically weak and inferior to other people.

A Common Dilemma

Richard's experience is quite common. Most of us have been taught to believe that our internal conversations and action patterns exist in our minds. Most of us have also been taught that our minds function like computers and that they become "programmed" with various thoughts, feelings, and beliefs which can be changed or "reprogrammed" if they are found to be defective.

As a result of these assumptions, once we identify an internal conversation or action pattern that is contributing to our stress, we often try to:

a) change our stress-producing beliefs;
b) get rid of our stress-producing action patterns;
c) control our thoughts;
d) control our emotions;
e) use other mind-control techniques, such as:
   1. positive thinking
   2. positive affirmations
   3. positive self-talk
   4. mental imagery

When these efforts fail, we feel much like Richard—discouraged, frustrated, and personally demoralized.

This frustration and demoralization does not have to occur. It results from a false understanding of ourselves as human beings, which arises from inaccurate mind-body theories that are no longer accepted by twentieth century thinkers.

In this chapter, I will attempt to show you that stress is not a mind-body phenomenon. While this insight is important, *it is not essential that you agree with it*. Since the arguments both for and against the mind-body view of human nature are quite complex, they may not be of interest to every reader. Therefore, I have relegated much of this discussion to Appendix C for those who wish to pursue it.

The Mind-Body Viewpoint

Most theories of human stress are based upon a mind-body model of human beings. This model, which has existed in one form or another for thousands of years, received its greatest impetus from 16th century French mathematician and philosopher Rene Descartes. Descartes, who is well-known for his statement "I think, therefore I am," proposed that all human beings consist of three different parts—an objective body, a subjective mind, and a spiritual dimension equivalent to the soul. For the past 300 years, this mind-body-spirit division has been one of the dominant social discourses in our society, much as the flat earth hypothesis was a dominant social discourse prior to the 15th century.

In recent years, a growing number of scholars, scientists, and other contemporary thinkers have begun to challenge this mind-body view. According to Fritjof Capra, noted physicist and author of two best-selling books, *The Tao Of Physics* and *The Turning Point*, many of our modern problems, such as inflation, international conflicts, and certain health-related problems, cannot be properly dealt with or understood in outdated Cartesian-Newtonian terms:*

> My intent has never been to criticize particular professional groups as such, but rather to show how the dominant concepts and attitudes in various fields reflect the same unbalanced world view, a world view that is still shared by the majority of our culture but is now rapidly changing. (*The Turning Point*, p. 17.)

Biolinguistics: A Recent Breakthrough In Our Understanding Of Human Stress

I believe we have reached a similar "turning point" in our knowledge of human stress, where old, outdated theories continue to dominate our thinking, even though a new, more accurate model has

---

* The mind-body viewpoint is part of a larger theoretical model—the Cartesian-Newtonian world view—which was named for its two leading contributors, Rene Descartes and Isaac Newton.

clearly emerged. This new model—which I call "Biolinguistics"—has been developing for many years.* Although few people know of it by this name, it is already beginning to have an impact on every major field of human study.

According to Biolinguistics, human beings do not consist of "a mind and a body." We consist of only one thing—a body—which has unique and remarkable capacities for language. (The term "Biolinguistics" comes from "Bio"=biology and "Linguistics"=language.) It is our biological capacities for language—i.e. speaking, listening, and coordinating our behavior linguistically—not our "mental" capacities that make us different from all other living creatures and from computers as well.

▶ NOTE: Modern scholars point out that Descartes would have been correct had he said "I *speak*, therefore I am" instead of "I think, therefore I am."

Stress Is Not A Mind-Body Phenomenon

The basic error of all mind-body theories is that they assume a separate "mental" domain inside human beings which doesn't really exist. In other words, in our efforts to understand why we think, feel, and behave as we do, we have mistakenly assumed that Descartes was right—that there is a "mind" inside each of us that is responsible for both our normal and abnormal functioning.

According to Dr. John Searle, Professor of Philosophy at the University of California at Berkeley, while our belief in the existence of the mind seems well-founded, it is actually incorrect. While no one doubts that human beings exhibit many abilities that appear to be "mental" in origin, Searle asserts that these abilities are actually produced by non-mental mechanisms. He offers the following analogy to illustrate this point: if we didn't already know what makes a clock run, we could assume (incorrectly) that since clocks and hourglasses both keep time, what makes a clock run are tiny grains of

---

* Prominent contributors to this perspective include philosophers Ludwig Wittgenstein, Martin Heidegger, and Hans George-Gadamer; linguistic scholars John Austin and John Searle; biologists Humberto Maturana and Francisco Varela; neurophysiologists Heinz Von Foerster and Gerald Edelman; psychotherapists Gregory Bateson and Paul Watzlawick, and many others.

sand that continually move around inside it. While this assumption is obviously absurd, Searle maintains we do the very same thing when we assume that our thoughts, feelings, moods, and behaviors are caused by "mental" factors that somehow exist within us.

► NOTE: Others have pointed out this is the same logical error as assuming the sun "rises" in the morning (the earth actually rotates), or that television screens contain "pictures" (they contain cathode-ray tubes that respond to varying electrical charges), or that computers store "information" (they store electrical impulses that are either in an "on" or 'off" configuration).

In addition, while most people believe that language is a product of the human mind, the reverse is actually true. Without language, Descartes could not have proposed his theory of the mind in the first place, and without language none of his followers could have agreed with him and disseminated his ideas.

Thus, many contemporary scholars and scientists are beginning to acknowledge that human language and human bodies clearly do exist, but that the human "mind" probably does not.

► NOTE: Advocates of the mind-body viewpoint have nonetheless contributed greatly to the relief of human problems and human stress. Their theories and treatment programs have helped millions of individuals. Even so, it may now be possible for them to achieve better results by acknowledging some of the weaknesses and inaccuracies of the mind-body view. Again, for a more detailed discussion of the arguments both for and against this popular viewpoint, see Appendix C.

Conversations And Action Patterns Exist In Our Bodies, Not Our Minds

While an in-depth discussion of Biolinguistics is beyond the scope of this book, a few key points are worth exploring. The first is that the conversations and action patterns that contribute to our stress *exist in our bodies*, not our minds.

Take the emotion of fear, for example. As we saw in the previous chapter, fear results not so much from events or circumstances that happen in our lives, but from the following conversations and action patterns which become triggered within us:

CONVERSATIONS THAT PRODUCE FEAR IN HUMAN BEINGS:

1) Something bad might happen.
2) Someone or something (including myself) may be hurt or harmed.
3) I don't have the power (control) to keep #1 or #2 from happening.
4) I should never feel afraid, since fear is a sign of weakness.

ACTION PATTERNS THAT PRODUCE OR MAINTAIN FEAR IN HUMAN BEINGS:

A) Remaining immobile ("freezing") in response to a fear-producing agent or situation;
B) Fleeing or avoiding the situation;
C) Trying to appear unafraid;
D) Not taking action to deal with the situation effectively.

While most people assume these fear-producing conversations and action patterns exist in their minds, these patterns actually exist deep within their bodies. They become "triggered" automatically—in response to certain events or situations—and they produce their effects without conscious thought or deliberation. Once these conversations and action patterns become "programmed" into our bodies, they are extremely difficult to change or eliminate.

EXAMPLE: Recall what happened when you first learned to ride a bicycle. At one time in your life, you didn't know how to ride a two-wheeled bike. Every time you placed your body upon one, all you could do was fall off. After hours and hours of trial and error, however, your body eventually became able to remain atop a bicycle without falling off. At first, you had to consciously attend to everything you were doing. But after a while, this "know how" became automatic—it began to be generated by your body without conscious reflection.

The reason bicycle riding becomes automatic for us is because our bodies physically change. Specific anatomic, physiologic, and other structural changes occur at many levels—especially, but not limited to, our brains and neuromuscular systems—which enable us to perform such complex new behaviors. Once these structural changes become established, they often remain in our bodies forever.

▶ NOTE: This is why people can get on a bicycle and ride it, even though they haven't done so for decades. While the structural changes that permit this activity became established in their bodies during their childhoods, these changes persist throughout their lifetimes. The same is also true for many of the conversations and action patterns that contribute to our stress, such as GOOD/BAD, RIGHT/WRONG, PERFECTIONISM, CONTROL, and many others. As we shall see later in this book, this realization can help us deal with the internal causes of our stress more successfully.

Conversations And Action Patterns Often Produce False "Realities" Within Our Bodies

The second key point of Biolinguistics is that many of our problems and conflicts arise from false or misleading "realities" that become triggered within us.

Consider the case of fear once again. Suppose a friend plays a trick on you one night by placing a plastic—but authentic looking—spider on your bed. As you prepare to go to sleep, you notice the spider and immediately become afraid. Why did *fear* occur in this situation? It occurred because each of the fear-producing conversations and action patterns noted earlier became triggered inside you, and because *your body automatically responded as if each of them was true*.

FEAR-PRODUCING CONVERSATIONS:

1) *Something bad might happen*—"the spider might bite me; it could be a poisonous spider;"
2) *Someone or something may be hurt or harmed*—"I could be hurt, get sick, or possibly even die!"
3) *I don't have the power (control) to keep #1 or #2 from happening*—"Once I am asleep, I won't be able to protect myself."

These conversations—and accompanying action patterns—became triggered in your body even though the spider was made of plastic. Thus, it was not the external reality of the situation that caused you to experience fear—it was the internal "realities" that became triggered within you.

▶ NOTE: This is how conversations such as GOOD/BAD, RIGHT/WRONG, and STUPID/SMART cause us to experience stress in the first place. They do so by:

a) giving us an *incomplete view* of the truth about life (e.g. seeing only the "bad" and ignoring the "good");

b) giving us a *distorted or inaccurate view* of reality (e.g. judging something to be "bad" or "wrong" when such is not the case);

c) causing us to "perceive" certain "realities" that are *not really there* (e.g. assuming someone's behavior was motivated by greed or stupidity, when other motives were actually involved.)

The same can be said about our stress-producing action patterns, such as NEEDING TO BE RIGHT, TRYING TO CHANGE OTHERS, FAILING TO MAKE REQUESTS OR DEMANDS OF OTHERS, and FAILING TO ASK FOR HELP. While each of these strategies is useful from time to time, each can also be inappropriate for some situations we encounter.*

EXAMPLE: Take the case of unexpectedly being fired from your job. Most people automatically respond as if this is a "bad," "awful," or "terrible" event. But these internal "realities" are not always true. After all, aren't many new job opportunities now available to you? Might you eventually find a job that is more to your liking? Don't some people ultimately benefit from being fired from their jobs by reevaluating their goals, priorities, and ambitions? Thus, while certain events in life can truly be tragic, *the amount of stress you experience from them will often be determined by the hidden conversations and action patterns that become triggered within you.* And while you may not be able to do much about the events or circumstances that happen to you, you can almost always do something about the internal causes of your suffering.

► NOTE: This point can be difficult to grasp. One reason for this is that everyone knows their internal "realities" are "correct" or "useful" much of the time. Also, we are well aware that ignoring certain internal "realities" can be fraught with danger. (Some spiders are real, and if they bite you, you can be harmed!) In addition, you may not always want to eliminate your pain and suffering—like when a loved one dies or becomes seriously ill. Thus, each individual situation you encounter must be evaluated on its own merits. Sometimes your internal conversations and action patterns will correspond to what is really happening in life, while at other times they may be far off the mark.

---

* While we usually think (and feel) that our internal conversations and action patterns are accurate and well-founded, they often turn out to be false and misleading.

Human Language Is A Social, As Well As An Individual, Biologic Phenomenon

Another key point of Biolinguistics is that human language is a social, as well as an individual, phenomenon. When we are born, our bodies are literally "dropped" into a sea of already-existing cultural and historical conversations, discourses, and customs. As we grow and develop, these social conversations and customs become "programmed" into our bodies. While we take this socio-linguistic conditioning for granted, it is essential for our normal growth and development.

Wolf Children

A dramatic example of what happens when we lack such sociolinguistic conditioning occurred in the early 1920s. After being abandoned in the woods as infants, two Hindu girls, one age five and the other age eight, were captured north of India. They were found living with a pack of wolves, who had apparently adopted them and raised them for several years. At the time they were found, both girls showed no signs of malnutrition or mental retardation. They appeared healthy and well, although neither one could speak and they both walked on all fours. The younger girl died shortly after being rescued. The older girl survived another ten years, but she never responded to human contact and she continued to prefer the company of dogs and wolves. She never learned to speak, except for a few simple words, and the people who cared for her reported that in no way did she impress them as being "human." These wolf children show us that without the presence of other users of language, even our brains and nervous systems cannot develop in the normal way. (Adapted from Maturana & Varela, *The Tree Of Knowledge*, pp 128-129.)

Language Also Affects Our Bodies

Biolinguistics not only explains how conversations and action patterns become "programmed" into our bodies, it also explains how both internal and external conversations affect our bodies as well. The following story illustrates this point.

TOM'S STORY

Tom was a 52-year-old, intelligent, likable, successful administrator who was referred to me for treatment. About six months before

I met Tom, he had suffered a mild heart attack. Prior to this, he was in very good health. He rarely got sick, he didn't smoke or drink, he wasn't overweight, he exercised several days a week, and his cholesterol level was perfectly normal. He had no family history of heart disease or other serious illness, and he had never been hospitalized. He had no complaints of stress or tension in his life, and he had no major conflicts, either at home or at work. His only medical problem was mild high blood pressure, which had been well-controlled with medication.

Needless to say, Tom was shaken to find out he had heart disease. For the first time in his life, he became worried about his health. With the permission of his cardiologist, he enrolled himself in a cardiac rehabilitation program offered at his local hospital. He also followed a strict low-salt, low-fat, low-cholesterol diet, and he exercised every evening, instead of only three days a week, as soon as he got home from work.

Despite following all these preventive guidelines, Tom began to feel worse rather than better. He became completely obsessed by the thought of having another heart attack. Although his cardiologist had assured him his heart was in good shape (a heart catheterization test had revealed no signs of extensive disease), this had little impact on Tom's obsessive preoccupation. He became extremely alarmed whenever he felt the slightest twinge of discomfort in his chest, and he was no longer the friendly, mild-mannered, confident person he used to be. He also became distant with his wife and children, and he frequently missed supper with his family, claiming he needed to exercise first before he could eat. His blood pressure was no longer under excellent control, and he had even developed a new health problem—palpitations of his heart—which only served to amplify his anxiety.

Tom's cardiologist believed these palpitations were mainly due to stress. When they failed to respond to medication, his doctor advised him to seek counseling.

During his first visit to my office, Tom readily admitted to me that he was driving himself "crazy" by being overly worried about his heart. "I just can't seem to control myself. Instead of getting better, I feel like I'm making myself worse, and I really don't know what to do about it."

As I listened to Tom speak, it became clear to me that his obsessive preoccupation was not really new for him. Rather, it was consistent with the way he had always related to problems in his life. For example, he believed that people should always strive to control themselves and everything that happens around them. He considered himself personally responsible for how others around him behaved, and he even boasted that his main job at work was to anticipate problems and prevent them through his own individual actions. These control-oriented patterns also appeared in his relationships with his wife, his children, and now with his body. Over the years, these patterns made Tom a valuable and successful employee. But they also may have placed a burden upon his heart, of which both he and his cardiologist were unaware.

In addition to listening to Tom speak, I was also able to observe his cardiovascular system on a minute-to-minute basis during each of our counseling sessions. With the aid of a computerized monitoring system developed by Dr. James Lynch and his colleagues at the University of Maryland Medical School, I was able to observe Tom's blood pressure and heart rate on a computer screen as we talked and worked together.*

Figure 3-1

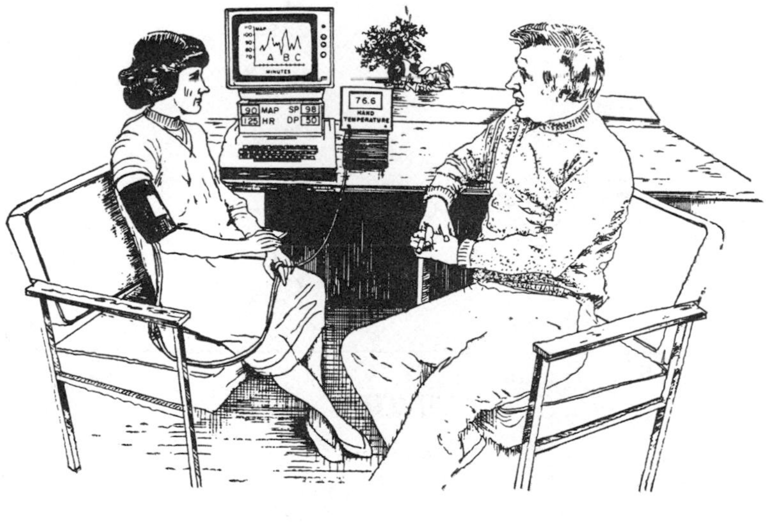

Dr. Lynch (right) treating a woman for migraine headaches.

* Dr. Lynch's group is one of the leading research teams exploring the role of language in human stress.

During our sixth counseling session, a dramatic illustration of the effect of language on the human body took place. In our session the week before, Tom had become aware of his tendency to automatically overreact—i.e. think the worst about—any minor chest sensation. This was a new insight for Tom, and he had spent much of the past week trying to keep himself from having such "catastrophic" thoughts. He was extremely pleased with the results he had achieved. He felt much less anxious and worried, and he had even begun to notice other areas of his life where similar patterns of thinking would automatically become triggered within him when something minor went wrong.

Here is what happened to Tom's blood pressure during our sixth counseling session:

Figure 3-2

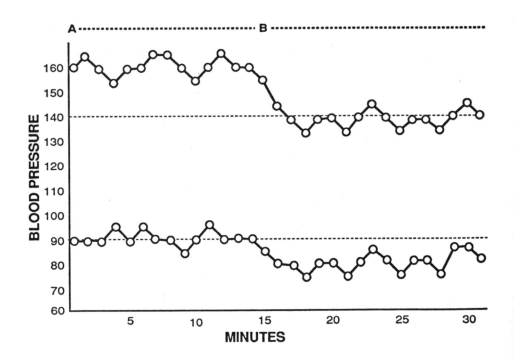

At point A, Tom began telling me about the success he was having trying to prevent (i.e. control) his negative thoughts from occurring. Even though he was feeling much better, his blood pressure remained abnormally high (normal = 140/90) during the entire time he was engaged in this conversation about "control."

At point B, I interrupted the conversation and shifted it in a different direction. I told Tom it was nice that he was feeling better, but there might be an even better way to deal with his negative thoughts. I suggested that instead of struggling so hard to prevent such thoughts from occurring, he could relax, let them occur, and just ignore them.

This was another new insight for Tom, and he seemed genuinely excited about it. He continued to talk and reflect upon this possibility for the next 15 minutes. As was the case from point A to point B, Tom did most of the talking while I listened to him and observed his cardiovascular responses (the computer screen was positioned so Tom could not see his readings).

What happened to Tom's body during this session was quite revealing. By simply changing the nature of our conversation from "needing to be in control" to "letting go of the need to control," I was able to produce a dramatic decrease in Tom's blood pressure. Within 2-3 minutes of abandoning the conversation of "control," Tom's blood pressure returned to normal and remained there for some time.

This example shows that human conversations not only arise from our bodies, but they can have profound effects upon our bodies as well.* Was it Tom's diet or genetic makeup that caused him to have a heart attack, or could his automatic conversation of "needing to be in control"—a conversation that is very prevalent in our society— have placed an unnecessary strain upon his heart and cardiovascular system? (At this point in time, no one knows the answer to this question.)†

---

* The well-known phenomenon of "voodoo death" is perhaps the most striking example.
† An interesting parallel: in ancient Chinese Medicine the heart pathway of the body is called the "Supreme Controller."

Implications

Here are some implications of this Biolinguistic model:

1. *Biolinguistics is a new way of understanding our "thoughts."* According to Biolinguistics, "thoughts" are not ideas in our minds— they are conversations that take place within our bodies. "Conscious thoughts" are conversations we are aware of. "Unconscious thoughts" are conversations in our bodies that we are not usually aware of.

2. *Biolinguistics is a new way of understanding our feelings, moods, and emotions.* Any body sensation we become aware of—such as pain, tiredness, nervousness, or warmth—can be called a feeling. "Moods" and "emotions," on the other hand, are specific types of feelings. Moods such as depression, irritability, and impatience, or emotions such as fear, anger, sadness, guilt, and joy, can readily be distinguished from each other.*

In human beings, both moods and emotions are primarily caused by hidden conversations and action patterns that have been triggered in our bodies.† For example, the internal causes of anger and guilt are listed below:

```
┌─────────────────────────────┐
│                             │
│           ANGER             │
│                             │
└─────────────────────────────┘
```

CONVERSATIONS THAT PRODUCE ANGER IN HUMAN BEINGS:

1) Someone did something they shouldn't have done.
2) Someone was hurt, harmed, humiliated, embarrassed, offended, disappointed, or otherwise inconvenienced by what was done.
3) Some person or persons (other than myself) were unilaterally (totally) responsible (to blame) for #1 and #2.
4) The offending person or persons should acknowledge what they did wrong, offer to make amends, and/or be punished.

---

* Moods actually differ from emotions in several ways. For one, they are often more subtle, pervasive, and difficult to change. For another, they are more culturally-determined and they often can affect large groups of people at the same time.
† While pre-verbal infants clearly experience emotions such as sadness and fear, these experiences are largely driven by language-mediated factors in older children and adults.

ACTION PATTERNS THAT PRODUCE OR MAINTAIN ANGER IN HUMAN BEINGS:

A) Failing to recognize how your own judgments, evaluations, and standards might not be valid for other people.
B) Failing to recognize how your own actions, past and present, may have contributed to what happened.
C) Justifying your anger, instead of looking within yourself for its internal causes.
D) Retaliating or seeking revenge, instead of openly and honestly dealing with what happened.

GUILT

CONVERSATIONS THAT PRODUCE GUILT IN HUMAN BEINGS:

1) Someone did something they shouldn't have done.
2) Someone was hurt, harmed, humiliated, embarrassed, offended, disappointed, or otherwise inconvenienced by what was done.
3) I am unilaterally responsible (to blame) for #1 and #2.
4) I should suffer (be punished) for what I did wrong.

ACTION PATTERNS THAT PRODUCE OR MAINTAIN GUILT IN HUMAN BEINGS:

A) Obsessing about what happened in order to heap additional blame and criticism upon yourself.
B) Failing to challenge your assumption that something "bad" or "wrong" actually took place.
C) Failing to recognize other people's responsibility for causing what happened or for any "hurt" or "harm" they experienced.
D) Leaving the situation incomplete—i.e. failing to take action to repair or compensate for any "damage" that was done.

► NOTE: The conversations which produce guilt and anger in human beings are very similar. The major difference is that conversations #3 and #4 shift directions. When we feel guilty, we assume we are unilaterally responsible (to blame) for something "bad" or "wrong" that happened. When we feel angry, the opposite assumption becomes triggered within us—someone else is to blame and we are the innocent victim. In the case of guilt, we believe we deserve to be punished. In the case of anger, we assume someone else should be punished.

THIS EXPLAINS WHY MANY PEOPLE ALTERNATE BETWEEN FEELINGS OF GUILT AND ANGER. As their internal conversations of unilateral blame shift from themselves to others, so do the emotions of guilt and anger which follow in their wake.

3. *Each mood or emotion is produced by specific internal conversations and action patterns that are essentially the same for all human beings.* Each of our moods and emotions is produced by a specific set of conversations and action patterns that becomes triggered in our bodies.

Figure 3-3

Invisible Conversation-Action "Mechanisms" For Human Moods and Emotions

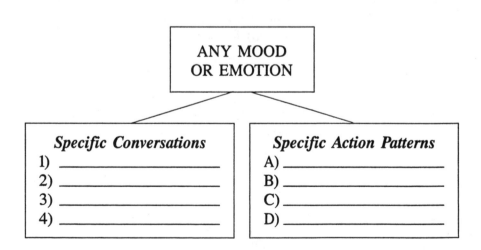

While cultural differences clearly exist, these internal "mechanisms" are remarkably similar for most human beings. For example, the emotion of sadness is generally produced by the following conversations and action patterns, regardless of individual or cultural differences in the meanings or interpretations of each:

SADNESS

CONVERSATIONS THAT PRODUCE SADNESS IN HUMAN BEINGS:

1) I have lost something.
2) What I lost is important.
3) I will never be able to replace what I have lost.
4) Without it, I can't be happy or content.

ACTION PATTERNS THAT PRODUCE OR MAINTAIN SADNESS IN HUMAN BEINGS:

A) Failing to challenge conversations 1-4.
B) Dwelling on the past and what was lost.
C) Withdrawing from your usual activities in life and/or failing to seek out other sources of happiness.
D) Being reluctant to communicate about your loss to others.

Because these internal mechanisms are similar for most human beings, we can train ourselves to know, in advance, which hidden causes *must be operating within us* whenever we are experiencing a particular mood or emotion. We can also use this knowledge to understand why other people feel the way they do. In other words, if someone else is feeling sad, angry, fearful, or depressed, they must be doing so for the very same reasons we would experience these same moods or emotions.

4. *Stress is not your fault!* The conversations and action patterns responsible for your moods, emotions, and other types of stress are not necessarily of your choosing. They become programmed into your body as a result of the conversations you are exposed to in your culture and in your family.

Some of these conversations, such as GOOD/BAD, RIGHT/ WRONG, CAUSE/EFFECT, and CREDIT/BLAME, are strongly ingrained in all human beings. Some linguistic authorities believe they may even be passed from individual to individual by genetic as well as socio-linguistic means.

Other conversations and action patterns are unique to certain geographic regions, cultures, or historical eras. Being born and raised in America, for example, means your body will be programmed with certain social and historical discourses that originated from our ancestors. In their highly acclaimed book, *Habits Of The Heart*, a team of sociologists headed by Robert Bellah outlined what they found to be the four main discourses underlying all of American life. According to these researchers, "cultures are dramatic conversations about things that matter to their participants, and American culture is no exception" (p.27). The four discourses they found to be associated with our unique character and identity as Americans are:

1) Individualism
2) Success
3) Freedom
4) Justice

The purpose of *Habits Of The Heart* was not just to extol the virtues of these cultural conversations, but to show how they cause us to experience certain problems and difficulties. For example, our belief in radical individualism often leads to the dissolution of family and community bonds and results in inner feelings of loneliness and isolation:

> American cultural traditions define personality, achievement, and the purpose of human life in ways that leave the individual suspended in glorious, but terrifying, isolation. These are limitations of our culture, of the categories and ways of thinking we have inherited, not limitations of individuals...who inhabit this culture. (p. 6)

5. *Your conversations and action patterns can make you "blind" to many truths about life.* Another benefit of Biolinguistics comes from recognizing that not only are the conversations and action patterns you inherit not of your choosing, they are frequently false and misleading. Even many long-standing scientific "facts" have turned out to be wrong many years later. William Osler, one of the most famous and respected physicians of the twentieth century, commented upon this phenomenon as follows:

> How eminent soever a man may become in science, he is very apt to carry with him errors which were in vogue when he was young—errors that darken his understanding, and make him incapable of accepting even the most obvious of truths.*

* From *The Collected Writings of Sir William Osler*, The Classics Of Medicine Library, 1985, volume 1.

6. *Internal conversations and action patterns are difficult to change or eliminate.* Another benefit of Biolinguistics comes from understanding that our internal conversations and action patterns are difficult to *change* or *eliminate*. This differs radically from our usual understanding. Once we assume something exists in our mind, we also tend to assume that we should be easily able to change, control, or eliminate it.

While it may be "normal" to want to change or eliminate your stress-producing patterns once you become aware of them, *you are actually expecting yourself to change or eliminate processes that are deeply ingrained in your body.* Just as it is impossible to "unlearn" how to ride a bicycle once your body has been programmed to do so, it is equally difficult to stop thinking negatively, stop perceiving events as threatening to your survival, stop judging and evaluating everything around you (including yourself), or otherwise change or eliminate patterns that have been part of your body for many years.

This also explains why new thoughts, ideas, and insights don't "stick" with us for very long. Unless our exposure to them is sufficient to alter our bodies, especially our brains and nervous systems, we will "forget" such new ideas very quickly. The type of "forgetting" is not due to inadequate "mental" effort on our part—it is a natural consequence of our existence as Biolinguistic organisms.

▶ NOTE: Another disadvantage of mind-body thinking is our belief that certain types of health problems are purely physical in nature—i.e. that they have little to do with our internal conversations, action patterns, or other ways in which we choose to live our lives (the story of Tom shows that the truth may be otherwise). This unfortunate assumption keeps many people from recognizing that they may have something to do with many of the physical problems they develop. (This subject is discussed in more detail in Chapter 12.)

7. *Internal conversations and action patterns are also difficult to stop or control.* Not only are our internal conversations and action patterns difficult to change or eliminate, they are also difficult to *stop* or *control*. When we feel angry, sad, fearful, or depressed, the conversations and action patterns that produce these emotions get triggered within us like "knee-jerk" reflexes. They are activated automatically by situations and events, and there is little we can do to keep this from happening.

Good News! You Don't Have To Stop, Change, Or Eliminate Your Internal Patterns

Even though you can't do much to change or eliminate your stress-producing patterns, you can learn to keep them from causing stress and tension in your life. In order to do this, however, it helps to know that they exist in your body, not your mind.

DAY 3: EXERCISES

1. *Imagine you sailed to the New World with Columbus in 1492. As a result, you learned that the earth is really round, not flat, as you had previously been taught to believe. Upon returning home, which of the following problems might you encounter when you tried to explain your new discovery to others? (Circle your responses.)*

  A. They would think you were crazy.
  B. They would accuse you of blasphemy.
  C. They would try to publicly discredit you.
  D. They would stop hanging around with you.
  E. All of the above

2. *Now imagine you just learned that human beings don't really have "minds." Which of the same problems do you think you would encounter if you tried to explain this new discovery to your family or friends?*

  A. They would think you were crazy.
  B. They would accuse you of blasphemy.
  C. They would try to publicly discredit you.
  D. They would stop hanging around with you.
  E. All of the above

3. *Here are some statements parents often say to their children. Check any you may have heard as a youngster:*

  ☐ "I'm sorry you were ever born."
  ☐ "You're no good."
  ☐ "You're lazy."
  ☐ "Why can't you ever do things right?"
  ☐ "That was a stupid thing to do."
  ☐ "You're never going to amount to very much."

4. *How do you think the above conversations would affect a child's:*

	Decrease	Increase	No Effect
A. Self-esteem	_____	_____	_____
B. Self-confidence	_____	_____	_____
C. Sense of trust	_____	_____	_____

5. *List three internal conversations or action patterns that you tried to change about yourself in the past but failed.*

Examples:

"I tried to stop thinking negative thoughts about other people."

"I tried to stop thinking negative thoughts about myself."

"I tried to be more organized."

(See Appendix A for further examples to choose from.)

A._____

B._____

C._____

6. *If you had known these tendencies were part of your body, not your mind, would you have still expected yourself to be able to change or eliminate them?*

A. ☐ YES ☐ NO
B. ☐ YES ☐ NO
C. ☐ YES ☐ NO

*　　*　　*　　*

Congratulations! You have just finished the most difficult part of this book. The reading gets easier from this point on, and the focus shifts from theory to practical application. Remember, you don't have to understand or agree with everything in chapters 1-3 to benefit from the coping method I will begin to discuss tomorrow.

DAY 4

THE ULTIMATE METHOD FOR COPING WITH STRESS

Which of the following coping strategies do you tend to use when you are troubled by "stress?":

☐ Ignore your "stress"
☐ Relax it away
☐ Exercise it away
☐ Drink some alcohol
☐ Take a tranquilizer
☐ Eat ice cream

☐ Smoke a cigarette
☐ Take a vacation
☐ Get a massage
☐ Take a hot bath
☐ Go shopping
☐ Go to sleep

While all of these strategies work from time to time, they rarely address the *causes* of your problems. As we have already seen, these causes lie mainly within you. The best way to cope with your stress, therefore, is to learn how to identify and deal with these internal causes effectively.

A Step-By-Step Approach

This chapter will introduce you to a step-by-step approach for coping with stress that I use in my own life and that I have taught to hundreds of patients in my medical practice. This method differs from stress management in several important ways:

1. It is a method for dealing with the *internal causes,* not just the symptoms, of your problems.

2. It is more *natural* and less *time-consuming* than stress management.
3. It can be used successfully with *any* type of stress.
4. It *empowers* you in other areas of your life as well.

In addition, unlike most stress management techniques, this method is *open-ended*. This means it doesn't tell you exactly what to think or exactly what to do. Instead, it gives you a *general approach* for solving any type of problem you encounter.

Here is the method in abbreviated form:

THE ULTIMATE METHOD FOR COPING WITH STRESS

STEP 1: *BE SPECIFIC*—Stop trying to deal with "stress" and identify the specific problem or problems that are troubling you.

STEP 2: *RELATE TO YOUR PROBLEMS AS "FEEDBACK"*— Consider that you may be partly the cause of any "stress" you are experiencing.

STEP 3: *IDENTIFY THE SPECIFIC CONVERSATIONS AND ACTION PATTERNS within you* that are causing your problem(s) to occur or persist.

STEP 4: *REMIND YOURSELF: THESE HIDDEN CAUSES EXIST IN YOUR BODY, NOT YOUR MIND.*

STEP 5: TAKE ACTION TO NEUTRALIZE THESE INTERNAL CAUSES—challenge stress-producing conversations, disrupt stress-producing action patterns, create stress-relieving contexts.

STEP 6: *IF YOUR "STRESS" DOESN'T DISAPPEAR, REPEAT STEPS 1-5 AND/OR GET COACHING.*

Consider the following example: One day, you ask a friend to do something important for you. Your friend agrees but doesn't follow through. When you find this out, you immediately feel "stressed." Here's how the method described above could help you cope with this problem:

Step 1: Be Specific!

Instead of trying to deal with "stress" per se, focus upon the specific problem or problems that are troubling you. In the example above, feeling "stressed" probably means you are angry.*

Step 2: Relate To Your Problems As "Feedback"

The next step is to consider your anger as "feedback." In other words, instead of assuming the other person's behavior (i.e. failing to do what was promised) is the major cause of your anger, *look within yourself* to identify its internal causes.

Relating to stress in this way gives you a special type of power and control. While you may have little direct control over external events in your life, you do have control over the conversations and action patterns that become triggered within you (the nature of this "control" will be discussed in Chapter 5).

Step 3: Identify The Specific Conversations And Action Patterns (Within You) That Are Causing Your Problems To Occur Or Persist.

From our Biolinguistic understanding of human moods and emotions, we already know the specific conversations and action patterns that produce anger in human beings (see pages 48-49):

Figure 4-1

The Internal Causes Of Anger In Human Beings

ANGER

Specific Conversations	*Specific Action Patterns*
1) _____	A) _____
2) _____	B) _____
3) _____	C) _____
4) _____	D) _____

* Each person experiences anger in his or her own way. Some people may not "feel" angry even though they are.

Let's examine the conversation part of this mechanism:

CONVERSATIONS:

1. *'Someone did something they shouldn't have done."* People should do what they promise. Therefore, it was definitely "wrong" of your friend to have done what he or she did.

2. *"Someone was hurt, harmed, humiliated, embarrassed, offended, disappointed, or otherwise inconvenienced by what was done."* At best, you may only have been disappointed; at worst, you could have suffered a serious consequence.

3. *"The other person (your friend) was unilaterally responsible (to blame) for their actions and any consequences you experienced."* This assumption of unilateral blame—and innocence on your part—is essential for the experience of anger.

4. *"The other person should acknowledge what he/she did wrong, offer to make amends, and/or be punished."* If the first three conversations above are assumed to be true, this conclusion logically follows.

In addition to these conversations, one or more of the following action patterns probably was triggered within you:

ACTION PATTERNS:

A. Failing to recognize how your own judgments, evaluations, and standards might not be valid for other people.

B. Failing to recognize how your own actions, past and present, may have contributed to what happened.

C. Justifying your anger, instead of looking within yourself for its internal causes.

D. Retaliating or seeking revenge, instead of openly and honestly dealing with what happened.

Step 4: Remind Yourself: These Hidden Causes Exist In Your Body, Not Your Mind

As you begin to identify the internal causes of your stress, always remember that they exist in your body, not your mind. This will keep you from feeling guilty, frustrated, angry, or depressed for repeatedly responding in such automatic ways.

Step 5: Take Action To Neutralize These Internal Causes.

Once you identify the internal causes of your anger, you can then neutralize them by using one or both of the following coping strategies:

1) *challenging* your stress-producing conversations;

2) *disrupting* your stress-producing action patterns.

If you apply these strategies correctly, your "stress" will quickly disappear without needing to use drugs, food, alcohol, physical exercise, meditation, biofeedback, or any other stress management technique.

▶ NOTE: At one time or another, everyone has used these coping strategies. For example, people will often say to me, "I just looked at my situation differently and my stress disappeared," or "I just took the bull by the horns and dealt with my situation, and in no time at all my stress went away!" Unfortunately, most of the time we use these strategies intuitively. We don't know how to use them consciously and intentionally, even though we are always capable of doing so.

Challenging Your Stress-Producing Conversations

As we learned in Chapter 3, much of our stress is caused by hidden conversations that produce false or misleading "realities" in our bodies. When you challenge and "disprove" a false internal "reality," most of the stress it is causing will quickly disappear. This well-known coping strategy has been advocated for many years. For example, cognitive therapists such as Aaron Beck and Albert Ellis have shown that "disputing" or "disconfirming" automatic thoughts and beliefs is an effective strategy for dealing with many types of depression (and other emotional problems as well). As we saw in Chapter 2, depressed people often suffer from a host of erroneous thoughts and beliefs, such as:

-"I'm not good enough."
-"I'm never going to amount to anything."
-"Nobody really cares about me."

-"Things are never going to get better."
-"Maybe it would be better if I were dead."

When people are helped to challenge and disprove these false internal "realities," their feelings of depression may be temporarily alleviated.

This same basic strategy can also be used with anger. In the example cited earlier, you became angry at your friend in large part because the following conversations became triggered in your body:

ANGER-PRODUCING CONVERSATIONS:

1. "Someone did something they shouldn't have done."
2. "Someone was hurt, harmed, inconvenienced, etc."
3. "The other person was unilaterally responsible (to blame) for #1 and #2.
4. "That person should admit he or she did something wrong, offer to make amends, and/or be punished.

If you examine and disprove any of these internal conversations, your anger will either lessen or completely disappear!

EXAMPLE A: Consider the first of these anger-producing conversations:

> Is it true your friend did something
> he or she shouldn't have done?

Suppose your friend was angry with you for something you did to them earlier. Perhaps you promised to do something and failed to keep your word, for instance. Might your friend's behavior—especially if it was unconsciously motivated—suddenly appear more understandable when viewed from this perspective?

► NOTE: What initially appears to us as "bad," "wrong," or "inappropriate" behavior often looks different once we appreciate the other person's point of view.

EXAMPLE B: What about the third anger-producing conversation?:

> Is it true your friend was unilaterally
> responsible (to blame) for what happened?

In other words, could you have played a role in causing his or her behavior? While this role will hardly ever be obvious to you, you may be able to detect it on further reflection. Here are just a few possible scenarios:

-As noted above, you might have done something to hurt, harm, or anger the other person, who is now getting back at you, either consciously or unconsciously.

-You might have known the importance of what you requested, but perhaps you didn't communicate this importance clearly.

-When your friend agreed to do what you asked, you may have sensed some hesitation, but you chose to ignore this.

-Perhaps your friend misunderstood what you wanted, and you didn't confirm their understanding.

If any of these scenarios were even partly true, then you, as well as the other person, had something to do with the way things turned out. Once you can see the role you played in the problem, your feelings of anger will usually subside.

EXAMPLE C: Has this ever happened to you: you're driving down a highway and another motorist slowly pulls out in front of you, causing you to slam on your brakes to avoid a collision? Don't you usually feel angry toward this person and accuse him or her of being "reckless" and "inconsiderate"? I used to get furious when motorists did this to me, until one day I noticed that I was usually driving 60-70 miles an hour whenever this occurred. As soon as I recognized my own role in causing the near-collision, I could no longer remain angry with the person who pulled out in front of me. In fact, I could remember similar times when I had done the very same thing, thinking I had plenty of time to get out into traffic only to find that the person bearing down on me was going much faster than I had estimated.

Disrupting Your Stress-Producing Action Patterns

In addition to internal conversations, many action patterns also contribute to our "stress." Depressed individuals, for example, often behave in ways that confirm their negative outlooks. They withdraw from social interactions, fail to ask for help, cut themselves off from sources of support, and refuse to go out in public until they are feeling better about themselves.

Some depression-prone individuals, however, have learned to go against (i.e. disrupt) their automatic behavior patterns. When they feel depressed, they don't necessarily follow what their body "tells" them to do. Often, they will force themselves to go out with other people. They may also force themselves to pay more attention to—and follow—other people's suggestions and advice. In any event, they will keep doing things in their lives regardless of how they feel.

EXAMPLE: I remember one young woman who suddenly stopped being depressed after three months of near total inactivity. When I asked her what had happened to turn things around, she said:

> One day I noticed myself thinking 'I can't go out and do things until I'm feeling better about myself.' After thinking this over for a while I suddenly realized 'That's a lot of bull!' So I got out of bed, got dressed, forced myself to go shopping, and I've been going out every day since.

With regard to the problem of anger, sometimes it is our actions or lack of actions—more so than our internal conversations—that cause this emotion to occur.

EXAMPLE: A patient once complained to me that he was having "a terrible time" with his auto mechanic. Every time he took his car in for repairs, either the job wasn't done right or something new would go wrong almost immediately. The problem was further complicated because the mechanic was his brother-in-law. When I asked why he didn't just change to a new mechanic, he replied, "I'm afraid of hurting my brother-in-law's feelings, and my wife would never forgive me." Thus, by continuing to take his car back to the same mechanic, he was behaving in a way that caused his problems to persist. No matter how much he dealt with his anger-producing conversations, his car wasn't going to run well until he took some different actions.*

* This example underscores that simply dealing with your "thoughts" and "cognitions" (i.e. your internal conversations) is not always sufficient to eliminate certain types of stress.

► NOTE: Additional tips on challenging your internal conversations and disrupting your behavior patterns will be presented in Chapter 6.

Stress-Relieving Contexts

A third important strategy for making stress disappear naturally is to create stress-relieving contexts. Contexts are *guiding principles or "meanings"* that we add to life. In addition to the contexts that occur for us automatically—i.e. the ones that have been "programmed" into our bodies—*we also have the ability to invent new contexts and guiding principles* that can help us reduce our "stress." This is the "good news" about being Biolinguistic. Even though we are programmed to view life in many inaccurate ways, we can use the creative power of language to compensate for our deficiencies.

EXAMPLE: Relating to stress as "feedback"—assuming you play some role in any stress you experience—is a context you can create. You can also choose to live in accordance with this principle, even if it goes against what you are normally programmed to do.

For dealing with anger, the following contexts are often very helpful:

ANGER-REDUCING CONTEXTS:

-"There is no such thing as a stressful situation."
-"Negative statements about other people are rarely true."
-"Negative statements about life are rarely true."
-"People always make the best decisions they can, given the information available to them at the time."

As you will learn in Chapter 7, these and other contexts can serve as powerful "antidotes" for the conversations and action patterns that cause your stress to occur.

Step 6: If Your Stress Doesn't Disappear, Repeat Steps 1-5 And/Or Get Coaching

The method we have been discussing can be graphically illustrated as follows:

Figure 4-2

THE ULTIMATE METHOD FOR COPING WITH STRESS

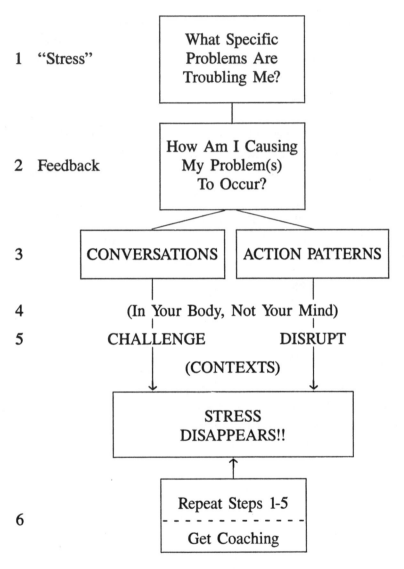

If you correctly execute the first five steps in this method, your stress will greatly diminish or completely disappear. If your stress doesn't go away, or if it only partially disappears, you may need to repeat one or more steps in the sequence.

Remember, one feature of this approach is that it is highly open-ended—i.e. it doesn't tell you exactly what to think or exactly what to do. It merely gives you a framework for dealing with your problems effectively. It's up to you to "fill in the blanks" each step along the way. This open-ended feature allows you to use this method successfully for any type of problem you encounter, but it also allows you to use the method poorly—to make false assumptions, select inappropriate strategies, or create foolish or unrealistic contexts. All these mistakes can be corrected as you go along. (The more you practice with this approach, the fewer mistakes you will make.)

EXAMPLE: Suppose you tried to use this approach to deal with your feelings of anger (in any situation). If you completed the first five steps but still felt angry, one of the following probably went wrong:

a) you weren't really angry but were experiencing some other negative mood or emotion, such as frustration, disappointment, or sadness; or b) you didn't identify the hidden causes of your anger correctly; or c) you may have thought you challenged or disrupted your anger-producing patterns, but in your heart you still believe they are justified; or d) other aspects of the truth about your situation still remain hidden from your view.

Sometimes you will be able to correct these mistakes by repeating steps 1-5 on your own. If you try this but still feel angry, *get coaching*. Find a friend or confidant and explain the situation to them. Since they may have a different viewpoint about what happened, they can often open your eyes to other interpretations or insights that might not have occurred to you.

Or you could ask the person involved—for example, the friend who forgot to do what you asked—to help you out. You could go to that person and say, "I'm really having trouble understanding what happened. Is there anything I may have done that hurt or offended you in the past? Were you upset with me for some other reason?" (These types of questions commonly emerge when you adopt a "feedback" perspective.) You'd be amazed how often this strategy pays off. When you give people the chance, they will usually—but not always—tell you how they feel.

Coaching, therefore, is another valuable strategy you can use to deal with your stress. It's value comes from recognizing that many of our internal conversations and action patterns are invisible to us.

These patterns are so much a part of the background of our thinking and behaving that it is often very difficult for us to spot them on our own. As I explain in Chapter 8 (Coaching), you don't always need to hire a professional to obtain such help. Many people in your life could serve as excellent coaches for you, provided you know how to select them and use them wisely. (The issue of how to select and use a coach wisely will also be explained in Chapter 8.)

Other Types Of Stress

In addition to anger, fear, sadness, guilt, worry, impatience, and other negative moods and emotions, the step-by-step method described in this chapter can be used to deal with:

a) relationship problems;
b) stress at work;
c) physical symptoms and illnesses;
d) financial stress;
e) the stress of raising children;
f) any other problem.

Let's look at a common example of relationship stress.

EXAMPLE: Suppose you are married or have been living with some-one, and you begin to lose your feelings of love and affection for that person. Suppose he or she begins to "grate on your nerves" or no longer appears as wonderful, witty, attractive, or sexy as before.

Most people tend to blame the other person for such problems. Perhaps they think they made a mistake and chose the wrong mate, or their partner changed, or maybe they just "fell out of love" or became attracted to someone else who appears to be more loving or desirable.

People who know how to win against stress, in contrast, wouldn't approach the problem in this way. First, they would get more specific. What *exactly* do they dislike about their partner? What specific behaviors do they find offensive? Has that person broken any major promises or commitments? Are feelings of anger, hurt, disappoint-ment, or fear involved? Is their partner aware of their negative feel-ings and concerns? How does their partner respond to such communications?

Next, they would relate to their loss of love and affection as "feedback." In other words, they would *look within themselves* to determine its primary causes. They wouldn't simply blame the other person, nor would they conclude that they had just "fallen out of love." Instead, they would look for conversations and action patterns within themselves that might have contributed to their change in feelings. These might include:

Conversations:

-GOOD/BAD
-RIGHT/WRONG
-CAUSE/EFFECT
-CREDIT/BLAME
-RESIGNATION
-CONTROL

Behavior Patterns:

-FAILING TO DEAL WITH "LITTLE" PROBLEMS
-TRYING TO CHANGE OTHERS
-FAILING TO MAKE REQUESTS OR DEMANDS OF OTHERS
-FAILING TO ASSESS THE COMMITMENT OF OTHERS
-FAILING TO ADMIT YOU MAY BE WRONG

Having identified these or other internal patterns, they would then try to challenge or disrupt them. In addition, they might also adopt one or more of the following relationship-enhancing contexts:

-"If I'm having relationship problems of any kind, I must be somehow creating these."
-"The best way to get love is to give love."
-"Whatever happens in life and in my relationships can be used to my advantage."

If none of these strategies improved their situation, they would ask for coaching. They would seek help from other people to identify additional hidden causes or other coping strategies they may have overlooked.

► NOTE: While some relationship problems may be primarily your partner's fault, most of the time both you and your partner share the blame equally. By following the step-by-step approach outlined in this chapter, either of you could improve your ability to recognize your own role in causing such relationship problems to occur. This awareness will greatly improve your chances of resolving such problems successfully.

Typical Questions And Concerns

Here are some of the typical questions and concerns people have when they are first introduced to this coping method.

Won't I Feel Worse If I Blame Myself For Causing My Stress?

The approach I have just described is very different from blaming yourself for being the cause of your stress. The truth about human beings is that we almost always contribute—in one way or another—to the "stress" we experience. This doesn't mean that external situations and events play no role at all. Clearly they do. But usually we can recognize these external factors without too much difficulty. In contrast, we often fail to recognize how our own internal conversations and action patterns also play a role. The aim of this step-by-step approach is to empower you to *identify* and *deal with* these internal causes more successfully. Since they exist to some degree in all of us, whether we notice them or not, there should be no shame, blame, guilt, or humiliation in acknowledging their presence.

Must I Use This Method To Deal With Every Type Of Stress?

You don't have to use this method to deal with every minor problem you experience. When I have a headache, for example, I usually try to ignore it. If that doesn't work, I might take Tylenol or aspirin. If I started having headaches every day, however, I would definitely use this approach, in conjunction with a good medical evaluation. Even if my headaches turned out to be due to some physical condition, I would still use the step-by-step approach outlined in this chapter to explore how I might have contributed to the development of this condition and, more importantly, how I might possibly be able to alleviate it. (This issue of how you can use this method to deal with physical symptoms and problems is discussed in Chapter 12.)

Should I Stop Using Exercise, Relaxation Procedures, Or Other Stress Management Techniques?

No. By introducing you to this alternative approach, I don't mean to imply that you should completely abandon stress management. You can combine both approaches or use either one alone. If all you want to do is deal with the symptoms of your problems, then stress management is an excellent way to go. But if you want to make your stress disappear naturally—and possibly learn to keep it from reoccurring—you must understand that stress management won't do this for you. The only way to do so is by learning how to recognize and deal with the hidden causes of your problems.

Should I Stop Taking My "Nerve" Pills, Tranquilizers, Antidepressants, Or Other Prescription Medicines?

No. Not right away, sometimes not at all, and certainly *not without first consulting with your physician or other health care provider.* While the method described in this book can help you get rid of your stress without using drugs, relaxation exercises, or stress management techniques, it often takes time before you can safely abandon your previous coping strategies. Prescription medications, such as tranquilizers, anti-anxiety drugs, anti-depressants, blood pressure pills, and sleeping pills, *should never be stopped or reduced* on your own. Some people may eventually be able to go off all drugs completely, while others may need to, or choose to, remain on medications for the rest of their lives.

How Will I Know If I've Used The Method Correctly?

There's a very simple way to know if you've used this method correctly:

> YOUR "STRESS" WILL EITHER LESSEN
> OR COMPLETELY DISAPPEAR!

You will feel much better, your actions will be more effective, and your life will improve in many other ways. In addition, you will know that you have learned something important about yourself, or about life, that will be useful for dealing with similar problems in the future.

How Does This Approach Differ From Cognitive Or Behavioral Therapy?

The method I describe in this chapter is similar in some ways to cognitive and behavioral therapy. Many of the conversations and action patterns I discuss, for instance, have been recognized by other people. In addition, both cognitive and behavioral therapists also work with people's bodies, not their "minds." The difference is that they often don't appreciate that's what they are doing. They also fail to educate their clients about the benefits of abandoning mind-body models.

Is There Any Scientific Evidence To Support This Coping Method?

While most previous studies have focused on stress management techniques, a recent study published in *Behavioral Medicine* compared the value of traditional vs. Biolinguistic interventions. This study involved 80 volunteers of a health maintenance organization (HMO) in the greater Boston area. All volunteers, who were referred by their physicians, suffered from high levels of stress or "psychosomatic" illnesses.

This study compared the effectiveness of three different group treatment approaches on reducing the number of patient visits to doctors as well as reducing both physical and psychological discomfort. Each group met one evening a week for 2-6 weeks, and all subjects were tested both before and 6 months after completing their respective programs. The three treatment approaches were: 1) giving people information about how to manage their stress (Information group), 2) using cognitive and behavioral exercises based upon a mind-body model (Mind/Body group), and 3) using cognitive and behavioral exercises based upon a Biolinguistic model (Ways To Wellness group). The Ways To Wellness program, which was developed several years ago by Dr. Matthew Budd of the Harvard Medical School, differed from the other two approaches in that it was designed to "help patients understand how language shapes the world that they see and how they can learn to see and interpret differently what is happening in the moment-to-moment state of their bodies."*

At the conclusion of this study, both the Mind/Body group and the Ways To Wellness group showed significant improvements in all three outcome measures (patient visits, physical discomfort, and psychological discomfort), whereas the Information group showed *no improvement* in any of these measures. The Ways To Wellness group, however, showed greater reductions than the Mind/Body group in the first two outcome measures and equal reductions in the third.

Additional Explanations

In the next four chapters, I will provide you with additional explanations of this step-by-step coping method. From time to time, you may want to review these four chapters to refresh your memory of the insights and tools they contain.

* From *Behavioral Medicine*, Winter 1990, p.167.

DAY 4: EXERCISES

1. A. *What do you do when one of the warning lights on the dash-board of your car begins flashing?*

_____

_____

_____

   B. *How does this compare to the way you deal with symptoms of "stress" when they begin to appear in your body?*

   ☐ I do the same.
   ☐ I do something similar.
   ☐ I do something different.

2. *Recall the last time you felt "stressed." Write down whatever you remember.*

_____

_____

_____

   A. *Imagine that external causes were largely responsible for the problem(s) you listed above.*

   ☐ Check here when you have done this.

   B. *Now, imagine that internal causes—conversations and action patterns within you—were largely responsible. (See Appendix A for specific examples.)*

   ☐ Check here when you have done this.

   C. *Now, imagine that both external and internal causes were jointly responsible.*

   ☐ Check here when you have done this.

3. A. *Think of three negative things about yourself that others have pointed out to you. (Write them down below).*

1. _____

2. _____

3. _____

   B. *Are you sure these are really "negative?"*

   1. ☐ YES ☐ NO ☐ NOT SURE
   2. ☐ YES ☐ NO ☐ NOT SURE
   3. ☐ YES ☐ NO ☐ NOT SURE

   C. *If any of your answers in part B were "yes," see if you can challenge or dispute your conclusion.*

4. A. *What do you think it takes to have a successful, long-term, loving relationship? (Check all that you believe apply).*

   ☐ Luck
   ☐ Finding the perfect mate
   ☐ Money
   ☐ Good sex
   ☐ Frequent communication
   ☐ Common interests
   ☐ Common values
   ☐ Having strong loving feelings for each other

   B. *How would you feel if you found out some of your answers were wrong?*

   ☐ I would feel terrible.
   ☐ I would feel stupid.
   ☐ I would feel excited.
   ☐ Regardless of how I feel, I would be interested.

DAY 5

IDENTIFYING HIDDEN CAUSES

The first three steps in the method described in Chapter 4 can be summarized as follows:

Figure 5-1

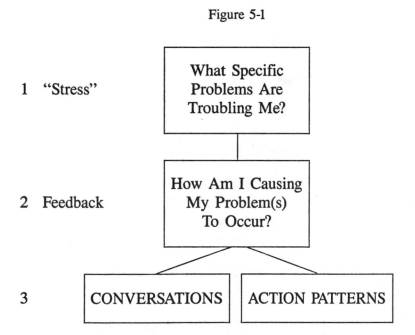

These three steps, which are the focus of this chapter, enable you identify the hidden causes of your stress. In Chapter 6, we will look at how to challenge your internal conversations and how to disrupt your stress-producing action patterns, once you have identified them.

Chapter 7 focuses on creating stress-relieving contexts, and Chapter 8 examines the importance of coaching as a strategy for winning against stress.

Step 1: Be Specific

The purpose of this step is to help you look at your problems more closely, separate them, clarify them, and focus upon them individually. Specifying your problems is not always easy. Over the years, I have found the following guidelines to be helpful:

• *Avoid non-specific terms.* Never define your problems as "feeling bad," "feeling upset," or "feeling stressed." These terms are much too vague. Whenever you feel "stressed," ask yourself if you are:

-feeling bad physically, emotionally, or both?
-feeling angry, sad, anxious, worried, or depressed?
-having financial problems, relationship problems, work-related problems, problems with your children, etc.?
-worried about something specific or everything in general?
-feeling "bad" all the time or just in certain situations?
-Etc.

The more specific you can be about your problems, the easier it will be to pinpoint their underlying causes.

• *Separate your problems into internal and external components.* Multiple problems, both internal and external, usually contribute to our "stress." Because we tend to "lump" our problems together, it is often very useful to consciously separate them.

▶ NOTE: This would be a good time to review the list of internal and external problems presented in Chapter 1 (see pages 6-7).

The problem "you made me angry," for example, can be separated into internal and external components:

a) the other person did what they did *(external);*

b) you responded by becoming angry *(internal).*

When you fail to make this distinction, you may find it difficult to deal with your anger successfully.

- *Separate what happens in life (facts) from your internal judgements, interpretations, and evaluations about what happened.*

EXAMPLE: Each of the following statements combines an external event or circumstance (fact) with a judgement or evaluation *added by the observing individual:*

-"The weather is terrible today." (The weather is what it is, and you judged it to be *terrible.*)

-"Someone did something wrong." (They did what they did, and you judged it to be *wrong.*)

-"Someone did something stupid." (They did what they did, and you judged it to be *stupid.*)

In addition to external events, things that happen inside our bodies, such as thoughts, feelings, moods, emotions, and other sensations, can also trigger judgments and evaluations:

-"I shouldn't be having these thoughts."
-"I shouldn't be having these feelings."
-"Maybe I'm having a heart attack."

Thus, separating your internal judgements and evaluations from other events that occur—both inside and outside your body—can also help you clarify the true nature of your problems.

- *Separate superficial problems from core issues and concerns.* Many of our superficial problems and conflicts arise from deeper issues and concerns that often go unnoticed. For example, spouses may have numerous superficial complaints about each other, which actually stem from deeper core issues such as:

-What is each person committed to in the relationship?
-What are each person's expectations of the other?
-What are each person's views about marriage in general?
-Does each person know what it takes to create a happy, loving, long-term relationship?

Unless these core issues are recognized and addressed, it may be difficult for couples to resolve many of the superficial problems that trouble them.

Step 2: Relate To Your Problems As "Feedback"

Most of us can easily recognize the external causes of our "stress." We are usually quite "blind," however, to the *internal* causes of our suffering. This second step is designed to help you compensate for this common type of blindness.

Instead of asking yourself "What external factors are causing my stress to occur?," you execute this step by asking:

> How Am I Causing
> My Problem(s) To
> Occur?

While this probably differs from what you normally tend to do, it is a powerful coping strategy that is used by many individuals.* It is also used, from time to time, by just about everyone.

EXAMPLE: Consider how you relate to the warning lights on the dashboard of your car. When one of these lights begins flashing, do you take your car to the nearest service station and ask for someone to disconnect the wires to the bulb? Of course not. The reason you don't behave in this way is because you automatically relate to these flashing lights as "feedback" signals—i.e. as helpful *warning messages*—that something else might be wrong with your car that is not immediately apparent to you.

When you "manage" or control the symptoms of your stress, on the other hand, you are essentially "disconnecting the wires to the bulb." You are ignoring the warning signs that something may be wrong with your own internal conversations and action patterns. Thus, when you deal only with the symptoms of your stress, you guarantee that many of your problems will continue to occur.

The best way to deal with any type of "stress," therefore, is to consciously choose to relate to it as "feedback"—as a useful warning message that hidden conversations and action patterns within you are contributing to your problems.

* "Feedback" approaches have been part of Eastern religions and healing systems for thousands of years.

Relating to "stress" in this way enables you to draw upon a special type of personal control. When most people try to deal with their stress, they do so in ordinary ways. They work very hard to change or control the circumstances of their lives—their environment; their job; the behavior of others; their own internal thoughts, feelings, and behaviors; etc. There are two major problems with this ordinary type of control: 1) this control is not always available to us; and 2) it can be physically and emotionally draining.

Choosing to relate to your stress as "feedback," in contrast, enables you to take advantage of a different type of personal control. This type of control is *extraordinary* because:

A) it is always available to you, regardless of your circumstances;
B) it is always within your power to utilize (it is not dependent upon the cooperation or permission of others);
C) it is aimed at the internal causes of your stress, not the external situations or causes of your problems.*

Extraordinary Personal Control

```
• Independent of circumstances

• Always within your power

• Internally focused
```

EXAMPLE: An interesting historical example of this type of control comes from concentration camp survivors. Stripped of the ordinary types of control available to most other people, some concentration camp inmates were able to cope by other means. Viktor Frankl, a psychiatrist who was imprisoned at Auschwitz during WWII, wrote about this phenomenon in a book titled *Man's Search For Meaning*. Frankl observed that many prisoners quickly lost faith in their ability to carry on:

> The thought of suicide was entertained by nearly everyone, if only for a brief time. It was born of the hopelessness of the situation, the constant danger of death looming over us daily and hourly, and the closeness of the deaths suffered by many of the others. (p. 27)

* Often, by gaining more control over the internal causes of your problems, you will find it easier to improve your external circumstances as well.

A few prisoners, however, managed to cope much better. Instead of worrying about their own predicament and survival, they chose to dedicate themselves to taking care of others:

> We who lived in concentration camps can remember the men who walked through the huts comforting others, giving away their last piece of bread. They may have been few in number, but they offer sufficient proof that everything can be taken from a man but one thing: the last of the human freedoms—to choose one's attitude in any given set of circumstances, to choose one's own way. . . .
>
> Even though conditions such as lack of sleep, insufficient food and various mental stresses may suggest that the inmates were bound to react in certain ways, in the final analysis it becomes clear that the sort of person the prisoner became was the result of an inner decision, and not the result of camp influences alone. Fundamentally, therefore, any man can, even under such circumstances, decide what shall become of him—mentally and spiritually. He may retain his human dignity even in a concentration camp. (pp-104.105)

Frankl is describing what I call extraordinary personal control. The best way to exercise this extraordinary type of control is to:

LOOK WITHIN YOURSELF TO IDENTIFY THE INTERNAL CAUSES OF YOUR PROBLEMS

► TIP: Don't expect to benefit from this approach right away. In fact, the first few times you try it, you may need to *pretend* you are the cause of your stress in order to discover its value. Later on, after you've had some success using this "feedback" approach, you won't need to pretend anymore—you will know from personal experience that it is an extremely useful perspective to adopt.

Step 3: Identify The Specific Conversations And Action Patterns Within You That Are Causing Your Problems To Occur Or Persist

Once the internal causes of your stress have been brought to your attention, you can then do something about them. As long as they remain hidden from your view, there is little you can do to deal with them effectively. While identifying your internal conversations and action patterns might seem like a formidable task, it is not really as difficult as most people think. Here are some suggestions that can make this step easier:

• *Use the master lists of conversations and action patterns located in Appendix A.* Whenever you experience any type of stress in your life, turn to this appendix. Here you will find two important lists which include most of the internal conversations and action patterns that cause stress to occur for human beings.*

► NOTE: When you scan these lists for the very first time, you can sometimes feel confused or overwhelmed. Many of the terms have not yet been explained, and the sheer number of causes can be difficult to take in all at once. Therefore, don't be concerned if you have such feelings or if you don't understand every item on these lists. By the time you finish the book, they will all be very familiar to you.

► NOTE: Also, don't be concerned about the amount of redundancy and overlap you notice on both of these lists. The conversation CREDIT/BLAME, for example, is actually a composite of three other conversations—GOOD/BAD, RIGHT/WRONG, and CAUSE/EFFECT—that are also listed separately. Similarly, UNREALISTIC EXPECTATIONS and NEGATIVE THINKING are category headings for a multitude of conversations, some of which are also listed separately.

You can use these master lists in several ways. For instance, as you discover which patterns occur for you most frequently, you can circle them or otherwise highlight them for future reference. When you return to these lists for help with a particular problem, you can focus in on your highlighted items first.

Another way to use these two lists is to convert each item into a question, or set of questions, for exploring any problem or conflict you are experiencing. Beginning with the list of stress-producing conversations, for example, you could ask yourself:

-Am I judging some event to be "bad" or "good" in any way?
-Am I assuming I am right and other people are wrong or vice versa?
-Do I believe I am a victim (effect) of my circumstances (cause)?
-Do I believe I am a victim (effect) of other people's behavior (cause)?
-Am I blaming myself or others for something that went wrong?

---

* Obviously, these master lists do not contain every conversation or action pattern that contributes to human stress, but they do contain the ones that are generally most common.

Conversations like "Perfectionism" and "Control" could prompt you to ask yourself:

Perfectionism

1) Am I expecting myself to think, feel, or behave perfectly in any way?
2) Am I expecting others to think, feel, or behave perfectly?

Control

1) Am I trying to change or control something that is difficult or impossible to control? (General)
2) Am I trying to change or control something *outside* of me that is difficult or impossible to control?
3) Am I trying to change or control something *inside* of me that is difficult or impossible to control?

...and so on. In my experience, once people begin to ask such focused questions, they are able to notice many patterns of thinking and behaving that previously escaped their attention.

• *Know which conversations and action patterns are most likely to be involved.* While the master lists in Appendix A contain 65 different internal causes, most of our stress results from a few common conversations and action patterns. For instance, when I begin to experience "stress" in my life, I usually look for the following conversations:

Good/Bad	Right/Wrong	Cause/Effect
Credit/Blame	Perfectionism	Control

| Unrealistic Expectations | Negative Thinking | Forgive/Punish |

I also look for the following action patterns:

| Failing To Challenge Internal "Realities" | Failing To Relate To Stress As "Feedback" | Failing To Clarify Agreements & Expectations |

| Failing To Assess Commitment Of Others | Failing To Admit You May Be Wrong | Failing To Ask For Help |

| Trying To Change Others | Trying To Control The Wrong Things | Invalidating Others' Opinions & Points Of View |

• *Use The Index Card Technique.* Another way to identify the internal causes of your stress is to use index cards, especially for your negative moods and emotions. In other words, if you are feeling angry, frustrated, anxious, or sad, you can use the Index Card Technique to remind yourself of the hidden causes of these feelings.

Here's how the technique works. Once you know the conversations and action patterns responsible for any mood or emotion, write these patterns down on an index card and carry the card around with you. (Removable cards for six common negative moods and emotions are located in Appendix D.) Whenever one of these moods or emotions occurs, pull out the appropriate index card and review its contents. This will remind you of the specific conversations and action patterns that *must have become triggered within you,* whether you are aware of them or not.

▶ TIP: It may not always be practical for you to look at your index cards when you are emotionally involved in a given situation. Once you are removed from the situation, however, take out your cards and review what happened earlier. This will help you better understand why you felt the way you did, even if your mood or emotion has already disappeared.

Remember, the Index Card Technique is only good for *observing* the hidden causes of your negative moods and emotions. It is *not* a technique for getting rid of these feelings, even though this sometimes happens just from gaining a better understanding of their causes.

• *Know which patterns cause certain types of problems to occur.* For instance, if you often end up with more work than you can handle, you are probably under the influence of conversations such as "I've got to do it myself" or "People can't be trusted" or action patterns such as FAILING TO DELEGATE, FAILING TO PRIORITIZE, or FAILING TO DECLINE REQUESTS OR DEMANDS FROM OTHERS. If you are frequently late for important meetings or events, it is likely you either lose track of time, underestimate your travel requirements, try to accomplish too many things before leaving, or FAIL TO ANTICIPATE UNEXPECTED BREAKDOWNS AND DELAYS. Similarly, if people become angry with you on more than an occasional basis, certain conversations and action patterns (within you) are probably contributing to this outcome. Maybe you are insensitive or domineering in your interactions with others. Or perhaps you have a pattern of FAILING TO KEEP YOUR PROMISES or of FAILING TO ADMIT YOU MAY BE WRONG. Thus, you can sometimes figure out the hidden causes of your stress by asking yourself "What types of patterns would be necessary to cause such problems to occur?"

Once you detect a link between a particular problem or outcome and a specific internal conversation or action pattern, you can draw upon this knowledge in future situations.

EXAMPLE: Years ago, when I first started my medical practice, I frequently became angry with my patients whenever they refused to follow my medical advice. This would especially occur if my advice was clearly beneficial—stop smoking, exercise more, lose weight, take this medicine exactly as prescribed—and it was either resisted or ignored.

One evening, an event took place that helped me realize how one of my own internal patterns contributed to this problem. On that evening, I received an urgent phone call while out having dinner with some friends. The call was from an elderly patient of mine who had recently recovered from a heart attack. He was beginning to experience chest pains again, and he wanted to know what I thought he should do. After questioning him at length about his pain, I concluded that it wasn't coming from his heart, but rather it was due to a hiatal hernia (a protrusion of the upper part of the stomach into the lower chest cavity) which he also had. I advised him to take some antacids after meals and at bedtime, but no matter how many times I repeated these instructions, he couldn't comprehend them or give them back to me correctly. After several more attempts, I finally became so angry and frustrated with this man that I yelled into the phone "I can't believe you're being so stupid right now; these are not difficult instructions so please pay attention!" Eventually, he got a piece of paper and wrote down my directions. I returned to my dinner, but the memory of this call continued to bother me.

A few days later, I realized that this man's difficulty remembering my instructions wasn't due to stupidity at all. Having just recovered from a heart attack, he was probably terrified by having chest pains again. It was fear, therefore, not stupidity, that had caused all the trouble. Viewing his behavior as "stupid" was an error on my part— an error that resulted from my own STUPID/SMART pattern of thinking which automatically became triggered within me in such situations. This internal pattern caused me to: 1) misperceive what was really happening for this man, and 2) respond in a manner that was harsh and inappropriate. (Had I recognized he was terrified, I would have empathized with his plight and could have done something to reassure him instead of failing to acknowledge his fear.)

As a result of this insight, I decided to view all future instances of anger toward my patients as a *feedback* that my own STUPID/SMART pattern had probably become triggered within me. This strategy worked like a charm. From then on, whenever I became angry with a patient, I used this as a signal to search for fear or some other concern that the person might not be expressing. Thus, by knowing that my anger was associated with my own STUPID/SMART pattern of thinking, I was able to "defuse" much of this anger whenever it occurred. I was also able to develop a greater understanding of, and appreciation for, the unspoken fears and concerns of my patients.

The Hidden Picture Analogy

Pinpointing the hidden causes of your stress is much like playing a hidden picture game in a children's magazine. These games consist of a picture that contains numerous hidden objects. A list of these hidden objects is included with the picture, and the purpose of the game is to identify each of the objects on this list. Most people find, when they are helped to focus their attention in this way, that they can locate all the hidden objects without too much trouble—although on several occasions I was sure at least one had been omitted!

Many of the strategies and tools presented in this book—such as the Index Card Technique and the Master Lists of conversations and action patterns in Appendix A—function just like the helpful list of objects at the bottom of these games. They tell you *exactly* what types of hidden patterns to look for, and if you search for these patterns hard enough, you will usually find they are there.

More About The Index Card Technique

Since the Index Card Technique is such a powerful and helpful tool, I want to make sure you know how to use it properly. For the purpose of this discussion, let's consider the emotion of *frustration*—a common source of stress and tension in our lives.

Here are the conversations and action patterns that cause frustration to occur in human beings:

FRUSTRATION-PRODUCING CONVERSATIONS

1) I am not succeeding.
2) I should easily be able to succeed in this situation.
3) If I just keep trying harder and harder, I will eventually succeed.
4) If I don't succeed, I must be dumb, stupid, weak, or incompetent.

FRUSTRATION-PRODUCING ACTION PATTERNS

1) Failing to recognize unrealistic goals and expectations.
2) Failing to challenge your definition of "success."

3) Failing to relate to your "failures" as "feedback."
4) Failing to admit: a) you may not know how to succeed, or
   b) you might need help from others.

▶ NOTE: Even if you are frustrated because other people are not succeeding—for example, your favorite sports team has been losing—the conversations and action patterns listed above still apply. If you didn't have *personal* goals and ambitions that were thwarted, other people's failures wouldn't bother you very much.

When I treat patients for frustration, I give them an index card with the preceeding conversations printed on one side and the corresponding action patterns printed on the other. I then teach them to use this card in the following manner:

EXAMPLE: Suppose you had never used a computer before, but one day you decide to teach yourself to do so. You go to a store, buy a personal computer, complete with software, and then try to use it by reading the accompanying manuals. In no time at all, you begin to feel frustrated. Whenever you make a mistake or can't get your programs to run correctly, you become very critical of either yourself or the computer.

What are your options for dealing with this problem? (If you don't like this computer example, substitute learning to play a new sport, perform a new job, or master any other task that requires skills you don't already have). Some of your options include: a) smashing the computer with an ax; b) yelling and screaming for a while; c) hitting a punching bag; or d) using some type of stress management technique. To use the step-by-step approach outlined in this book, however, you would first have to admit that you are not suffering from "stress" at all. Rather, you are suffering from *frustration,* a very specific emotion with specific internal causes. You would then need to look within yourself to pinpoint these hidden causes. Here's where the Index Card Technique comes in handy:

1) Instead of yelling, screaming, or venting your feelings of frustration, take out your index card for this emotion and review its contents. Begin with the conversation side of the card and read each statement carefully. As you do this, confirm that you are indeed looking at, or responding to, your situation in exactly the ways stated on the card:

Q: *Am I automatically assuming I am not succeeding?*
A: "YES—I am clearly not succeeding at getting my programs to run. I am also not succeeding at learning to use my computer."

Q: *Do I expect that I should easily be able to succeed?*
A: "YES—I thought it would be easy to learn how to do this, especially with the help of the manuals. I've succeeded at other tasks that were much more complicated, and besides, even a four-year old can learn to use a computer."

Q: *Do I believe that if I just keep trying harder and harder I will eventually succeed?*
A: "YES"—If at first you don't succeed, try, try again. Isn't this the way everyone ultimately succeeds? I've used this strategy successfully in the past, so why shouldn't it work again?"

Q: *When I don't succeed, do I interpret this to mean I must be dumb, stupid, weak, or incompetent?*
A: "YES"—I suppose I automatically make these assumptions, even though I know they probably aren't true.

▶ NOTE: Even though you know "intellectually" that a particular conversation is not really true, that conversation can still become triggered in your body. Unconscious conversations in your body frequently take precedence over your conscious thoughts and beliefs.

2) After confirming each statement on the conversation side of the card, turn the card over and do the same for each action pattern listed:

Q: *Have I examined my goals and expectations to see if they are realistic?*
Q: *Have I examined the appropriateness of my definition of "success?"*
Q: *Am I relating to my lack of success as a "failure" instead of "feedback?"*
Q: *Have I acknowledged that I may not know how to succeed or that I could possibly benefit from the help of others?*

3) Once you complete such a review, *you will know exactly why you feel frustrated.* It's not just because your computer didn't run correctly, but rather because you interpreted and responded to this event in a particular way. Whether you are frustrated about not being able

to use a computer, operate some other mechanical device, play tennis, control your child's behavior, or get your point across while communicating with another person, you always feel frustrated for the same internal reasons. You feel frustrated because *the specific conversations and action patterns listed on your frustration card became triggered in your body and because your body automatically responded as if each of them was true.*

For example, frustration commonly results from:

-unrealistic goals and expectations;
-faulty definitions of "success;"
-Trying harder and harder without changing or correcting your
 ineffective strategies;
-Being overly critical of yourself, your competence, or your self-worth.

A Game Plan For Success

Learning to identify the hidden causes of your stress (Steps 1-3) is not a skill you develop overnight. It can be acquired, however, with practice, patience, and persistence. Here is a game plan for developing this skill that has worked very well for most of my patients:

1) *Begin By Practicing With The Index Cards Located In Appendix D.* There are two good reasons to begin with these cards. First, the problems they cover—specific moods and emotions—are easy to recognize and focus upon. Second, the underlying conversations and action patterns have already been worked out for you. I recommend you start with one, two, or three index cards—depending upon which moods and emotions you experience most frequently—and that you carry these cards around with you at all times.

2) *Use Your Index Cards To Sharpen Your Skills As An Observer.* Don't be in a hurry to get rid of your stress right away. In the beginning, you need to spend most of your time becoming a better observer of the internal causes of your stress. Attempting to do more at this stage would be like trying to play basketball before you learned how to shoot or dribble. Therefore, keep using your cards to practice observing your internal conversations and action patterns, whether or not your stress goes away.

3) *Observe Other Consequences Of Your Internal Conversations And Action Patterns.* Besides producing your negative moods and emotions, your internal conversations and action patterns also produce other undesirable outcomes. If you tend to seek revenge whenever someone makes you angry, for example, start paying attention to the consequences of this pattern. When you do "get even," is your life made richer or fuller by taking such action? Does seeking revenge produce any new problems or difficulties you now have to deal with? Does it create counter-retaliation from the other person which then requires further retaliation on your part?

EXAMPLE: The movie "Tin Men" was based upon this latter phenomenon. In this movie, two strangers, played by Richard Dreyfuss and Danny DeVito, who happen to be in the same line of work (aluminum siding sales) collide one day in a minor car accident. Each blames the other for causing the accident to occur. Each also feels compelled to retaliate. This leads to a series of senseless retaliations and counter-retaliations which escalates until both lives are nearly in ruin. When the movie ends, one can't help but remember the trivial incident that started it all, along with the obvious and non-obvious conversations that produced both men's behavior:

-"He did something really bad (wrong) to me."
  (Non-obvious conversations: GOOD/BAD; RIGHT/WRONG)
-"He was to blame and I was an innocent victim."
  (Non-obvious conversations: CAUSE/EFFECT; CREDIT/BLAME)
-"A real man wouldn't let this go unavenged."
  (Non-obvious conversation: MY VALUE AS A PERSON IS
  DEPENDENT UPON . . .)

4) *Practice Observing The Same Hidden Patterns In Other People.* Often it is easier to see hidden patterns by observing someone else, rather than yourself. Remember, the conversations and action patterns listed on your index cards are universal for most human beings. For instance, if a friend or lover becomes angry with you, you can be sure they did so for the following reasons: 1) they interpreted whatever you said, did, or didn't do as something you shouldn't have done; 2) they felt hurt, harmed, humiliated, embarrassed, offended, disappointed, or inconvenienced by what you did or didn't do; 3) they considered you to be unilaterally to blame for their hurt or disappointment; and 4) they want you to admit you were wrong, offer to

make amends, and/or be punished. Since you are less likely to be *consumed* by the emotion of anger when someone else is feeling it, you will often find it easier to recognize these underlying assumptions. In addition, since you usually will have a different perspective on the events that occurred, you will have access to information the other person lacks. Thus, you may easily recognize that some or all of the internal "realities" that are fueling the other person's anger aren't really true. In this way, you can practice understanding how the conversation-action mechanism of human anger works, and if you do this often enough, the insights you gain will spill over into your own self-observations.

▶ WARNING: Never point out what you observe about other people when they are in the midst of being angry. You could end up seriously injured in the process. A previous girlfriend taught me this lesson. Whenever she became angry with me, I would try to point out how she was misperceiving the truth about what really happened. Every time I did this, she became even angrier. The more I persisted, the angrier she became until finally she threw something at me. A day or two later she would invariably apologize, admitting that everything I had said was true. The next time I tried to be "helpful" when she was angry, I still had to duck another flying object. Eventually, I wised up. "Maybe I should let her work things out on her own," I said to myself, "instead of trying to help her with my new-found powers of observation." I strongly recommend you heed this advice yourself.

5) *Once You Become Aware Of Your Stress-Producing Conversations And Action Patterns, Don't Try To Change Them Or Get Rid Of Them.* Many people make this common mistake. In the first place, you can't get rid of your automatic conversations and action patterns even if you wanted to. As we've already seen, they don't exist like "thoughts" in your "mind" that can be easily changed. They are Biolinguistic processes that are deeply ingrained in your body. These patterns of thinking and behaving are going to get triggered within you, no matter what you try to do, so you might as well accept this fact and save yourself a great deal of wasted time and effort.

Secondly, you don't need to change or get rid of your internal conversations and action patterns in order to make your stress disappear.

The purpose of identifying them is not to get rid of them—which is impossible—but to learn how to defeat them without needing to change them or eliminate them at all.

6) *If At First You Don't Succeed, Don't Get Discouraged.* Remember, learning to recognize the hidden causes of your stress is not easy. Like learning to ride a bicycle, you will probably "fall off" many times in the beginning. If you relate to these failures as feedback, however—as useful indicators that you didn't do things quite right—you can transform them into valuable components of your game plan for success.

▶ TIP: If you have difficulty applying any of the strategies or tools presented in this chapter, or in other parts of this book, wait until you've finished reading the entire volume and then try again. Later discussions might clarify certain concepts for you. If you continue to have trouble, ask for help. Take this book with you and seek out a friend, family member, or professional counselor. Ask that person to read over the part you are having trouble with and see if they can help you determine the source of your difficulty. If they can't help, keep looking until you find someone who can. In my experience, most people can learn to use the method outlined in this book, provided they don't give up too quickly.

Learning To Identify The Hidden Causes Of Your Stress

A GAME PLAN FOR SUCCESS

- Begin With The Index Cards In Appendix D
- Develop Your Skill As An Observer
- Notice The Consequences Of Your Patterns
- Observe Other People
- Don't Try To Get Rid Of Your Patterns
- Don't Give Up

If you follow this game plan, and if you practice with the strategies and tools presented in this book, you will gradually improve your ability to recognize the internal causes of your stress. Once you know how to bring these causes out into the open, you will then be in position to do something about them.

DAY 5: EXERCISES

1. *Think of a financial problem you encountered in the past. Which of the following advantages could you have gained by adopting a "feedback" perspective? (Check all that apply.)*

☐ You could have gained more control over your own internal conversations about money, budgeting, saving, spending, etc.

☐ You could have gained more control over your own internal action patterns such as FAILING TO DO YOUR HOMEWORK/RESEARCH, FAILING TO DEAL WITH "LITTLE" PROBLEMS, FAILING TO ASK FOR HELP, FAILING TO ACKNOWLEDGE YOUR WEAKNESSES, ETC.)

☐ You could have reviewed similar financial problems you experienced in the past to identify recurrent behaviors or other problematic tendencies.

☐ You could have asked other people for help if you weren't able to identify your internal patterns.

☐ You could have learned something valuable about how to keep yourself out of similar problems in the future.

2. *Think of a relationship problem you encountered in the past. What advantages could you have gained by relating to this problem as "feedback"—i.e. by assuming that you, in addition to the other person, might have caused it to occur?*

_____

_____

_____

3. *Think of a work-related problem you encountered in the past. What could you have gained from viewing this problem as "feedback"?*

_____

_____

_____

4. *Recall a time when you were worried about something. What do you suppose were the hidden conversations and action patterns that produced this worry within you? (Hint: think in terms of GOOD/BAD and CAUSE/EFFECT.)*

THE WORRY-PRODUCING CONVERSATIONS WERE:

1. _____

2. _____

3. _____

4. _____

THE WORRY-PRODUCING ACTION PATTERNS WERE:

A. _____

B. _____

C. _____

D. _____

(Don't be concerned about the "correctness" of your responses; just write down your current thoughts and impressions.)

DAY 6

MAKING STRESS DISAPPEAR NATURALLY

So far, we've examined the first three steps in the ultimate method. In this chapter, we will focus on steps 4 and 5.

Step 4: Remind Yourself: The Hidden Causes Of Your Stress Exist In Your Body, Not Your Mind

This step will remind you that challenging your internal conversations and disrupting your internal action patterns does not change or eliminate your automatic tendencies. Fortunately, you don't need to change them or eliminate them in order to make your stress disappear naturally. You can use other coping strategies—such as the ones I will discuss in this chapter—that are based upon the knowledge your stress-producing patterns will continue to be triggered within you, probably for the rest of your life.

Step 5: Take Action To Neutralize Your Internal Causes

As we learned in chapter 4, the two main strategies for doing this are:

1) *Challenging* your stress-producing conversations;
2) *Disrupting* your stress-producing action patterns.

Figure 6-1

How To Make Stress Disappear Naturally

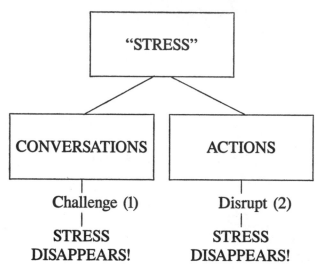

Once you learn to master these two strategies, you will be able to make most types of stress disappear whenever you want.

▶ NOTE: Depending upon the type of "stress" you are experiencing, you will sometimes need to focus on your internal conversations, while at other times you will need to address your internal action patterns. You may also need to do both, since conversations and action patterns frequently play a combined role in most types of stress we experience.

Challenging Your Hidden Conversations

When you challenge and disprove a faulty internal conversation, you can make whatever "stress" it is generating quickly disappear.

EXAMPLE A: Suppose you are feeling angry because the conversation "someone did something they shouldn't have done" became triggered in your body. If you are able to challenge and disprove this internal "reality," some or all of your anger will immediately vanish.

EXAMPLE B: Suppose you have a tendency to judge certain events as "bad," "awful," or otherwise devoid of value. If internal conversations such as these are causing you to suffer, challenging their validity can often make you feel much better.

There are three parts to challenging a stress-producing conversation:

1) Identifying it correctly;
2) Doubting its validity;
3) Destroying any false "realities" it has created in your body.

EXAMPLE: Computer frustration

Ted had the computer problem we discussed in the previous chapter. After buying a computer from a local store, he assumed he would learn to use it by reading the accompanying manuals. Whenever he ran into trouble, he immediately became frustrated and critical of himself. Sometimes he would get so frustrated that he had to walk away from the computer to compose himself emotionally.

After a few counseling sessions, Ted discovered that hidden conversations and action patterns within himself were creating most of his frustration. One of these conversations was:

• *"I should easily be able to succeed in this situation."*

Even though Ted had no previous training in the use of a computer, he was repeatedly "attacked" by this hidden expectation. Once he learned to identify this conversation, however, he was easily able to neutralize it. As soon as he felt frustrated, he would recall this hidden conversation and challenge its validity—"Now wait just a minute, I'm a beginner at this and I should be learning from my mistakes instead of expecting them not to occur." Every time he did this, *his frustration instantly disappeared.* If it returned a few minutes later, he would repeat the same process and his frustration would go away again. Thus, while he could not prevent this stress-producing conversation from becoming triggered in his body, *he could take steps to neutralize it every time it did.*

EXAMPLE: Low Self-Esteem

Low self-esteem results from self-demeaning conversations and action patterns that become programmed into people's bodies when they are very young. These can include conversations that the person is dumb, stupid, weak, lazy, no good, ugly, mean, selfish, clumsy, shy,

or moody. They can also include action patterns such as FAILING
TO MAKE REQUESTS OR DEMANDS OF OTHERS, FAILING
TO ACKNOWLEDGE YOUR STRENGTHS & ABILITIES, and
TRYING TO CHANGE YOURSELF. Throughout a person's life,
he or she can become convinced that these self-demeaning conversations (and action patterns) really are true, even though they rarely
are.

In order to "cure" yourself of low self-esteem, you must repeatedly
challenge these negative internal conversations (and related action
patterns). You must literally *declare war* upon them and recognize
how they rob you of your confidence, competence, and self-respect.
Rather than automatically agreeing with them, you must start to doubt
their validity. Then, you've got to search for evidence that contradicts
or "disproves" them.*

► TIP: For a short but excellent book on self-esteem see Nathaniel
Branden's *How To Raise Your Self-Esteem* listed in the Suggestions
For Further Reading section.

EXAMPLE: Fear (Anxiety)

Once you doubt the validity of a stress-producing conversation, you
must then destroy any false "realities" it has created in your body.
To destroy a false "reality," *you must challenge and disprove the
premises upon which it is based.* Let's look at the emotion of fear
(anxiety) to see how this can be done.

In Chapter 3, we saw that the emotion of fear can be produced by
a plastic spider. This occurs, in large part, because the following
conversations become triggered in our bodies:

CONVERSATIONS THAT PRODUCE FEAR IN HUMAN
BEINGS:

#1-"Something bad might happen."
#2-"Someone may be hurt or harmed."
#3-"I don't have the power (control) to keep #1 and #2 from
     happening."
#4-"I should never feel afraid, since fear is a sign of weakness."

---

* This is why you can't easily convince people they are worthy or "O.K." Unless they learn to recognize and challenge the invisible conversations (and action patterns) that have become established in
their bodies, there is little they, or anyone else, can do to raise their self-esteem.

As soon as we find out the spider is made of plastic, however, our fear *instantly disappears*. This occurs because each of the first three fear-producing conversations is automatically disproved by this new information:

#1-"Something bad might happen."—FALSE
#2-"Someone may be hurt or harmed."—FALSE
#3-"I don't have the power to keep #1 and #2 from happening."—FALSE

But what if you found a real spider crawling on your bed one night? Could challenging your internal conversations make this type of anxiety disappear? The answer is yes. If you successfully challenge and "disprove" any one of your fear-producing conversations, your fear will either lessen or completely disappear. Let's see how this can happen.

Conversation #1. Is it true that if a live spider is crawling on your bed something bad will inevitably happen to you? Not really. You haven't been bitten yet, and there's a very good chance you will keep this from happening. Statement #1, then, could easily be disproved, thereby reducing some or all of your triggered anxiety.

Conversation #2. Is it true you will be hurt, harmed, or injured? Here again, this depends on whether the spider bites you. It also depends—as long as the spider is not poisonous—on how you respond to such events. Some people are unafraid of bee stings, for example, because they view such events as trivial annoyances. Other people, including those who have had serious allergic reactions to bee-stings, might view such events with dread or horror.

Conversation #3. Is it true you don't have the power to keep #1 and #2 from happening? Again, this depends on your situation. If you are awake, alert, and free to move about, this conversation isn't true. You do have the power to control the situation. But if the spider runs away and hides so you can't remove it from your bedroom, you might continue to feel afraid, since once you go to sleep, you would not be able to protect yourself.

Conversation #4. The statement "I should never feel afraid, since fear is a sign of weakness" also comes in to play in many situations. It usually doesn't need to be challenged, however, since disproving any one of the other fear-producing conversations usually makes your fear go away.

There are times, however, where challenging statement #4 may be necessary.

EXAMPLE: Several years ago, I worked with a female police officer who had been taken hostage and held at gunpoint during a convenience store robbery. During her eight-hour ordeal, she not only managed to keep her composure, but she eventually convinced the gunman to surrender his weapon to her. Upon leaving the store, however, she vomited and began shaking uncontrollably. Her behavior was witnessed by several high-ranking police officials who had arrived upon the scene. A few days later, instead of receiving a commendation for bravery, this woman received an unofficial reprimand for "conduct unbecoming a police officer."

While the first two fear-producing conversations were appropriate for her situation—something "bad" could have happened to her and she could have been hurt or harmed—the third conversation—"I don't have the power to keep #1 and #2 from happening"—was disproved by the eventual outcome.

▶ NOTE: Sometimes our stress-producing conversations really are true and can't be disputed regardless of how hard we try. Most of the time, however, one or more of them will usually be inaccurate, as the above example demonstrates.

The fourth conversation also became a source of stress for this woman. Long after the event was over, she continued to feel embarrassed and ashamed about her display of emotion. This caused her to doubt her ability to continue as a police officer. Once she was helped to challenge and disprove her erroneous belief that fear is a sign of emotional, moral, or psychological weakness, her embarrassment and shame rapidly disappeared.*

The Barrister Technique

One way to challenge your internal conversations is to look for evidence that contradicts their apparent validity. I call this the Barrister Technique, since lawyers are trained to argue many sides of a given case, not just the one that appears to be true.

---

* Unfortunately, this inaccurate belief was still held by many of her colleagues and superiors. She also needed to learn how to deal with these external factors as well.

Whenever you find an internal conversation that is causing you to suffer, pretend you are a lawyer who has been hired to argue against it. No matter how "true" you believe your internal "reality" is, assume there may be other facts or arguments that could support a different conclusion.

EXAMPLE A: If you believe someone intentionally did something to hurt or harm you, put this conversation "on trial" and begin to "cross examine" it. Are you sure this was the person's true motive? Have you questioned him or her about your suspicion? Were any other explanations offered? How else might a skilled attorney cast doubt upon your assumption?

EXAMPLE B: Suppose you are convinced that you are a worthless, unattractive, or incompetent individual. Are these internal conversations really true? Are there people who know you who would be willing to "testify" on your behalf? Are there areas of life where you do have competence? Are you being excessively hard on yourself? Are you over-generalizing from a few minor events?

▶ TIP: If you find this technique difficult to use, you probably believe that your internal "realities" are always valid. Remember, this is what causes your stress to occur in the first place (see the Blindness and Certainty parable on page 15). If you really want to learn how to win against stress, you will have to find a way around your deep-seated assumptions of certainty. There is no simple advice I can give you for doing this, except to point out that recognizing your certainty as a problem is the first important step.

Flipping To The Opposite Reality

Another way to challenge your internal conversations is to use a technique I call Flipping To The Opposite Reality. To use this technique, take any stress-producing conversation (or action pattern) and "flip" it over—i.e. change it—to its opposite. Then, *assume this opposite "reality" is also true* and begin to look for evidence to confirm its validity.

EXAMPLE: Suppose something happens that looks very "bad" to you. And suppose you feel "stressed"—e.g. sad, angry, frustrated, or tense—as a result. Try Flipping To The Opposite Reality, by assuming that the event in question might in some way be "good," and *see what you notice when you look from this perspective.*

More often than not, you will uncover aspects of the event—or what you could have done in response to it—that truly are consistent with this opposite reality. Looking for positive aspects of being fired from your job—ending up with a better job, being happier and more fulfilled, etc.—is just one example.

While this technique might seem foolish or even dangerous at first, something quite amazing happens when you try it out. You begin to discover that most of the opposite realities you start out imagining really do turn out to be true! They were there all along, you just couldn't see them because of the dominating influence of your usual perspectives. Thus, by forcing yourself to examine these opposite realities, you can often compensate for much of the blindness your internal patterns produce.

► NOTE: It's important to remember this is *only a technique*. I am not suggesting you should believe that all "bad" things are really "good" or that all "stupid" things really are "smart." What I am suggesting is this: if you automatically assume something is bad or stupid (or good or smart), *sometimes your automatic assessments will not be completely accurate.* One good way to test for this possibility is to consider the opposite interpretation and see what you notice when you look from this perspective. Sometimes you will find that these opposite perspectives are not appropriate. But you will be amazed at how often they illuminate aspects of your situation that are very real, but that you don't normally appreciate.

The Anatomy Of An Argument

Consider the problem of arguing with another person. Most arguments arise because each party believes he or she is "right" and the other person is "wrong." These RIGHT/WRONG realities automatically become triggered in each person's body. If each person knew all the facts, however, each would have to admit there is some degree of validity to the other person's point of view. But both people remain blind to this possibility because of the passion of the moment. Each keeps communicating to the other "you are definitely wrong here and I am definitely right."

One good way to deal with this common problem is to *assume the other person is "right" rather than "wrong" whenever you find yourself in a heated argument.* By "flipping" to this opposite reality you may be able to recognize some of the merits of the other person's position. When either party in a heated argument legitimizes the other's point of view, the argument loses its intensity and both people can usually work out their differences in a spirit of cooperation, partnership, and mutual respect.

► NOTE: For a more detailed discussion of why this technique works, see Appendix B.

Always Try To Challenge Your Stress-Producing Conversations

Not all of your internal conversations are inaccurate or misleading. You wouldn't want to walk around doubting everything you think or believe, or "flipping" every internal "reality" to its opposite counterpart. But you should consider doing this for any conversation that is contributing to your "stress."* Here, for example, are just a few of the internal conversations we frequently need to challenge:

```
┌─────────────────────┐
│                     │
│  CREDIT/BLAME       │
│                     │
└─────────────────────┘
```

When good things happen, we look for someone to credit. When bad things happen, we look for someone to blame.

Assigning credit or blame to one element of a complex interactive process usually makes us blind to other elements that also play a role. This is why quarterbacks, running backs, and other football players refuse to take credit for their individual performances—"I couldn't have done it without our offensive line" or "it was a total team effort; all 40 players contributed." While fans and reporters like to think in terms of individual credit or blame, most athletes know this is not how things really happen.

---

* This is because the likelihood that one (or more) or your internal conversations or action patterns will be inaccurate is very high in such instances.

PERFECTIONISM

Perfection is highly valued in our society. We admire flawless performances and abhor even trivial mistakes. From the time we are very young, we are taught that being "good" and doing things "right" are ways to acquire our parents' love and respect. Unfortunately, once these perfectionistic patterns become established in our bodies, they can easily become triggered in situations where they aren't appropriate.

Therefore, we should often "talk back" to our perfectionistic tendencies. We should challenge them, debate them, and look for the many flaws inherent in their logic. For example, many people feel anxious when speaking to a group (I know, because I used to be one of them). One reason for this anxiety is our perfectionistic expectations. We believe any mistake or imperfection on our part will cause our audience to think poorly of us. We even prepare for our talks in a perfectionistic manner, trying to rehearse every detail of what we are going to say.

The truth about public speaking, however, is different from our assumptions. No matter how well we perform, it is difficult to please every listener. Some people will love what we say, some will be indifferent, and others will dislike our remarks, our style, or perhaps our appearance. Also, when we try to be perfect, we lose spontaneity and create distance between ourselves and our audience. In addition, we can sabotage our performance by too much preparation. Experienced speakers know that the best way to prepare for a talk is not to rehearse every phrase or sentence. As long as they are clear about the major points they want to deliver, and as long as they have the knowledge and experience to defend them adequately, they know that their talks will usually be successful.

HOPE

RESIGNATION

When we are "hopeful," we expect good things will somehow happen for us. When we are resigned, we have the opposite expectation—nothing good can happen no matter what we, or anyone else, tries to do.

▶ NOTE: People who are resigned often create "evidence" for their belief by failing to act at all or by adhering to strategies that have been unsuccessful in the past.

Experience has shown us, however, that hoping and wishing rarely make things happen. Experience has also shown us that we can usually solve most of the problems we face, provided we have the knowledge, skills, and determination to do so. Thus, our internal conversations of HOPE and RESIGNATION are frequently inaccurate. Instead of accepting them at face value, as we normally tend to do, we should always try to challenge them whenever they appear.

Challenging Your Conversations Is Not "Positive Thinking"

Challenging your stress-producing conversations is not the same as positive thinking. With positive thinking, you attempt to overpower a negative thought, feeling, or belief by forcing yourself to think in a positive manner, while suppressing or avoiding any thoughts to the contrary.

When you challenge a stress-producing conversation, on the other hand, *you don't try to suppress it, avoid it, or overpower it in any way.* Instead, you face it by bringing it out into the open, where you can critically evaluate it and determine its appropriateness.

▶ NOTE: When you successfully challenge a conversation that is producing a false *negative* "reality" in your body, a more *positive* reality will usually emerge. But both the *process* and the *results* are very different from positive thinking. For example, when you try to convince yourself you are not angry when indeed you are, you do nothing to disprove the internal "realities" that are producing this emotion. They will continue to operate in—and affect—your body, whether or not you are aware of them. In contrast, when you identify, challenge, and then disprove the internal conversations that are producing your anger *(a different process),* you are not only freed to think and feel more positively, but your body is also released from the physiological consequences of these conversations *(a different result).*

Challenging Your Conversations Is Not "Pollyanish" Thinking

Many people fear that strategies like the Barrister Technique and Flipping To The Opposite Reality are exercises in naive, unrealistic, or pollyanish thinking. If a plane crash occurs, killing hundreds of individuals, most people would be reluctant to think anything "good" had just happened. Similarly, if you lose your job, if your children get into trouble, if you become seriously ill or disabled, or if your world otherwise begins to collapse around you, you might also think it unrealistic to view such events in anything other than a negative light.

While there are many situations—such as the plane crash example—where our negative conversations are indeed appropriate, hindsight has taught us that positive outcomes still can occur even from the most tragic of events. While we don't like to focus on these possibilities, especially during times of our own or others' misfortune, they are there nonetheless. For example, the death of a loved one is rarely a "positive" event, unless the person was terminally ill and suffering unbearably. But such events often lead to positive changes in other people's lives—e.g. surviving friends and relatives begin to take better care of themselves, or they take greater precautions to avoid certain dangers, or they might become motivated to contribute to the welfare of others who are afflicted with similar problems. An unwanted divorce sometimes results in one or both partners having a much happier life. And there are many instances where the onset of a serious illness, such as a heart attack, stroke, or even cancer, has turned out to be a "positive" event in an individual's life. Thus, when we actively challenge our automatic assessments of GOOD/BAD, RIGHT/WRONG, and many others, we are not necessarily being foolish or naive. Most of the time we are being *more realistic,* because this strategy allows us to recognize other aspects of reality that normally escape our view.

The Value Of A Biolinguistic Understanding

It's important to understand that no matter how many times you successfully challenge your internal conversations, *you do not change or eliminate them.* Since these patterns of thinking are deeply ingrained in your body, they will continue to reassert themselves and cause mischief in your life. Thus, the beneficial effects of challenging your stress-producing conversations (and action patterns) are often only temporary. You can still exercise a great deal of control over these recurring patterns, however, by repeatedly challenging them every time they appear.

► TIP: Challenging your internal conversations is similar to playing the Space Invaders video game. This game involves shooting down rows of descending spacecrafts as they try to attack your home base. No matter how many times you destroy these relentless invaders, they keep reappearing at the top of your video screen. They never go away, just as your hidden conversations (and action patterns) remain in your body forever. Therefore, as in the Space Invaders video game, you must be prepared to deal with your stress-producing patterns over and over again, no matter how many times you successfully "shoot them down."

Here is an example from my own life that demonstrates the value of this understanding.

EXAMPLE: Many years ago, before I met my wife, Christina, I fell in love with a woman I desperately wanted to marry. We had an intense romantic relationship for several months, but when it came to the question of marriage, she wanted no part of a long-term commitment. When I tried to force the issue, she became angry with me and terminated the relationship.

For weeks after the relationship ended, I felt sad and depressed. I forced myself to go to work, but I was frequently bothered by uncontrollable crying spells. Eventually, I decided to do something about my suffering. Guided by my knowledge of Biolinguistics and by my understanding of the causes of human sadness (see page 51), I set out to identify the hidden causes of my misery. I quickly discovered that the following conversations—all examples of Negative Thinking—were always in the background of my thinking whenever I felt sad:

```
Negative
Thinking
```

-"I can't go on without her."
-"I'll never find anyone as nice, pretty, or intelligent as she was."
-"I'll never fall in love again."
-"Something must be wrong with me."
-"I'll never get married."
-"I'll always be alone."

As soon as I recognized these hidden conversations, I knew intellectually that none of them was true. Knowing this, however, *didn't keep them from attacking me,* nor did it stop my body from reacting "as if" they were really true. But from then on, I was able to challenge these hidden conversations every time they became triggered within me. Each time I began to feel sad, I would remember these conversations and remind myself:

-"She's not the only woman in the world, you know."
-"I can live without her since I was doing pretty well before I met her."
-"This is not the end of my romantic possibilities."
-"She did have her faults—some big ones in fact."
-"In the long run, I'll probably be thankful we didn't get married."

Each time I did this, *my sadness disappeared.* But a short while later, it would come back again. Each time it did, however, I was able to make it disappear once again by using this same basic strategy.

This went on many times each day. But instead of viewing my inability to eliminate these internal thoughts and feelings as a sign of personal failure, I knew from Biolinguistics that this was *exactly what should be happening.* I knew that challenging and disproving my internal conversations once, twice, or even a hundred times would not necessarily free me of their influence. I knew they could (and would) come back to disturb me, but I also knew that I had the ability to neutralize them every time they did.

▶ NOTE: While repeatedly challenging your internal conversations doesn't change them or get rid of them, it may start to build new conversations in your body, alongside your old, established ones. These new conversations are usually very "weak" at first. They are also rapidly extinguished if not reinforced repeatedly. Over time (usually months or years), these new conversations can become established in your body as well. In this way, events that triggered only your old, stress-producing patterns in the past may begin to trigger new, stress-relieving conversations at the very same time.

Disrupting Your Stress-Producing Action Patterns

The purpose of disrupting your stress-producing action patterns is the same as challenging your stress-producing conversations—to make your stress disappear naturally without needing to use drugs, relaxation exercises, or stress management techniques.

EXAMPLE: Joan discovered that much of her stress resulted from a common behavior pattern—TRYING TO SOLVE OTHER PEOPLE'S PROBLEMS. She grew up in a family where both of her parents were alcoholics. The oldest of three children, Joan spent most of her childhood protecting and comforting her two younger siblings. As an adult, she was attracted to people who frequently got into trouble and who looked to her for support. At times, Joan found this very satisfying. But often it left her feeling physically and emotionally drained. As Joan learned to recognize the role TRYING TO SOLVE OTHER PEOPLE'S PROBLEMS played in her life, she saw that she did have the power to choose whether to follow this pattern or not. Prior to this recognition, she had no choice at all—the pattern did the choosing and Joan felt obliged to obey it. Now, she obeys it only when she wants, and by learning to disrupt this one internal pattern, she was able to substantially reduce the amount of the stress in her life.

▶ NOTE: The key to dealing with your stress-producing action patterns is to recognize that you *cannot make them go away* or keep them from becoming triggered within you. They will invariably become activated, so it is best to accept this fact and learn to use the following coping strategies to deal with them effectively:

DISRUPTING YOUR AUTOMATIC BEHAVIOR PATTERNS*

STRATEGY #1 Simply ignore them
STRATEGY #2 Do the exact opposite
STRATEGY #3 Attach riders to them
STRATEGY #4 Deputize others
STRATEGY #5 Adopt pattern-busting disciplines

---

* Each of these strategies can also be used with your internal conversations as well.

Let's look at these strategies in more detail.

STRATEGY #1 Simply Ignore Them

If you've ever tried to lose weight, you're familiar with this strategy. To lose weight, you must consciously disrupt your automatic overeating patterns. This means ignoring certain urges to eat that become triggered in your body. If you are watching television, for example, and a commercial triggers you to want candy, ice cream, or some other "fattening" food, you can simply ignore these urges and do nothing instead.

This strategy doesn't require you to change or eliminate your automatic eating tendencies. Nor does it require you to work very hard to keep them from becoming activated. As long as you are prepared to ignore them when they occur, you can easily disrupt them and keep them from sabotaging your plans.

STRATEGY #2 Do The Exact Opposite

Another way to disrupt a habitual action pattern is to do the *exact opposite* of what your pattern would have you do. If you are feeling depressed, for example, and your natural tendency is to stay home and feel sorry for yourself, consider doing the opposite instead. Visit a friend, go to a movie, go to a gym and exercise—do just about anything except what your pattern would have you to do.

► WARNING: Some people with severe depression could possibly be made worse by using this strategy. Also, there may be times when it is quite appropriate for people to withdraw from social contact for one reason or another. Thus, each person must weigh the risks and benefits of this and other coping strategies on an individual basis.

As we have seen, this same strategy—in the form of Flipping To The Opposite Reality—works equally well for your internal conversations.

EXAMPLE: A dentist I had been counseling came in for a session after returning from a week at the beach. Even though he and his wife had enjoyed a wonderful vacation, he was upset with himself for making *three* wrong turns on the drive home. After repeatedly stating that this was "dumb" and "stupid" of him, I asked him if his "mistakes" could have been intentional in some way: "Were there any reasons you might have *wanted* to make wrong turns?" After thinking this over for a moment, he laughed and said, "You know, I was saying to my wife on the way home that we had such a great time I really didn't want to get back to my office." Once he looked at his behavior from this perspective, he saw that making wrong turns was not necessarily dumb on his part.

STRATEGY #3 Attach Riders To Them

When a bill is proposed by a committee under our system of government, riders or amendments can be attached to it by other representatives. These riders don't change the original bill itself, but they add other features or restrictions that can significantly alter its impact.

We can use a similar strategy to deal with our stress-producing behavior patterns. While we may not be able to change or eliminate them, we can decide to add creative "riders" to them. Deciding to exercise whenever you have an urge to eat is one type of rider you can add to an automatic behavior tendency. Deciding to apologize every time you become angry with, or yell at, someone is another. Deciding to use your index cards whenever you feel anxious, guilty, sad, or frustrated is a third. There is no limit to the number of creative, stress-reducing riders you can add.

STRATEGY #4 Deputize Others

Another way to disrupt your stress-producing action patterns is to involve other people. Instead of trying to monitor your behavior yourself, you can deputize others to help you with this task. For example, if you frequently talk down to your employees (or other people), ask them to support you in correcting this habit. Ask them to signal you whenever you are acting in this way, or have them apply a consequence—one that you have agreed upon in advance—whenever you slip into this automatic behavior pattern.

This strategy accomplishes several important things. For one, it reduces the pressure on you to monitor and control your own behavior patterns, which can be difficult. For another, it takes advantage of the fact that other people can frequently spot your behavior patterns better than you can. It also helps to strengthen your relationships with these people by allowing them to support you and by giving them some control over patterns they sometimes find offensive.

▶ TIP: As we will see·in Chapter 10, this strategy is very useful in our intimate relationships, where each of us has patterns that are often very destructive. When we deputize our partner to help us deal with our internal relationship-destroying patterns, we can achieve greater success than when we try to deal with them on their own.

STRATEGY #5 Adopt Pattern-Busting Disciplines

Pattern-busting disciplines can also be very helpful. Certain hobbies, exercises, and other regular activities can help you loosen the hold some of your ingrained behavior patterns have over you.

Hard-driving executives, for example, can reduce their "hurry-up" tendencies by engaging in slow-paced hobbies such as fishing, model building, or oil painting. People who spend most of their time in intellectual pursuits, such as medicine, law, and other professions, can engage in non-intellectual leisure activities, such as mowing the lawn, listening to music, or chopping wood.

▶ NOTE: Eastern disciplines, such as meditation and Tai Chi, have recently become popular in the West because they force us to abandon our "normal" competitive modes of being. By practicing these disciplines on a regular basis, we can train ourselves to "let go" of some of our automatic tendencies.*

In addition, once you identify a specific conversation or action pattern that gets you into trouble, you can design a specific discipline to help you counteract it. Suppose you find it difficult to make requests or demands of others, for instance. What discipline could you invent to help you beat this pattern? Perhaps you could set up a game for yourself where every day you ask two people to do something for you whether you need them to or not. You could also decide to reward yourself every time you go against your automatic tendency.

The Causes Of Human Worry

Once you know how to use the two main coping strategies discussed in this chapter, you can make most types of stress disappear whenever you want. Most forms of worry, for example, can be made to disappear by either challenging their underlying conversations or disrupting their underlying action patterns.

---

* These disciplines are not nearly as powerful when they are used primarily as stress management or relaxation techniques.

Figure 6-2
Making Worry Disappear

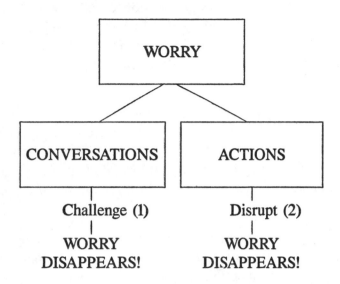

Here are the conversations that produce worry in human beings:

WORRY-PRODUCING CONVERSATIONS:

1) Something bad might happen.
2) Someone or something (including myself) may be hurt or harmed.
3) If I worry hard enough (think real hard, feel real bad, focus my attention on a problem, etc.), I can keep #1 and #2 from happening.

When we worry, we *fear* something bad will happen—to us or to someone or something we value. When our children are in trouble, for instance, we worry about their welfare (and ours as well). The same would be true if someone close to us became sick, or if we ourselves experienced some type of illness or crisis.

Thus, worry and fear are intimately related. You can see this from the first two worry-producing conversations above. Recall that these are the same conversations that produce fear in human beings (see page 28). It is the third conversation—about control—that distinguishes worry from fear. When we are afraid, we automatically assume we have *little or no control* over something bad that might happen to us. When we worry, on the other hand, *we unconsciously assume that we do have control,* even though this may be illusory.

EXAMPLE: Suppose you loan your car to someone with the clear understanding that you need it returned by 6 PM. If 6 PM arrives and your car does not, you might get concerned. By 8 PM you will definitely be concerned, and by 10 PM you will probably be worried. You may be preoccupied by thoughts about what might have happened, or you may find it difficult to concentrate on anything else until this situation is resolved.

Why does worry occur in such situations? Part of the answer is that each of the conversations listed above becomes triggered in your body, and because your body responds *as if* each of them is true. Even though there may be nothing you can do to prevent something bad from happening, your body may still respond *as if you do have this magical power.*

In addition, certain worry-producing or worry-maintaining behavior patterns also become triggered within you. These go hand-in-hand with the previously mentioned conversations:

ACTION PATTERNS THAT PRODUCE OR MAINTAIN WORRY IN HUMAN BEINGS:

A) Trying to magically influence situations or events through internal gyrations—thoughts, feelings, body movements, compulsive ruminating, etc.

B) Indulging in worrying instead of taking effective action to clarify and deal with your problem or situation.

C) Trying to clarify or deal with a problem or situation yourself, when you may lack the necessary skill or experience to do so.

D) Failing to seek help from others who do have the ability to determine if you have a problem and/or help you solve it.

▶ NOTE: Worrying sometimes can help you take more effective action to deal with a problem or situation. For example, if worrying that you didn't study well for an upcoming test causes you to change your study habits and achieve a better score, then worrying did have a positive outcome. But most of the time people worry *instead of taking action* ("If I just worry hard enough my problems will be solved") or they worry to such a degree that it detracts from, rather than improves, their performance.

The most important thing to recognize about worry, however, is that:

> ### WORRYING IS OFTEN LIKE
> ### DOING A "RAIN DANCE"

If you go outside and think real hard, make yourself feel miserable, or shake your body vigorously, eventually it will rain. Any cause-effect relationship between this external event and your internal thoughts, feelings, or body gyrations is purely coincidental. You can delude yourself into thinking, however, that worrying did make a difference. When you "worry yourself sick" because your car has not been returned or because your children have not come home on time, and when both come back in good condition, *your body may conclude* that it was worrying that kept them safe. This will cause you to worry once again, whenever a similar problem or situation arises in the future.*

There is a fourth conversation that also contributes to worry in human beings:

4. If I didn't worry, it would mean I don't truly *care.*

This conversation places us in a "catch-22." If worrying and caring are intimately related, then giving up our worry means we must be heartless, cruel, or self-centered individuals. In other words, in order to prove we care about someone or something, *we must show that we worry about it*—i.e. we must go along with the socially-accepted "rain dance" and deny that our worry is often based upon magical, illogical thinking.

The best way to deal with this hidden cause of worry is to recognize that worrying and caring (or being concerned) are independent phenomena. You do not have to worry about people in order to prove you care about them. You can also be genuinely concerned about a problem or situation without spending all your time worrying about it, especially when this doesn't improve anything.

---

* While most people say they never reason in this way, they fail to understand that their bodies can unconsciously engage in such illogical reasoning.

How To Make Worry Disappear

Once you understand the conversation-action mechanism that produces human worry, you can attack its hidden causes from either direction. You can challenge your worry-producing conversations or disrupt your worry-producing action patterns, whichever is most appropriate for your situation:

Figure 6-3

*How Understanding The Hidden Causes Of Worry Can
Help You Make Worry Disappear*

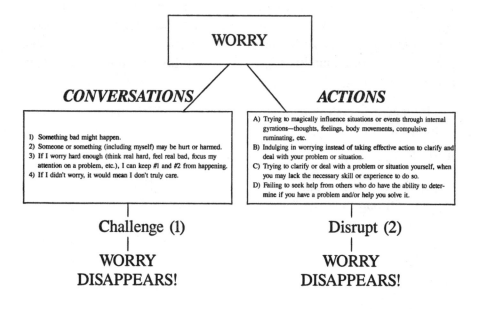

Some forms of worry are caused mainly by our internal conversations. These conversations usually take the form of: a) exaggerated or unfounded fears, or b) magical types of control. When we worry about a nuclear holocaust, for example, we often exaggerate the chances such an event will happen. When our loved ones are ill and we worry about their fate, we are often guilty of magical, illogical thinking—assuming that our worrying will protect them from harm.

The best way to deal with these worry-producing conversations is to challenge their validity:

- Is something bad really likely to happen?
- Will someone (including myself) truly be hurt or harmed?
- Are my fears and concerns well-founded or are they based upon inaccurate information or unrealistic assumptions? In other words:

Do I Really Have A Problem?	vs.	Am I Imagining A Problem?

- If you really do have a problem, are your assumptions about your ability to influence it realistic, or are you mainly doing a "rain dance" without acknowledging this fact?

Other forms of worry are caused by our behavior.

EXAMPLE: I recently counselled a young, gay man who was worried about getting AIDS. He was active sexually, but he was unwilling to limit his sexual partners, wear a condom, or practice other safe-sex habits. In his case, conversations were not the major cause of his worry (something bad could happen to him and he could be hurt or harmed). His worry was being produced mainly by his actions. In order to feel less anxious and more secure, he would need to disrupt some of his favored behavior patterns.

Sometimes, our worry-producing conversations and action patterns cannot be challenged or disrupted, no matter how hard we try. This usually means our worry is *appropriate.* A healthy respect for the dangers of AIDS is quite appropriate in this day and age. Or when threats of terrorism are made, it may be prudent to restrict your travel to certain parts of the world. Most of us can usually sort out *inappropriate* from appropriate forms of worry, and we can always make the inappropriate varieties disappear as discussed above.

Issues Related To Dealing With Your Internal Conversations And Action Patterns

The two main coping strategies outlined in this chapter work very well, provided you use them correctly. In order to do this, it helps to reflect upon each of the following issues:

1. **Commitment.** Knowing how to deal with your internal conversations and action patterns and actually dealing with them are two different things. The first requires knowledge, the second requires commitment and action. Thus, in order to benefit from the strategies outlined in this chapter, you must be committed to practicing them regularly.

Once you embark upon such a course, negative thoughts and feelings such as "This isn't working," "I'm too uncomfortable," "It's too much trouble," or "I'll never be any good at this," will invariably occur. These internal conversations—and the feelings they produce—can be very compelling. In order to learn how to win against stress, you must be prepared to withstand these and other obstacles—including the behavior and opinions of others—that might try to weaken your resolve.

2. **Change In Others.** Just as you can't easily change or eliminate your own automatic tendencies, don't expect others to be any different. It's important—and often stress-relieving—to remind yourself that other people are Biolinguistic organisms too. When you ask them to change one of their habitual patterns and they agree to do so, you must understand they will find it difficult to keep such a promise. They won't be able to change overnight, and despite their sincere intentions, they will occasionally revert to previous automatic tendencies.

3. **Design.** Another issue involves how well you design your pattern-busting strategies.

EXAMPLE: Years ago, I decided to change my habit of not wearing my seat belt. Prior to this decision, I rarely remembered to put my seat belt on, and even when I did remember, I talked myself out of doing it most of the time. My first attempt to change this long-standing pattern failed because I had a very poor game plan. My goal was to always remember to put my seat belt on, and whenever I forgot to do this, which was often, I felt defeated and demoralized. Eventually, I came up with a better game plan. Instead of trying to always remember to put my seat belt on, I changed my goal to *always putting my seat belt on whenever I remembered to do so.* This was a game I could win every time. When my usual pattern of forgetting asserted itself, I no longer felt like a failure, since my goal was to put my seat belt on *only when I remembered.* The more I played and won this game—by ignoring my internal excuses for not putting my seat belt on—the more I began to remember to do it! Now, I wear my seat belt 99% of the time, and I continue to get value from playing and winning this game every day.

4. *Temporary Incompetence.* Whenever you decide to challenge or disrupt one of your old, established patterns, you will be stepping into unfamiliar territory. At first, you may not have the skills or knowledge to function very well. But as time goes on, you usually become more successful. Thus, in order to train yourself to use these new coping strategies, you must be willing to accept a certain amount of incompetence, at least in the beginning.

Unfortunately, most of us hate to feel incompetent. Even though we know that temporary incompetence is a natural part of growth and development, we tend to avoid this state at all costs.

EXAMPLE: Workaholics are generally so afraid of temporary incompetence that they are reluctant to reduce their compulsive work schedules. They are so convinced that their productivity will decline if they take time off for recreation or relaxation that they are rarely willing to test this assumption. Those workaholics who do place reasonable limits on the amount of time they allow themselves to work often find out that their productivity remains high or sometimes even improves.*

Challenging Or Disrupting Your Internal Patterns May Not Feel Comfortable

One more thing you should know about challenging your internal conversations and disrupting your internal action patterns is that *you probably won't feel comfortable* when you use these two strategies. This discomfort can be understood from a Biolinguistic perspective.

Remember, your stress-producing conversations and action patterns are part of your body, not your "mind." Each is connected to hundreds of other internal "realities" that also exist in your body. Thus, disproving one of your hidden conversations or disrupting one of your automatic behavior patterns is not a trivial event. Your identity as an individual, even your whole understanding of life in general, can sometimes be shaken in the process.

* There are many other factors in addition to fear of incompetence that contribute to "workaholic" behavior.

This partly concludes our discussion of Steps 4 and 5 in the ultimate method. Tomorrow, you will see how creating certain contexts can also help you eliminate "stress."

DAY 6: EXERCISES

1. *Choose two conversations from the list of stress-producing conversations in Appendix A. Write your choices down below.*

_____

_____

   A. Think of a time in your life when one or both of these conversations were probably true.

   B. With regard to the same two conversations, think of a time when each appeared to be true, but later turned out to be false.

2. *Choose two action patterns from the list of action patterns also in Appendix A. Write your choices down below.*

_____

_____

   A. Think of a time when each of these action patterns worked to your advantage.

   B. Now, think of a time when each of these very same patterns caused you to suffer.

3. *For each of the conversations listed below, "flip" to its opposite "reality" and write this opposite "reality" down in the space provided (don't be concerned if you disagree with these opposite statements):*

   EXAMPLE: "The person who caused this traffic jam must be an imbecile."
   Opposite: "The person who caused this traffic jam probably isn't an imbecile."

A. "I am responsible (to blame) for something bad that happened to someone else."

_____

B. "I am not responsible (to blame) for something bad that happened to someone else."

_____

C. "I will never be able to replace what I have lost."

_____

4. *Follow these instructions exactly as they are stated:*

   A. *Think about ripping this page out of your book, but don't do anything in response to this thought.*

   ☐ Check here when you have completed this task.

   B. *Think about wanting to skip ahead to Chapter 10 (before reading Chapters 7, 8 & 9), but don't act on this desire.*

   ☐ Check here when you have completed this task.

   C. *Think about turning to page 155 in this book. Now, keeping this thought clearly in mind, turn to page 60 instead.*

   ☐ Check here when you have completed this task.

DAY 7

STRESS-RELIEVING CONTEXTS

In addition to the conversations and action patterns that are programmed into our bodies, we can also invent new conversations and action strategies to help us relieve our stress. I call these conversations and action strategies "contexts" to distinguish them from positive thoughts, positive affirmations, positive forms of "self-talk," or other cognitive interventions.*

A context is very different from a positive thought or affirmation. It is a powerful linguistic act that opens up new possibilities for observation and action. For example, the Declaration Of Independence contains conversations and behavioral guidelines that opened up new forms of social interaction. These "contexts," which formed the backbone for our freedom-oriented society, continue to dominate our thinking and actions even today. Similarly, Martin Luther King, Jr.'s, "We shall overcome" was another powerful context that changed the course of American history. So was John F. Kennedy's declaration, "We will send a man to the moon by the end of the decade."

* The term "context" has been employed by several leading researchers and authorities on human behavior. Dr. Robert Shaw, a psychiatrist in Berkeley, California, has established a new form of psychotherapy called Contextual Therapy, which is based upon this principle. Also, psychotherapists Bill O'Hanlon and James Wilk wrote a book titled Shifting Contexts (1987), in which they talk about the interrelationships between language, meaning, and behavior in all forms of psychotherapy.

These created contexts were more than positive thoughts, wishes, hopes, or aspirations. They were powerful linguistic acts that altered the "reality" in which many people lived. As you will learn in this chapter, you too possess this same linguistic capability. You can invent new conversations and action strategies that alter the "realities" in which you live. In fact, you can create many useful contexts that can empower you in your life or that can serve as effective antidotes for your previous socio-linguistic conditioning.

Human Beings Are Context-Creating Organisms

As Biolinguistic organisms, we live our lives contextually. This is to say we are always adding "meaning" and "significance" to everything that happens to us—including everything that happened in the past or that we envision happening in the future. Most of the time, we add these meanings unconsciously, by virtue of the internal conversations and action patterns that were previously established in our bodies. But language also gives us the power to invent new conversations and action strategies anytime we want. These *self-created* contexts can have any meaning we choose. They can be positive or negative, vague or precise, short or long, simple or complex. They can also be realistic, unrealistic, or even nonsensical, as many psychotic patients demonstrate.

For example, each of us, if we wanted to, could make the following declarations:

-"I am the world's best tennis player."
-"I am not very romantic."
-"I'm pretty good at most things I do."
-"I can leap tall buildings at a single bound."

We can also choose to behave in ways that are consistent with these invented realities. Sometimes we will be able to actualize the realities we declare, while at other times we will not be able to do so. Regardless of the eventual outcome, we do have the power—through language—to invent such realities anytime we choose.*

* The freedom we have, via language, to invent ourselves newly and to consciously influence our future development was the main message of the European Existential Movement, which began in France in the late 1940s.

Stress-Relieving Contexts

Some created contexts can be very stress-relieving. In general, these are contexts that:

- empower you to be more successful in some area of life;
- allow you to "see" certain aspects of reality that you are normally blind to;
- enable you to compensate for your previous socio-linguistic conditioning.

EXAMPLE: Take the statement "I'm O.K., You're O.K.," for instance. This context was popularized in 1969 by Thomas Harris in a book by the same title.* This book became an instant best-seller because many of us have been programmed to believe we are "not O.K." and that other people are "not O.K." either. Much of this negative programming stems from our early childhood experiences. It can even be fostered by loving, caring parents, who were unaware that their repeated efforts to correct us and reprimand us could have such unwanted effects.

If, later in life, we discover that this negative programming is not really true, there is little we can do to change it or eliminate it from our bodies. But we do have the power to invent a new context for our lives, namely "I'm O.K, You're O.K.," to help us compensate for our previous conditioning.†

▶ NOTE: We can also make declarations that close, as well as open, possibilities for observation or action. Take the context "People can't be trusted," for example. This declaration closes down certain types of interactions with other people. It also produces certain moods—especially the mood of distrust—which strongly influence our relationships with others.

Contexts such as "I'm O.K., You're O.K." or "Negative conversations about myself (or others) are rarely true" are powerful coping options that are always available to us. They can provide us with many important benefits, such as:

* See *I'm O.K., You're O.K.*, Harper & Row, New York, New York, 1969.

† I prefer to use the broader context "Negative conversations about myself (or others) are rarely true." This context functions just like "I'm O.K., You're O.K.," but it can also be used to counter a wide variety of other negative assessments.

- Helping us compensate for many of the "blind spots" our internal patterns produce;

- Empowering us to be more successful in life;

- Enabling us to be happy and satisfied, regardless of our circumstances;

For example, some created contexts can enable you to "win" in life no matter what happens to you. A writer once commented that ever since he became a professional, it was hard for him to get upset about anything "bad" that happened to him. "When you're a writer," he said, "nothing bad can happen anymore—it's all material." Thus, no matter what happened, either inside or outside his body, he had a context for relating to it that immediately transformed it into something useful.

Johnny Carson is another example. Most comedians depend upon the strength of their material. If their jokes are good, they do well; if their jokes are rotten, they bomb. Carson, on the other hand, operates from a completely different context. If his jokes are good, he makes people laugh; if his jokes are rotten, he also makes people laugh. Thus, no matter what type of joke he tells—a good one or a bad one—he has a context for relating to his audience that usually enables him to "win" as a comedian.

Other created contexts help by alleviating some of the blindness our internal conversations and action patterns produce. For example, the context "When I think someone (including myself) is wrong, that person may actually be right" is a powerful stress-relieving context that is always available to us. Its stress-relieving capability stems from helping us overcome our tendency to automatically judge other people (or ourselves) as being "wrong" when this is not always the case.

▶ NOTE: It is also possible to create foolish or unrealistic contexts, or to use potentially stress-relieving contexts in dangerous or inappropriate ways. For example, assuming that other people are "right" every time you believe them to be "wrong" is not the thing to do in ALL situations. Occasionally, this could cause you to experience even more stress. But most of the time this coping strategy will reveal hidden aspects of a problem or situation that are not usually obvious to you.

The Power Of Created Contexts

While positive thoughts, positive affirmations, and positive forms of self-talk can sometimes function as self-empowering tools, created contexts, in general, are much more powerful. Ghandi, for example, forced the British to leave India on the basis of a single context—the idea of non-violent resistance—which he created and maintained as the central guiding principle for his life.

The reason contexts are more powerful than thinking positive thoughts is because they do something more than simply allow a difficult problem or circumstance to be looked at in a different way. They also have the power to alter one's existence so that the reality one linguistically envisions eventually becomes an actual reality in life.

Let me share an example from my own life to illustrate this important point. Many years ago, I used the power of created contexts to change myself from a person who hated running (and exercise in general) to a person who now thoroughly enjoys the act of running. As a result of harnessing this linguistic power, I have since completed five major marathons, including two Boston Marathons, and I have also taught hundreds of other people to enjoy the sport of running as well.

Prior to my understanding of created contexts, however, I hated the act of running. Whenever I tried to run on a regular basis, I felt stiff, sore, and completely exhausted. I was physically able to run about a mile, but only with a great deal of pain and discomfort. I was absolutely certain that anyone who ran on a regular basis had to be disturbed, and that anyone who ran a marathon had to be a masochist. The three things I knew for sure about running were: 1) I was not a runner; 2) running was no fun at all; and 3) I clearly lacked the discipline and willpower to run on a regular basis.

Then, one day, something very strange occurred. I started to wonder "what if there was a natural runner inside of me that I had been suppressing? What if running really wasn't an unpleasant activity, but it was me who was making it painful in ways that I was not consciously aware of?"

While I actually didn't believe this was true, the idea was so intriguing that I was eager to check it out. So I decided to run a marathon (26.2 miles) and train for it in a way that was easy, enjoyable, and as pain-free as possible.

My first step was to "invent" the appropriate contexts that might empower me to achieve my goals. After a great deal of thought and experimentation, I settled upon the following guiding principles:

Context #1: "I do have the ability to enjoy the act of running."

Context #2: "If running isn't enjoyable for me, I must be somehow making it unpleasant."

As a result of creating and *living from* these self-selected contexts, which were very different than positive thoughts or affirmations, I was able to manifest the realities they suggested. Specifically, I used these contexts to uncover more than 30 different ways in which I had been programmed to automatically—i.e. unconsciously—turn running into a painful, unenjoyable activity.

One of the first patterns I uncovered was my automatic tendency to push myself very hard—at near-maximum speed—whenever I went for a run. I remembered that my mother had always told me "if it doesn't hurt, it probably isn't good for you." This "no pain; no gain" conversation had clearly become programmed into my body, where it influenced my approach to running even though I was unaware of it. No wonder I always felt sore and uncomfortable!

Once I became aware of this hidden pattern, however, I was able to neutralize it by designing my own running strategy. I reduced my speed to a leisurely, relaxing pace, and I decided to stop and walk whenever I felt the slightest bit uncomfortable. When my feelings of discomfort completely disappeared, I would begin to run again, making sure to stop and walk each time they reappeared. After a while, I was able to run farther and farther without having to stop.

Within one month of adopting my two created contexts, I was able to run five miles with ease. Within three months, I was able to run twenty miles with hardly any pain or discomfort. In December, 1979, I ran 26.2 miles in 3 hours and 48 minutes. I felt terrific during the entire race, except for the last half mile when I developed a cramp in my side. That evening, I went to a party and danced until midnight. The next day, I woke up feeling refreshed and energetic, although both my legs were stiff and sore.

The point of this example is not that I was able to run a marathon, but rather that two simple contexts enabled me to do it. Despite having no proof or evidence for the "realities" they suggested, I was able to actualize those realities in a real and tangible way.

25 Stress-Relieving Contexts

Starting on the next page is a list of twenty-five stress-relieving contexts that have already been tested and that can help you eliminate much of the stress you experience. I frequently use each of these contexts myself, and they have also been of value to many of my patients.

► NOTE: It is important not to think of these contexts as "truths" in and of themselves. Instead, it is best to consider them as "corrective lenses" that you can temporarily "put on" to compensate for your blindness or to reveal certain truths about yourself or about life that you are not accustomed to seeing. Also, do not expect to fully understand or make use of these contexts at this point in the book. As you read about them further, their value will become more apparent.

Twenty Five Stress-Relieving Contexts

Everything in life is always working.

True responsibility means neither
credit nor blame.

There is no such thing as a stressful
situation.

There is no such thing as a stressful
occupation.

However I am feeling is exactly how
I should be feeling.

Anything that happens can be
used to my advantage.

If I'm feeling "stressed" in any way, I
must be somehow creating my problems.

If I'm feeling unhappy or dissatisfied, I
must be somehow creating my unhappiness.

If I'm having relationship conflicts, I
must be somehow creating these problems.

If I'm having financial difficulties, I
must be somehow creating these problems.

The best way to get love
is to give love.

Negative conversations about myself
are rarely true.

Negative conversations about others
are rarely true.

Negative conversations about life
are rarely true.

When I think someone (including myself)
is wrong, that person may actually be right.

When I think someone (including myself)
is right, that person may actually be wrong.

Happiness and satisfaction are always
available to me regardless of my circumstances.

The past does not determine the future.

Successful people often ask for
help.

People are capable of solving their own
problems and difficulties.

People naturally want to contribute
to other people.

People always make the best decisions they
can, given the information available to them.

Life can be a win-win proposition.

The state of my body has much to do
with the way I am living my life.

None of the statements above is
always true.

These contexts can be used as powerful antidotes for many of the internal causes of your stress. Some of these antidotes can be applied to any type of stress, whereas others are geared to particular problems or situations.

By no means am I implying that these are the *only* stress-relieving contexts available to you. Hundreds of others contexts and guiding principles can also be of value. If you learn to master these specific ones, however, you will be way ahead of most other people.

You will also find it easier to benefit from other stress-relieving principles that you might subsequently encounter during your lifetime.

Let's examine a few of these contexts in more detail.

EVERYTHING IN LIFE IS ALWAYS WORKING

This context is the antidote for internal conversations such as "Things aren't working," "Life isn't working," "My life isn't working," or other similar conclusions. While life often appears not to be "working," this is seldom truly the case.

There is another legitimate perspective in which "life is always working" regardless of how things turn out. When a lion kills a zebra, for example, we could say that life isn't working very well for the zebra. But without such predator-prey interactions, the entire ecological balance of our planet would be disrupted. Thus, when a lion kills a zebra we could also say that life is working, even if we dislike the outcome.

Similarly, if you are unhappy or unsuccessful, you could argue that life isn't working as it should. You could also argue that life is working exactly as it should, in the sense that when you don't do what is necessary to achieve happiness or success, you should not be surprised when happiness or success eludes you.

NOTE: The problem with assuming "life isn't working" is that it shields you from acknowledging your own responsibility in the matter. It enables you to falsely blame life for your suffering and misery, instead of looking within yourself to determine your own internal causes.

TRUE RESPONSIBILITY MEANS NEITHER CREDIT NOR BLAME

In our society, "responsibility" is synonymous with either credit or blame. As we have already seen, such either/or viewpoints are frequently misleading. For example, we usually play some role—direct or indirect—in almost everything that happens to us. While we are not usually aware of the role we play, this role exists nonetheless.

► NOTE: Arguing that human beings are not responsible—at least in part—for most of the things that happen to them is like arguing that baseball catchers have nothing to do with successful pitching performances. When a baseball team wins a "no-hitter," for example, the pitcher becomes the focus of attention. He is treated as if he produced the no-hitter all by himself, even though we all know that the catcher and many other players also played a role. Sometimes, the role of the catcher is even more important, but much less noticeable, than that of the pitcher. Thus, instead of arguing which one was really responsible—the pitcher or the catcher—it would be much more accurate to acknowledge that both were necessary for the event to have occurred.

Thus, by creating the context "True responsibility means neither credit nor blame," you can make it easier to acknowledge your own role in causing whatever happens in your life without needing to feel guilty, remorseful, or unilaterally to blame.

► NOTE: Guilt, remorse, and blame all result from viewing responsibility from an either/or perspective.

THERE IS NO SUCH THING AS A FRUSTRATING SITUATION

As we saw in earlier chapters, external events only trigger our emotions; they don't directly cause them to occur. Thus, there is no such thing as a frustrating situation—only situations that trigger frustration-producing conversations and action patterns within us.

By declaring to yourself "There is no such thing as a frustrating situation," you can remind yourself that the main causes of your emotions lie within you. Thus, instead of blaming your situation for the way you feel, you can begin to identify and take charge of your own internal causes.

THERE IS NO SUCH THING AS A STRESSFUL OCCUPATION

The same can be said for "stressful" occupations. While some occupations are generally more stressful than others, it is not necessarily true that they are *inherently* stressful. Many physicians, for example, believe that medicine, by nature, is a highly stressful occupation. My own experiences as a physician, along with the experiences of many of my colleagues, show this widespread belief is not really true.

It all depends on how you relate to your job or profession. If you approach the practice of medicine in a self-sacrificing, perfectionistic, dogmatic manner, you will probably find that it is very stressful. But if you honestly assess your strengths and weaknesses, if you are flexible in your attitudes and beliefs, if you know when to be perfectionistic or take control and when these behaviors are not really necessary, and if you understand the limitations of science and medical knowledge, you can practice medicine today with little stress or tension.

ANYTHING THAT HAPPENS CAN BE USED TO MY ADVANTAGE

This is the "half-full vs. half-empty" situation. Life is certainly full of unexpected twists, turns, problems, and difficulties. Many of us tend to automatically respond to such problems in a negative, pessimistic manner. When you create the context "Anything that happens can be used to my advantage," you can keep yourself from getting stuck in these negative, pessimistic outlooks. The more you assume that advantages and opportunities are lurking in every "disaster," the more you will find that they really do exist.

HOWEVER I AM FEELING IS EXACTLY HOW I SHOULD BE FEELING

Most of us believe we should always be in control of our thoughts and our feelings. We also believe there are "right" ways and "wrong" ways to feel in certain situations. As we have already seen, however, it is not always possible to control your emotional reactions. Certain situations will trigger emotions within you, but these emotional reactions are not really "wrong" since your body has been programmed to respond as such. Thus, whenever you are triggered to feel sad, angry, anxious, or depressed, you are probably feeling exactly the way you should be feeling, given your existence as a Biolinguistic organism.

This context should never be used as an excuse for indulging or wallowing in your triggered feelings. To the contrary, I argue in this book that you can learn to make most of your negative moods and emotions disappear whenever you want. Thus, the purpose of this declaration is not to condone your triggered reactions, but to keep you from feeling guilty, stupid, weak, or incompetent for experiencing them in the first place.

Another way this context can be of value is when your triggered feelings are indeed appropriate for your situation. When someone close to you dies, for example, it's normal to feel sad or depressed. When you are genuinely concerned about your safety or welfare, it is normal to feel afraid. And if someone does something nasty or cruel to you, it's normal to feel hurt or angry. In these and other situations, declaring to yourself, "However I am feeling is exactly how I should be feeling," may keep you from ignoring or devaluing your legitimate reactions.

IF I'M FEELING "STRESSED" IN ANY WAY, I MUST BE SOMEHOW CREATING MY PROBLEMS

This is just another way of reminding yourself to relate to your stress as "feedback."

▶ NOTE: The principle of "feedback" is so important that I have stated it four different ways in the list of twenty five contexts beginning on page 130.

Our normal tendency is to automatically assume that something other than ourselves is responsible for our stress. Either life is going wrong, or other people are doing something wrong, or our bodies are malfunctioning, etc. The last thing we consider is that we may be the source of our own pain and suffering. People who know how to win against stress, on the other hand, frequently adopt this self-empowering context.

While many people are concerned that adopting this context might cause them to experience even more "stress," the opposite usually occurs.

NEGATIVE CONVERSATIONS ABOUT MYSELF (OR OTHERS) ARE RARELY TRUE

You should always be suspicious of any negative conversation about yourself or other people. While these conversations often appear to be true, they can usually be found to be inaccurate on closer inspection.

The best way to deal with such negative conversations is to declare over and over again that "Negative conversations about myself (or others) are rarely true." This may keep you from judging yourself or others too harshly. It can also help you focus on the positive qualities both you and others possess. Thus, when you hear yourself saying things like: "I shouldn't be feeling this way," or "I shouldn't have done what I did," or "I must be stupid," or "That's just the way I am," you should always assume that the real truth is not being told. You should also be skeptical when you hear other people make similar comments.

How To Make Use Of A Stress-Relieving Context

A great deal of confusion exists today about how to use the stress-relieving contexts discussed above. Most of this confusion stems from:

- Failing to understand this strategy from a Biolinguistic perspective;

- The need for courage and wisdom in using this approach;

- The use of such contexts as linguistic "stepping stones" for taking more effective coping actions.

The Biolinguistic Perspective

It's important to remember that the conversations and action patterns which produce most of your stress are located in your body, not your mind. This means they get triggered automatically—i.e. you don't have to think of them or create them in order for them to appear.

A stress-relieving context, on the other hand, is not usually established in your body. It will not occur for you automatically, so you must consciously create it or *it will not exist for you.* Moreover, once you create a stress-relieving or self-empowering context, it will vanish almost immediately. It does not persist in your body—and hence your awareness—for very long. This means that all stress-relieving contexts must be continually *recreated.*

▶ NOTE:This is very different from our usual expectation. Once we understand something or have a new insight, we usually expect such insights to carry over into the future. While they can indeed be useful to us in our future endeavors, they will not appear *automatically* unless we do things to "remember"—i.e. recreate—them.

After months or years of creating certain contexts, they may become established as permanent parts of your body. This often requires much practice and repetition, however. If you are programmed to view life negatively, for example, it may take thousands of instances of creating opposing contexts before you automatically begin to see things more positively. Until this transition occurs, you must actively and consciously create your positive contexts over and over again.

One problem this introduces is that in order to benefit from a stress-relieving context you must literally "make it up." This can sometimes confuse people since making up a context can seem like naive or "make-believe" thinking.

In a book titled *Healing Fiction,* psychotherapist James Hillman argues that much of the success of therapy depends upon such useful "fictions." According to Hillman, our usual perceptions of reality have already been distorted by our own unconscious fictions, stories, and limiting declarations. To become aware of these fictions and to *consciously participate in designing new ones* is what successful psychotherapy is all about. In the publisher's preface to Hillman's book, George Quasha sums up the author's central theme as follows:

> The 'sickness' of our lives has its source in our fictions. . .(and) our fictions can be 'healed' through willing participation. . .(p. ix.)

Thus, when we make up something that *really is true*—but not normally apparent to us—we are not necessarily engaging in "make-believe" thinking. For example, pretending you are "lovable" or you are a "worthy" human being is not necessarily fantasizing. By consciously assuming such "realities" about yourself, you can actually empower yourself to identify and overcome some of the conversations and action patterns that keep you from recognizing their validity.

Courage

Making up a context and having the faith to live from it requires a great deal of courage. Courage is required because many stress-relieving contexts go against the popular wisdom of society. Many of these contexts will be considered foolish or unrealistic by your peers, including family members, co-workers, and friends.

Thus, to create and maintain these stress-relieving contexts, you must be prepared to withstand the criticisms and taunts of others.

Courage is also required to challenge certain beliefs that are generally accepted by experts. In order to win in many areas of life, you must often be willing to question certain elements of professional dogma and to chart your own course when you find these to be in error.

EXAMPLE: All of the assertions I make about stress in this book are actually examples of created contexts, including:

- "Stress is not inevitable."
- "Stress is just a word."
- "Stress is always caused by conversations and action patterns that become triggered within us."
- "Stress is not a mind-body problem."
- "The best way to deal with stress is not to manage or avoid it, but to identify and deal with its underlying causes."

Each of these notions contradicts prevailing thought in our society. Each also contradicts many of the thoughts, beliefs, and automatic behavior patterns that were previously ingrained in our bodies. Thus, in order to become a winner against stress, you must have both the courage and the commitment to adopt such alternative viewpoints, even though others may strongly disagree with you.

Still another type of courage is needed because created contexts are not a function of proof, evidence, or previous personal experiences. *You do not need proof that a context is "true" before you begin to use it.* In fact, the proof almost always comes later, after you have tried out the new context and found it to be effective.

► NOTE: A stress-relieving context need not be true itself in order to be useful. The context "I am the cause of any stress that occurs for me" is not completely true. Neither is its counterpart "I am not the cause of any stress that occurs for me." As a created context, however, the first of these contexts is enormously self-empowering. Why? Because it enables us to compensate for the latter conversation, which frequently gets triggered in our bodies. Thus, even though a created context may not be true itself, it may still be useful if it helps us to recognize an important, but neglected, truth about life.

We are usually very reluctant, however, to embrace a new idea or theory unless we have proof of its validity beforehand. Even though many important scientific discoveries began as nothing more than intuitive "hunches" on the part of their originators, we continue to operate as if we *must have proof* before we can adopt a self-empowering context or guiding principle.* It takes another type of courage, therefore, to embrace a stress-relieving context without first having proof, evidence, or the endorsement of other people.

Wisdom

In addition to courage, it also takes wisdom to use this coping strategy. Not only must you have some idea about which created contexts have the potential to be stress-relieving, but you must also be able to distinguish when it is appropriate and when it is not appropriate to use them. As I mentioned earlier in this chapter, certain winning contexts can be used in foolish or even dangerous ways. They are not to be believed as "truths" that always hold. Each problem or situation must be evaluated individually to determine if it would be useful to invoke such coping strategies.

► NOTE: Most of the time—probably more than 80-90%—you can assume that you will indeed benefit from adopting these contexts. As long as you understand this will not always be the case, you will probably be able to recognize those times when it would be unwarranted to use this coping strategy. For example, the context "There is no such thing as a stressful occupation" should not be used to remain in a job that is totally unsatisfying to you or that may be damaging to your health or well-being. Its intent is to help you look at the ways in which you might be contributing to your job-related stress, and if this proves to be helpful in any way, then it was a useful context for you to have created. If it doesn't prove useful, or if it makes your problems worse, you should quickly abandon it and look for other coping alternatives.

* For example, when Einstein proposed that E=mc2 in 1905, there was no scientific proof to confirm his suspicion. It was not until twenty years later that the first scientific experiment was devised to confirm this generally-accepted law of the universe.

Stepping Stones

You can avoid many of the unwise or inappropriate uses of such contexts by remembering they are merely "stepping stones" for taking new types of actions to resolve certain types of problems you experience in your life. If they don't help you act in more effective ways, and if they don't result in tangible, desired results, then don't waste your time entertaining them for very long.

For example, the context "Anything that happens can be used to my advantage" is worthless—and sometimes harmful—unless you interact with a problem or event in such a way that actualizes this reality. The context itself is merely a stepping stone you can use to take new types of actions that are consistent with this declaration.

Again, this in one of the major ways in which created contexts differ from positive thoughts, affirmations, or "self-talk." For a context to be stress-relieving, it does not have to be couched in positive terms. Sometimes it may resemble a positive-sounding statement, but other contexts may be negative or even neutral in their tone.

THE IMPORTANT FEATURE OF A STRESS-RELIEVING CONTEXT IS NOT WHETHER IT IS POSITIVE OR NEGATIVE, BUT WHETHER IT REVEALS CERTAIN ASPECTS OF LIFE THAT ARE NORMALLY NOT APPARENT TO YOU.

The context "I'm O.K., you're O.K.," for example, is only empowering if it reveals a truth about life—i.e. about you and others—that is hidden from your view. If you and other people are truly not "O.K." or lack the capacity to manifest this reality, then creating this context would be of very little value. In order to function as an antidote for stress, therefore, every winning context must be consistent with a possible truth about life.

Your Previous Programming Isn't Going To Go Away

One of the important secrets to winning against stress is to know that your internal, stress-producing conversations and action patterns are not going to go away just because you become aware of them or just because you temporarily create a context to reverse whatever blindness they have produced. They will continue to exist within you and create mischief in your life. But even though you can't change them or eliminate them, you do have the power to nullify their stress-producing effects.

Summary Of The Key Points Of This Chapter

The major points covered in this chapter are:

1. While language causes most of our stress to occur, we can also use language to overcome many of the limitations of our automatic tendencies.

2. Through language, we can "invent" stress-relieving contexts that can serve as "antidotes" for our internal conversations and action patterns.

3. These antidotes are contextual declarations, not positive thoughts, affirmations, or "self-talk."

4. As contextual declarations, they reveal aspects of reality that we don't normally see or that we are capable of actualizing if we take appropriate action.

5. As human beings, we also have the power to create foolish, unrealistic, or non-actualizable contexts or to use potentially stress-relieving contexts in foolish or dangerous ways.

6. The ability to create and utilize stress-relieving contexts is one of the major coping strategies that can help us become life-long winners in our battle against stress.

DAY 7: EXERCISES

1. *How many specific contexts can you find in the following passage from the Declaration Of Independence?:*

. . .We hold these truths to be self-evident, that all men are created equal, that they are endowed by their Creator with certain unalienable rights, that among these are life, liberty and the pursuit of happiness. . .

CONTEXTS = _____

2. *Which of the following contexts have been programmed into your body?: (Check all that might possibly apply)*

☐ "I am not O.K."
☐ "I am not very lovable."
☐ "I will never be a success."
☐ "I am incapable of being happily married."
☐ "I don't have what it takes to win against stress."

3. *Which of the following contexts would be foolish, unrealistic, or difficult for you to actualize?: (Check all that fit this description)*

☐ "I can do anything I want to do whenever I want to do it."
☐ "I can abuse my body and not pay a price."
☐ "I can abuse other people and not pay a price."
☐ "I should always be able to control my thoughts and feelings."
☐ "I am superior to most other people."

4. *Which of the following contexts would probably empower you?: (Check all that fit this description)*

☐ "You don't always get what you want."
☐ "If you want to have a friend, be a friend."
☐ "Do unto others as you would have others do unto you."
☐ "The best way to get love is to give love."
☐ "Life can be a win-win proposition."

5. What is the distinguishing feature that makes each of the statements in Question 4 more than just a positive thought, positive affirmation, or positive form of ''self-talk''?

_____

_____

_____

DAY 8

COACHING

"Coaching" is another powerful strategy for winning against stress. Since most of our stress is caused by internal conversations and action patterns that are difficult for us to "see," we can compensate for our blindness by allowing others to "coach" us.

Coaching is actually a context you create. It combines two of the stress-relieving contexts I listed in the previous chapter:

Coaching: A Created Context

"IF I'M FEELING 'STRESSED' IN ANY WAY, I MUST BE SOMEHOW CREATING MY PROBLEMS."

"IF I CAN'T FIGURE OUT HOW I AM DOING THIS, I SHOULD ASK OTHER PEOPLE FOR HELP."

Creating this context is the final step in the ultimate method. It can enable you to successfully deal with any type of stress that doesn't go away with the first five steps.

Examples Of Coaching In Everyday Life

Whenever I can't get my stress to go away naturally, I always assume the problem lies *with me*, not with the method outlined in this book. The first thing I do is repeat the first five steps, looking for errors or omissions I may have made. If my stress still doesn't go away, I will usually ask for coaching.

EXAMPLE: When a professional baseball player has a hitting slump, he will usually look within himself to determine the cause. He will try to figure out what he is doing wrong and then make corrections. If he fails to solve his problem, he will call upon others—coaches, teammates, family members, friends—anyone he believes might help him to succeed.

Similarly, if you want to excel in any sport or game, it's nice to have a coach to help you. Many amateur athletes also use this strategy. Bill Cosby, for example, has a tennis coach who tours with him on a regular basis. Other people hire golf coaches, ski instructors, racquetball coaches, and the like.

People also rely upon coaches in other areas of life. There are business coaches (called consultants), financial coaches, relationship coaches, child-birth coaches, computer coaches, book-publishing coaches, fitness coaches, weight loss coaches, and so on.

I have personally benefitted from many different coaches in my life. In high school and college, I was fortunate to have a number of excellent athletic coaches. During my medical school and residency training, I had several key mentors who contributed to my development. I have also received "coaching" from experts in communication skills, relationship skills, and counselling techniques.

I have also served as a coach for many individuals. I have done stress-related coaching, business and management coaching, marital and relationship coaching, weight loss coaching, and exercise coaching.

What amazes me the most about coaching is how reluctant people are to use it, especially when they are suffering from stress. There seems to be a pervasive, negative attitude about this strategy, even though it can be very beneficial.

One reason we are reluctant to take advantage of coaching is that we confuse it with psychotherapy. To ask for help with a stress-related problem makes many people feel they are weak, incompetent, or mentally ill. These feelings result from widespread misconceptions about what coaching is and how it differs from psychotherapy.

Coaching Vs. Psychotherapy

► NOTE: The comments that follow are not intended to be critical of psychotherapy or psychotherapists. Many therapists function as highly effective coaches and vice versa. My primary aim in this discussion is to point out that "coaching" and "psychotherapy" are two different activities. In other words, when a psychotherapist is "coaching," he or she is doing something slightly different than when he or she is doing therapy that does not involve coaching. I also want to point out that the helper-helpee relationships for coaching and psychotherapy are also different. These distinctions are important because many people who are not psychiatrists or psychologists can function as excellent "coaches" for you and other people. When you don't understand how these two activities differ, you will not know when and how to use them appropriately.

Coaching and psychotherapy differ in a number of ways. First of all, psychotherapists tend to view people from a disease-oriented perspective. Their job is to diagnose "illnesses" and treat individuals accordingly. Coaches, on the other hand, do not operate from disease-oriented or disability models. They view people as capable and able, lacking only in knowledge and instruction, and consider their job as bringing out the true "champion" within individuals.

Secondly, the goals of coaching are never vague, imprecise, or potentially conflicting. When you enter psychotherapy, both you and your therapist will often be unclear about the outcomes to be achieved. You may have a vague sense of being unhappy or "unwell" and an equally vague sense that you would like to change. As therapy proceeds, you may get clear about your goals, only to find that some of them clash with the goals your therapist has in mind.

When you ask for coaching, however, both you and your coach are always clear about what is to be accomplished: "I want to learn to win at tennis," "I want to play golf and shoot below par," "I want to double my business profits," or "I want to learn how to stop yelling at my children." Such well-defined goals are at the heart of every coaching relationship. They are never vague or imprecise, and they are always shared by all parties involved. While you may occasionally disagree about the best way to achieve your stated goals, both you and your coach will always be aiming at the same objectives.

A third way in which coaching differs from psychotherapy is that past history, past events, and past personal performances are not that important to a coach. Psychotherapists, in contrast, often place a great deal of emphasis on the past. Coaches are much more present and future oriented. Their concern is not so much what went on in the past, but what you want to have happen now. While your past may explain your previous level of performance, it does not necessarily limit what you can achieve in the future.

Another difference between coaching and psychotherapy is that coaches mainly engage in *pointing* and *empowering*, not theorizing. The function of a coach is to help you see where you are blind. A baseball player, for example, cannot see the fine points of his swing or batting stance when he is focusing on a ball coming toward him at 90 miles an hour. An experienced coach, on the other hand, can observe certain flaws the player may not notice. If a problem is detected, the coach brings it to the player's attention—by pointing to it— and then suggests several ways to correct it.

EXAMPLE: In 1989, The Baltimore Orioles signed a promising young pitcher named Ben McDonald to a professional contract. McDonald was one of the best college players in recent years. A few days after signing his contract, he traveled to Baltimore to audition for manager Frank Robinson and several Oriole coaches. To McDonald's surprise, Robinson correctly yelled out "curve ball" or "fastball" just before McDonald released every pitch. The manager and his staff had studied films of McDonald's delivery and had spotted certain movements that "tipped off" the pitch he was planning to throw. By pointing out these movements to the astonished rookie, Robinson made him aware of certain unconscious habits that he was previously blind to. This is the type of "seeing" and "pointing" that is the hallmark of effective coaching.

Psychotherapists, on the other hand, frequently theorize (this is why there is so much disagreement in the field). When coaches speak and point, however, there is rarely disagreement. Once a problem has been spotted, it can usually be recognized by everyone. Good coaches, therefore, rarely engage in supposition. They observe you in action, point out what you are doing wrong, and communicate with you in a way that enables you to improve your performance.

The role of both parties in a coaching relationship also differs from the client-therapist relationship in psychotherapy. For coaching to be successful, you must agree to empower your coach. This means *surrendering* to your coach's wisdom and judgement and following his or her instructions explicitly. Your coach, in turn, must be willing to assume such a leadership role. Many psychotherapists, however, are trained to be passive. They are very willing to assist you with your problems, but they consider you to be one who primarily directs the process.

Good coaches, on the other hand, rarely encourage you to "do your own thing" or "find your own way." To the contrary, they often take the position "it's my way or the highway." Your job, therefore, is to find a competent coach you can trust and then *surrender to his or her guidance.* Often, this will require you to trust his or her opinion more than you trust your own.*

This requirement to turn over control of your life to another human being is another major obstacle that keeps us from benefitting from coaching. It can cause us to refuse to ask for help altogether or to enter into coaching relationships with little intention of giving up control. Surrendering to your coach, therefore, is one of the most difficult, yet important, things you must do.

► NOTE: What stops most of us from surrendering to another person is distrust—not distrust of our coach, but distrust of ourselves. We fear that if we give up control to someone else, this person could abuse us. While this could happen, we don't trust that we can protect ourselves if it does. Surrendering to the will of another person doesn't mean we give up all of our critical faculties. It just means we acknowledge that our own ideas and strategies are insufficient to achieve our goals and that if we truly want to succeed, we will have to let others help us.

The final way in which coaching differs from psychotherapy is that both you and your coach always know how the process is going. Since the goals are clear from the outset, both people know if results are being produced. If they are not, adjustments must be made.

---

* Several popular movies have been made about the nature of the coaching relationship, including The Karate Kid (Part I), The Color Of Money, and Hoosiers.

In coaching, the burden for such adjustments rests mainly with the coach. In psychotherapy, the failure to make progress is often blamed on the client. A coach will usually look within himself or herself whenever things are not going well.

Examples of Successful Coaching

Coaching is an excellent strategy for dealing with many types of "stress." Often, all that people need to solve a difficult problem or conflict is a shift in their perspective of what's really going on.

EXAMPLE #1—TRIED, CONVICTED, AND SENTENCED

A 35-year-old woman came to see me for depression, guilt, and marital distress. "During the first five years of our marriage," she said, "we were as happy as any couple could be." Then, her husband decided to open his own business and she agreed to support him. At first the business went well, but then sales dropped off and expenses started to escalate. As the business did worse, both she and her husband increased their efforts to turn things around. They poured all of their savings into the failing venture; they took a second mortgage on their house; and they both borrowed money from their respective friends and relatives. After months and months of struggle and effort, the wife finally concluded that the business was not going to survive. She refused to ask her friends and family members for additional loans, and she communicated to her husband that she was no longer hopeful about their chances for success. She also told him that he would be very wise to close the business down.

The husband, on the other hand, refused to admit defeat. He continued to focus every waking hour on the business. When the business eventually failed and the couple was forced into bankruptcy, the husband's behavior changed. He withdrew from the relationship and started to have an affair. He also became abusive toward his wife, picking fights with her over trivial or manufactured issues.

Eventually, the wife came to see me because she was feeling hurt and depressed. She loved her husband very much, and she felt guilty and partly responsible for the failure of his dream. After listening to her story, however, I could see that she was not in touch with the truth about what happened. Her reluctance to go deeper into debt to support a failing venture was not inappropriate or wrong of her, and it in no way justified the punishment her husband was giving her. In his own heart, he had tried her, convicted her, and sentenced her for her crime, when in fact she had little to do with the demise of the business.

This coaching was all she really needed. Once she recognized that her own internal conversations of "wrong-doing" and "unilateral blame", which were strongly reinforced by her husband, were not completely accurate, she was able to deal with her feelings of guilt and depression more easily. She also stopped agreeing with her husband's accusations, and she began to confront him about his behavior in the relationship. Eventually, the husband acknowledged that he was indeed blaming her for the failure of his business, and that this was wrong and unfair of him, since his own poor decisions were largely responsible for his downfall. He ended his short-lived affair, forgave his wife for withdrawing her support, and they ultimately started a new business together which was much more successful.

EXAMPLE #2—THE POISONED APPLE

Jake, who was divorced, had been living alone for more than ten years. Then he met Janet, a vivacious, attractive young woman who recently came to work for his company. Janet went out of her way to make friends with Jake. They soon started dating and eventually began living together. All went well for about a year until Janet complained that she was bored with the relationship. She told Jake she wanted to date other men, and a short while later she moved back into her old apartment. She continued to see Jake on a regular basis at work, but all she wanted from him was a friendly relationship.

Needless to say, Jake was devastated by Janet's sudden turnaround. He longed to be with her and broke into tears whenever he saw her at the office. He blamed himself for the failure of their relationship, even though Janet had been married and divorced three times before, and even though he had done everything he could think of to please her and make her happy. He came to me for counselling because he was finding it difficult to get over her and because he wanted to stop feeling sad whenever he saw her at the office.

After working with Jake for one or two sessions, I could see why he was having trouble. While he was very willing to acknowledge his own problems as a relator, he never mentioned a word about Janet's deficiencies in this area. After all, she was so lovely, personable, and attractive that he was certain it must have been his fault the relationship failed.

What Jake had not seen was that Janet had a long-standing problem with commitment. She was easily attracted to men, but when this initial attraction wore off, so did her commitment. Jake had actually sensed this about her when they first met, but he was so enthralled with her that he ignored his "gut" reaction.

The coaching I offered Jake was to repeatedly create the context that Janet was like a poisoned apple—attractive and alluring but deadly to eat. Whenever he saw her at work, he was to consciously remind himself of this image. I even told him to place an apple on his desk every day, just to remind himself of this association. When I saw him two weeks later, he was greatly improved. The coaching had worked wonders, and he was no longer despondent about the breakup of the relationship.

EXAMPLE #3—BARKING UP THE WRONG TREE

Before I met my wife, Christina, I had a series of failed romantic relationships. I usually became attracted to women who were not very interested in me, but whom I eventually hoped to win over. When yet another of these relationships failed, I called a friend who specialized in relationship counselling. I spoke with her by phone for about twenty minutes, after which she said something to me that changed my life dramatically. She said, "You know, it sounds like you keep picking women who aren't really interested in you or who don't share your goals and ambitions in life. Why don't you make things easy for yourself by finding a woman who would be truly thrilled to be your partner?"

I can't tell you how dumbstruck I was by this simple communication. I had never considered that finding a compatible mate could be so easy. But it made sense to me, so I decided to give it a try. Within a month I met Christina, and a few months later we were engaged to be married.

The point of these examples is that coaching need not be complex, nor does it always require a prolonged period of time. One

critical observation or comment can sometimes be all that is needed. Obviously, many of life's problems cannot be solved so easily.
But more often than not, you can benefit greatly from the advice
and guidance of others.

How To Find And Utilize Different Kinds Of Coaches In Your Life

Coaching is one of the most abundant resources available to human
beings. Good coaches exist everywhere around you. All you have
to do is know how to: a) spot them; b) enlist their support; and
c) use them wisely. In the remainder of this chapter, I will focus
on each of these issues.

You Don't Always Need A Professional

To benefit from coaching, you don't always need a professional.
While professional coaches get paid for what they do, many people
in your life might be willing to coach you for free, especially if you
ask them for help and allow them to support you.

What To Look For In A Coach

Suppose you are having a relationship problem, a work-related
problem, or some other type of problem that you haven't been able
to resolve. And suppose you want to call upon a friend, family member, or associate to coach you. Here are some of the qualities you
should look for in a coach:

1) *Has the person mastered the type of problem you are having?*
Don't ask a 300 lb. person to coach you to lose weight. Ideally, you
want someone who has personally solved a similar problem or who
knows what it takes to do so. Look around for people who handle
problems like yours very easily. You can even ask your friends "Do
you know someone who's good at dealing with problem X?"

2) *Does the person have a track record of successfully helping others?*
While a successful track record isn't essential, it can be helpful. Some
people can handle certain problems well themselves but can't communicate to others what they know or what they did. Be sure to check
out your potential coach's record of success as tactfully as you can.

3) *Is the person good at "seeing" and "pointing" or are they prone
to theorizing and hypothesizing?*

From your initial conversations, you can usually tell if someone has what it takes to coach you. Since "seeing" and "pointing" are what your coach will need to do, you should be able to get a feel for whether the person is oriented this way.

4) *Is the person trustworthy?*
You should feel that you could put your life in your coach's hands and you would be taken care of. If you get any hint of the opposite feeling, look for someone else.

5) *Is the person willing to work with you?*
When you find someone who meets your criteria, ask them to become involved. Tell them the specific problem or problems you are having and the specific outcomes you want to achieve. Then, ask if they would be willing to work with you to help you achieve your goals. If they say "yes" or "perhaps," then ask what they would expect of you. When both of you reach agreement on these terms, you have created the foundation for a successful coaching relationship. If, on the other hand, you detect any unwillingness or hesitancy on the other person's part, don't force the issue. Promising to coach someone is a huge responsibility. Therefore, you should only work with people who are excited about your goals and who have a decent chance of helping you to succeed.

6) *Does the person have a higher estimation of you and your abilities than you do yourself?*
Most people believe they will never solve their problems. Since they've tried many times in the past and failed, they have no reason to expect any other outcome. You want a coach, therefore, who can see through your pessimism, who has confidence in your ability, and who knows you can succeed regardless of your beliefs to the contrary.

7) *Does the person tend to see things differently than you do?*
The last thing you want is a coach who thinks and sees things exactly as you do. What you need is someone who can help you break out of the conceptual "box" you've been living in. For example, if you have trouble sticking to an exercise plan because you buy into any excuse that conveniently comes along, you don't want a coach who will sympathize with you. You want someone who is rarely stopped by excuses, who doesn't care how good your arguments are, and who will hold you to your exercise agreements no matter what you say or do.

How To Enlist A Coach's Committed Partnership

To enlist a coach's partnership you can either: 1) pay them, or 2) ask them to volunteer. Either way, you've got to assure them you are serious about achieving your goals. More importantly, you've got to convince them that you are willing to surrender to their guidance and support. The best way to do this is to promise this explicitly. Say to the person "Look, I really want you to coach me and I give you my word I will do whatever you say." Then stick to this promise as best as you can. This is what most coaches truly want to hear. They do not like trying to help someone who is going to fight them and resist them every step of the way.

▶ NOTE: You can even get coaching without asking for it directly. If you find someone who is proficient or expert at something, you can tap that person's wisdom in many ways. You can follow them around to learn what they think and do. You can read any books or articles they may have written. You can attend their public lectures and workshops. You can even invite them to speak to your club or organization. As long as you have the desire to be coached in a particular area of life, you can always find people who can help you succeed.

How To Use Your Coaches Wisely

The most important thing to remember about coaching is that *the outcome is largely dependent upon you*. The critical factors are:

- How badly do you want to solve your problem or develop a particular skill?
- Are you willing to invest the time and energy required?
- Are you truly open to the thoughts and ideas of others?
- Are you willing to be brutally honest (if necessary) about both your strengths and your weaknesses?
- Are you willing to surrender to the wisdom and guidance of another?

If the answers to these questions are all affirmative, you will find it easy to benefit from coaching.

This concludes our discussion of the six major steps in the ultimate method. In the next five chapters (9-13), I will show you how this same step-by-step approach can be used to deal with any type of "stress" you encounter.

DAY 8: EXERCISES

1. *Go to a video store and rent one of the following movies: a) The Karate Kid, Part I; b) The Color Of Money; c) Hoosiers. Even if you have seen the movie before, watch it again, recalling what you have learned about coaching from this chapter.*

☐ Check here if you agree to do this.
  By when will you do this: _____

2. *Think of three current problems in your life for which you could benefit from coaching.*

A _____

B _____

C _____

3. *Think of a time when you asked someone for help but refused to follow their advice. Write down your justifications for refusing.*

_____

_____

_____

_____

4. *Think of a time when you tried to help someone else, but that person refused to surrender to you. Did you address this issue of surrender with them? Write down whatever you remember.*

_____

_____

_____

_____

5. *Write down three things you have learned about coaching from your observations of professional coaches and athletes (in any sport).*

A _____

B _____

C _____

DAY 9

NEGATIVE MOODS AND EMOTIONS

The six-step method we have just examined can be used to deal with any type of "stress" you encounter. It can help you deal with emotional distress, relationship conflicts, stress at work, stress-related physical complaints, financial stress, and many other problems. This chapter focuses on the first of these problem categories: negative moods and emotions.

How To Eliminate Negative Moods And Emotions

Everyone experiences negative moods and emotions from time to time. Emotions such as anger, sadness, fear, guilt, frustration, and worry are very common, as are moods such as depression, apathy, irritability, boredom, and resentment. The secret to dealing with any negative mood or emotion is to follow the step-by-step method outlined in Chapter 4:

STEP 1—Be Specific!

Every negative mood and emotion has internal conversations and action patterns that cause it to occur. In order to pinpoint these causes, you must first identify the specific mood or emotion you are experiencing.

Saying you are "stressed," "upset," or "emotionally exhausted" is not sufficient. When you use these terms, you are probably suffering from one or more of the following specific problems:

Figure 9-1

*Negative Moods And Emotions**
(Check the ones that bother you frequently)

☐ Anger	☐ Hostility
☐ Annoyance	☐ Humiliation
☐ Apathy	☐ Impatience
☐ Boredom	☐ Insecurity
☐ Depression	☐ Jealousy
☐ Despair	☐ Loneliness
☐ Dissatisfaction	☐ Panic
☐ Embarrassment	☐ Powerlessness
☐ Fear/Anxiety (Acute)	☐ Resentment
☐ Fear/Anxiety (Chronic)	☐ Resignation
☐ Frustration	☐ Sadness
☐ Grief	☐ Shame
☐ Guilt	☐ Worthlessness
☐ Hopelessness	☐ Worry

Distinguishing which of these moods and emotions you are experiencing at any point in time is not always easy. The following guidelines may help you with this task:

A) *The "Big Three" Negative Emotions*

Most emotional distress results from three basic emotions: FEAR, SADNESS, and ANGER. One way to clarify your feelings, therefore, is to ask yourself:

> What am I feeling most right now—
> FEAR, SADNESS, OR ANGER?

* This list does not include every negative mood or emotion.

Once you answer this question, you can further clarify your problem as follows:

ANGER

FRUSTRATION—Anger at yourself.

RESENTMENT—Low-grade anger over an extended period of time (lack of forgiveness).

HOSTILITY—Tendency to express or act out angry feelings easily.

IMPATIENCE—Anger about time (hurry-up syndrome).

ANNOYANCE—Mild form of anger.

IRRITABILITY—Tendency to become angry over trivial events.

FEAR

ACUTE ANXIETY/PHOBIAS—acute fear reactions precipitated by specific situations, objects, or events.

INSECURITY—sense of impending loss or disaster.

WORRY—excessive concern about the possibility of negative outcomes.

JEALOUSY—a combination of insecurity, worry, and sometimes anger about the possible loss of something you value to someone else.

EMBARRASSMENT—fear that a humiliating secret will be revealed to others.

PANIC—an acute sense of impending doom or disaster (e.g. "I'm going to have a heart attack," "I'm going to become paralyzed," "I'm going to die!," etc.).

CHRONIC ANXIETY—a chronic sense of insecurity, worry, jealousy, embarrassment, or any other fear without a discrete precipitating event or circumstance.

```
┌─────────────────────┐
│                     │
│       SADNESS       │
│                     │
└─────────────────────┘
```

GRIEF—loss of something valued.

DISSATISFACTION—loss of happiness or satisfaction.

DEPRESSION—loss of self-esteem, self-confidence, and optimism about the future.

DESPAIR—loss of the will or desire to live.

HUMILIATION—loss of social acceptance by others.

HOPELESSNESS—loss of hope regarding the future.

POWERLESSNESS—loss of confidence that you can personally influence a problem or situation.

RESIGNATION—loss of confidence that you or anyone else can influence a problem or situation.

LONELINESS—loss of someone to love, communicate with, or relate to.

APATHY—loss of desire, enthusiasm, and initiative.

BOREDOM—loss of excitement, loss of interest.

SHAME—loss (real or imagined) of esteem in the eyes of others.

WORTHLESSNESS—loss of self-esteem, self-worth.

GUILT—loss of self-esteem due to self-punishment for a real or imagined crime or offense.

B) *Your Most Obvious Feelings May Not Be The Only Ones*

Another problem with identifying your moods and emotions is that some of your feelings are not always obvious. "I'm feeling angry," for example, may mean you are angry, but it may also mean you are feeling hurt, disappointed, insulted, or betrayed. Similarly, when you are "anxious" you are usually afraid. But sometimes anxiety can also mean you are angry. This is because intense feelings of anger can make you afraid of hurting another person or being hurt yourself.*

Thus, while some of your feelings may be very apparent, they may not be the only ones that are causing you to feel "stressed."

C) *Moods And Emotions Can Change Very Quickly; They Can Also Occur In Rapid Succession*

Suppose you are at work one day and you begin to feel frustrated about not being able to accomplish some task. And suppose your frustration quickly leads to anger, which causes you to scream and yell and throw your papers on the floor. The next thing you know, everyone in the office is looking at you, and you begin to feel embarrassed and guilty for disturbing their work as well. As you reflect upon your behavior, you begin to feel ashamed and suffer a temporary loss of self-esteem.

This example illustrates two things you've probably already noticed:

1. *Your moods and emotions change from time to time.* Some may persist for days, months, or even years while others can come and go in an instant.

2. *Your moods and emotions often occur in rapid sequences.* The appearance of one emotion triggers the appearance of another, which then triggers another—all in a very short period of time.

This latter phenomenon can also make it difficult to identify your moods and emotions precisely. Often, you will not be aware of each individual mood or emotion in a sequence. In the example above, frustration, anger, embarrassment, guilt, and shame all occurred in rapid succession, each being produced by its own set of hidden conversations and action patterns:

* Some negative moods and emotions can affect you even though you may not be aware of them. This is particularly true for anger.

Figure 9-2

Each Mood Or Emotion In A Sequence Is Caused By Its Own
Specific Conversations (C) and Action Patterns (A)

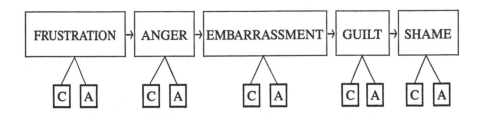

When complex sequences such as these occur, you don't have to deal with every component of the chain. Usually, all you have to do is focus on the first or last emotion. If you go back to the first negative emotion (frustration) and deal with it successfully, none of the other emotions would have arisen. Or, if you deal with the last emotion (shame), much of your "stress" will also go away.

The following sequences of moods and emotions occur very frequently:

FRUSTRATION——ANGER
You become frustrated by failing to accomplish some task, and this causes you to get angry at yourself or at others around you.

ANGER——GUILT
You react angrily toward other people, then immediately feel guilty when they seem hurt or rejected.

ANGER——RESENTMENT (ANGER OVER TIME)
You become angry with someone then hold on to your anger long after the precipitating event is over.

FEAR/SADNESS/ANGER——EMBARRASSMENT——SHAME
You react with fear, sadness, or anger to a situation, then feel embarrassed for reacting in this way, which causes you to feel ashamed for both your initial reaction and the embarrassment that followed it.

IMPATIENCE——ANGER——GUILT

You get impatient with someone, which causes you to get angry with them. When you see their hurt reaction, you feel guilty for having responded in such a harsh manner.

GUILT——DEPRESSION

You feel so guilty about something that you begin to ruminate about it. You criticize yourself severely and then begin to feel worthless and depressed.

D) *Pay Attention To What Triggered You*

While external events don't cause your emotions to occur, you should still pay attention to the circumstances that trigger you. These can provide you with valuable clues about the specific feelings you may be experiencing.

Suppose someone insults you, for example, and you are left feeling "tense" or "upset." By recognizing the circumstances under which such feelings occurred, you can deduce that you are probably feeling angry, hurt, or both. Or suppose you are feeling "stressed" after someone close to you dies. Given the nature of the precipitating event, it's likely you are sad or possibly angry. Thus, when you aren't sure which particular mood or emotion is bothering you, take a good look at the events or circumstances that triggered you.

STEP 2—Relate To Your Negative Moods And Emotions As Feedback

Once you identify a specific mood or emotion to work on, the next step is to consider it as "feedback." This means assuming that you—not what happens to you or the behavior of other people—are the primary cause of the way you are feeling.

Take the emotion of frustration, for example. As we saw in Chapter 5, frustration is not directly caused by the problems and obstacles we encounter in life, nor is it caused by our failure to accomplish a particular task. Frustration always results from the following conversations and action patterns that become triggered within us:

CONVERSATIONS THAT PRODUCE FRUSTRATION IN HUMAN BEINGS:

1) I am not succeeding.
2) I should easily be able to succeed in this situation.
3) If I just keep trying harder and harder, I will eventually succeed.
4) If I don't succeed, I must be dumb, stupid, weak or incompetent.

ACTION PATTERNS THAT PRODUCE OR MAINTAIN FRUSTRATION IN HUMAN BEINGS:

A) Failing to recognize unrealistic goals and expectations.
B) Failing to challenge your definition of "success."
C) Failing to relate to your failures as "feedback."
D) Failing to admit: a) you may not know how to succeed, or b) you might need help from others.

Choosing to relate to frustration as "feedback" enables you to recognize and deal with these internal causes. If, on the other hand, you blame your circumstances or external events for your emotions, you will find it very difficult to make frustration, or any other negative emotion, quickly disappear.

Step 3—Identify The Hidden Conversations And Action Patterns (Within You) That are Causing Each Of Your Negative Moods And Emotions To Occur Or Persist

As we have already seen, the internal causes of your feelings will not be obvious to you. Thus, you must do something to bring them into the open. The Index Card Technique is one good way to do this. Once you have an accurate index card for any negative feeling, all you have to do is refer to this card and presto—the invisible causes of your feelings will be brought to your attention.

In Appendix D, you will find copies of index cards for six of the most common negative moods and emotions (anger, frustration, worry, guilt, fear, and sadness). These copies can be cut out and pasted on actual index cards for your personal use. (You can also obtain a free set of pre-printed cards from Breakthru Publishing by returning the coupon, with a self-addressed envelope, located on page 289.)

► TIP: Think of your index cards as being similar to the handy "help screens" included with most computer programs. Whenever you encounter a problem with one of these programs, you can call up a help screen that reminds you of important information that is not normally visible to you. In much the same way, whenever you want to recall the hidden causes of any negative mood or emotion, you can use your index cards to make these causes apparent.

As you begin to use these cards, you may sometimes disagree with the statements they contain. If this occurs, ASSUME THE INFORMATION ON YOUR CARDS IS MORE ACCURATE THAN YOUR OWN THOUGHTS OR OPINIONS. Each of these cards has been tested with hundreds of individuals. Each has also been reviewed by expert psychologists, psychiatrists, and other knowledgeable professionals. Remember, emotion-producing conversations and action patterns operate in your body whether you agree with them or not. Even though you may know intellectually that one or more of the statements on your card is not true, your body may respond as if they actually are. Thus, if a particular mood or emotion has become triggered within you, each of the causes listed on your card has probably become triggered within you.

STEP 4—Remember, These Hidden Causes Exist In Your Body, Not Your Mind

Before trying to do something about these hidden causes, you should always remind yourself that they exist in your body, not your mind. This may keep you from feeling stupid, weak, or incompetent for reacting in such automatic ways. Remember, it isn't your fault you were programmed to think and respond in certain ways, and it's also not your fault that you can't get rid of such ingrained tendencies.

STEP 5—Take Action To Neutralize The Internal Causes Of Your Moods And Emotions

Once you are aware of the internal conversations and action patterns that are causing your feelings to occur, you can then take action to neutralize any unwanted effects these internal patterns produce. As we have seen, you can do this by:

1) *Challenging your stress-producing conversations*
2) *Disrupting your stress-producing action patterns*
3) *Creating stress-relieving contexts*

As we discussed in Chapter 6, you can put conversations such as GOOD/BAD, RIGHT/WRONG, CREDIT/BLAME, and STUPID/SMART on trial by pretending you are a lawyer who has been hired to argue against them. You can also "flip" each conversation to its opposite reality (discussed in Chapter 6 and Appendix B).

Consider the conversations and action patterns that produce frustration, for example. When you are frustrated, is it always true you are *not succeeding?* Sometimes the answer will be "yes," but often it should be "no." When Thomas Edison was asked how he kept going after failing more than 900 times before inventing the light bulb, he allegedly replied "What failures?" Each time one of his prototypes didn't work out, he learned something valuable that eventually helped him succeed.

Similarly, if you are frustrated with a particular project or task, is it always true that you should *easily be able to succeed?* Could you be lacking certain insights or skills that are necessary for success? If succeeding is dependent upon the cooperation of others, do those individuals have both the commitment and skill to get the job done? If not, then why are you expecting to succeed when these crucial ingredients are missing?

And is it always true *that trying harder* and harder is the best way to succeed? Sometimes this may be the case, but other times you may need to try "smarter," not harder. Instead of doing more and more of what already hasn't worked, you may need to step back and find out what you are doing wrong.

In addition to challenging your hidden conversations and disrupting your stress-producing action patterns, you can also create emotion-dissolving contexts. The following contexts are often very helpful for dealing with frustration and other negative moods and emotions:

-EVERYTHING IN LIFE IS ALWAYS WORKING—when you have unrealistic goals, impossible criteria for success, or when you lack the know-how, skill, or support to succeed, failure is exactly what should result.

-EVERYTHING THAT HAPPENS IN LIFE CAN BE USED TO MY ADVANTAGE—the obstacles or roadblocks you encounter can often be turned into benefits if you are resourceful and creative enough to use them in this way.

-THERE IS NO SUCH THING AS A STRESSFUL SITUATION—
Remember, situations themselves are never frustrating. Therefore, you should always search for hidden conversations and action patterns within you that are causing your frustration or other moods and emotions to occur.

-NEGATIVE CONVERSATIONS ABOUT MYSELF ARE RARELY TRUE—whenever you don't succeed at something, you are not necessarily stupid, weak, or incompetent. Always be suspicious of such negative generalizations. They are almost never true, even though your body may react as if they are.

STEP 6—If Your Stress Doesn't Disappear, Repeat Steps 1-5 And/Or Get Coaching

Whenever you fail to make a negative mood or emotion disappear, repeat steps 1-5, looking for errors you may have made. If that doesn't work, get coaching. Whatever you do, don't invalidate the method. If you are honest, persistent, and open to help from others, you can almost always discover what it takes to make your negative feelings disappear.

► TIP: You can even use this step-by-step approach to deal with any negative moods or emotions that arise from failing to use the method successfully. If you begin to feel angry, frustrated, guilty, or depressed for failing to make your negative feelings go away, you can use your index cards to uncover the hidden causes of these reactions. Most of the time, such feelings result from faulty assumptions, unrealistic expectations, or inappropriate use of the method we have been discussing.

The Truth About Forgiveness

Before moving on to consider stress in our interpersonal relationships, let's consider the issue of forgiveness. Much has been written and said about forgiveness throughout the ages. Despite this advice, we still find it difficult to forgive. While we may say the words "I forgive you" or "let's forget the past," still, in our hearts, we find this hard to do.

Forgiveness is tied to the emotion of anger. In order to forgive, you must "let go" of any anger or resentment that has been triggered within you. Most people find this difficult for two main reasons:

1) They don't understand what "letting go" really means;
2) They don't understand what causes their anger to occur in the first place.

As we have already seen, the causes of anger and resentment lie mainly within us. They are anger-producing conversations and action patterns that become triggered in us automatically. Often, they produce false internal realities that have little correspondence to the truth about what really happened. For example, automatic conversations such as "someone did something they shouldn't have done" or "I was hurt or harmed by what happened" or "the other person was unilaterally to blame for what occurred" are frequently incorrect. As a result of these mistaken realities, we conclude that a "crime" has been committed and that someone should apologize, offer to make amends, and/or be punished. When none of these things occur, we find it difficult to forgive.

There is no way you can let go of your anger or truly forget the past *as long as such false anger-producing "realities" remain unchallenged within you.* You cannot pretend all is forgiven when you are certain that: a) you were seriously harmed; b) the other person (or yourself) was unilaterally to blame; and c) this person should have done something different.

ONE SECRET TO TRUE FORGIVENESS IS TO CHALLENGE YOUR ASSUMPTION THAT A "CRIME" WAS ACTUALLY COMMITTED.

The best way to do this is to assume that the automatic assumptions that are maintaining your anger and resentment are probably false or misleading. Once you challenge and disprove these false internal realities, your anger and resentment will quickly disappear.

▶ NOTE: Even when a true crime, such as a theft or murder was committed, it is still possible—although not easy—to forgive the offending party. This can sometimes be done by challenging your automatic assumption that the person should have known better or should have behaved in a different manner.

In *You'll See It When You Believe It,* psychologist Wayne Dyer comments about forgiveness as follows:

Learning to forgive involves learning to correct the misperceptions you have created with your own thoughts. Once you have your thoughts clear. . . .you will get yourself to the point where forgiveness is no longer something you must practice. (p.249)

Dyer also points out:

The belief that others should not have treated us the way that they did is, of course, the ultimate absurdity. The universe is always working just the way it is supposed to, and so is everything in it, even the things that we have judged to be wrong, improper, cruel, and painful for us and others. . . . . .Instead of being angry at the way we were treated, regardless of how horrible we have assessed it to be, we need to learn to view that treatment from another perspective. They did what they knew how to do, given the conditions of their lives. (p.249)

EXAMPLE: Mark, a 45-year-old man, came to see me because he was still very angry with both of his parents, even though his father was dead. As a young child, he was confined to a sanatarium for more than a year because of rheumatic fever. He vividly remembered how his parents had "abandoned" him at the door of the sanatarium and how they had only visited him on rare occasions. He had concluded that this was a betrayal of their love for him—a betrayal which, even as an adult, he could not bring himself to forgive.

After several counselling sessions, I urged Mark to visit his elderly mother to check out his assumptions. He was instructed to share his feelings and memories with her and ask her what she remembered about the events at the time. He returned from this trip with a completely new perspective. He learned that both his mother and father were extremely upset about placing him in the sanatarium. They only consented because of extreme pressure from their family doctor, who believed that confining Mark to such a facility was the only way to save his life. Both of his parents felt terribly guilty and depressed about this decision, and they stayed away from the sanatorium because it was too painful for them to witness their son's unhappiness. When Mark finally realized that his parents had not "betrayed" or "abandoned" him, he was filled with compassion and empathy for their predicament. His anger and resentment immediately disappeared, and he no longer needed to forgive them for what had happened. Ironically, one or two additional counselling sessions were needed to help Mark forgive *himself* for unjustly blaming his parents for so many years.

The moral of this story is that if you are trying to force yourself to forgive another person (or yourself), this isn't true forgiveness. True forgiveness is more like an undoing. It is a willingness to challenge and disprove any anger-producing realities that become triggered within you. Once you see the truth about what really happened—including aspects of the truth that weren't initially apparent to you—your anger and resentment will usually disappear.

▶ NOTE: Since we are Biolinguistic organisms, our anger and resentment may reappear from time to time, even though we may have sincerely forgiven what happened in the past. Each time this happens, however, all we have to do is remind ourselves of the truth we discovered, and our anger and resentment will disappear once again.

Summary

Regardless of which negative mood or emotion you are experiencing—anger, frustration, worry, guilt, fear, etc.—you can always make such feelings quickly disappear by using the method described in Chapter 4. The more you learn to use this approach, the less you will need to rely upon drugs, cigarettes, alcohol, food, relaxation exercises, or other time-consuming stress management techniques.

DAY 9: EXERCISES

1. *Think of a time when you were very angry. Write down your reasons for believing you were innocently victimized by another person's actions.*

_____

_____

_____

2. *Using the same example, write down how you might have contributed to the events that occurred.*

_____

_____

_____

3. *Which of the following internal conversations are involved in producing the moods and emotions listed below? (Put a check in the appropriate column if you think the conversation is involved.)*

	GOOD/BAD	RIGHT/WRONG	CAUSE/EFFECT	CREDIT/BLAME
A. Fear				
B. Sadness				
C. Anger				
D. Impatience				
E. Guilt				
F. Worry				
G. Boredom				

4. *Think of a time when someone was angry with you. Write down how they must have been thinking or behaving, either consciously or unconsciously, to feel the way they did.*

_____

_____

_____

5. *Which of the following contexts might be useful for dealing with feelings of loneliness? (Check all that apply.)*

☐ Everything in life is always working.
☐ However I am feeling is exactly how I should be feeling.
☐ If I'm having relationship problems, I must be somehow creating these.
☐ The best way to get love is to give love.
☐ Negative conversations about myself are rarely true.

DAY 10

STRESS IN RELATIONSHIPS

Relationship problems are another type of "stress" we all experience from time to time. Conflicts can arise with our spouse, parents, children, friends, co-workers, employees, bosses, or even with total strangers.

As common as our relationship problems are, we often misunderstand what causes them to occur. Much of the time they come from hidden conversations and action patterns within us, not from the behavior or attitudes of others. Often, however, we don't notice the role our own internal patterns play.

In addition, most people are confused about what it takes to create happy, successful, long-term interpersonal relationships. This is another hidden cause of our stress, which I will address in the second half of this chapter.

How To Deal With Relationship Stress

The secret to dealing with any relationship problem is to use the six-step method outlined in Chapter 4:

How To Deal With Relationship Problems

Step 1: DEFINE YOUR PROBLEMS(S) SPECIFICALLY—"My husband never talks to me," "My boss hates my guts," "I can't stand to be around X for more than two minutes," or "I'm in love with Y, but he/she isn't interested in me."

Step 2: RELATE TO EACH OF YOUR RELATIONSHIP PROB-
LEMS AS FEEDBACK—assume you are partly the cause
of the problem.

Step 3: IDENTIFY THE SPECIFIC CONVERSATIONS AND
ACTION PATTERNS within you that are causing your
relationship problems to occur or persist.

Step 4: REMIND YOURSELF that these hidden patterns EXIST
IN YOUR BODY, not your mind.

Step 5: TAKE ACTION TO NEUTRALIZE THESE HIDDEN
CAUSES—challenge your stress-producing conversations;
disrupt your automatic behavior patterns; create relationship-enhancing contexts.

Step 6: If your relationship problems don't improve, REPEAT STEPS
1-5 AND/OR GET COACHING.

EXAMPLE: Consider the case of Laura and Steve. Laura came to
see me because she was tired of her husband Steve's uncaring
behavior. The couple had been fighting about this problem for years,
but no matter how much Laura complained, Steve refused to give
her the type of attention she wanted.

My first step in treating Laura was to help her define her problems more specifically. This involved showing her that her problem
could be divided into two separate parts:

PROBLEM #1: "My husband doesn't care about me anymore."

PROBLEM #2: "My husband doesn't do certain things I want him
to do no matter how much I ask."

Next, I helped Laura view each of these problems as feedback.
Instead of assuming that Steve was the sole cause of these problems,
I asked her to consider that she might also be playing a role in bringing
them about.

From this new perspective, Laura was able to recognize some of
the conversations and action patterns within her that were contributing
to her difficulties. Regarding her first problem—"my husband doesn't
care about me anymore"—she eventually discovered that she was
wrong about this conclusion. Steve did care about Laura very deeply.
He just didn't show his love for her in the ways she expected. For

Laura, there was a "right" way and a "wrong" way to show a wife that you cared. Even though Steve did many things that from his perspective showed he loved her, Laura couldn't appreciate these expressions because they didn't fit her standards. She had formed a negative judgement about Steve—"he doesn't care anymore"—which kept her from recognizing the truth about his feelings.

As Laura began to deal with this internal conversation, she was able to challenge and disprove the false "reality" it created within her. She began to notice that Steve did express much love and concern for her, and this helped her feel better about the future of their relationship.

With regard to her second complaint—"Steve doesn't do what I want him to do no matter how much I ask"—Laura also found the feedback perspective to be helpful. By asking herself how she might be contributing to this problem, she recognized the following issues, which had previously escaped her attention:

a) By assuming Steve didn't care about her anymore, she repeatedly interacted with him in a negative, resentful fashion. Given that Steve could feel her blame and anger, why should he try to please her when he knew she would never be satisfied?

b) Because Laura wanted Steve to behave in ways that were contrary to his nature, she spent much of her time trying to make him into someone different. This caused Steve to resist her even more.

c) Instead of praising and rewarding Steve for the few loving things he did the way she wanted, Laura constantly put him down for not doing these things more often. She noticed that her parents did the same thing to her when she was young, and she didn't like it much either.

d) Even though Steve found it difficult to give Laura what she wanted, he was not incapable of making certain changes. By assuming he would never come around, however, Laura stopped herself from exploring other ways to ask for what she wanted—ways that might work better for Steve and motivate him to want to do what she asked.

As Laura learned to free herself from each of these hidden patterns, she began to feel more hopeful about her marriage. Steve noticed this change in Laura too, and his own behavior began to improve spontaneously.

▶ NOTE: Had Steve come in for treatment, with or without Laura, I would have used the same approach with him. I would have helped him discover the ways in which he, not Laura, was causing their marital problems to occur. Since each partner generally plays a role in any relationship problem or conflict that occurs between them, both can usually benefit from adopting a feedback perspective.

Relationship-Destroying Patterns

Many of us assume that our relationships should work out just by virtue of our inherent goodness and kindness. Our thinking goes something like this: "Human beings are naturally loving, caring, committed individuals who only need to find the right kind of partner to live happily ever after."

The truth about human relationships is often the opposite, however. Most of us have been programmed to fail in our interpersonal relationships. If we follow our automatic tendencies, we will eventually destroy any union that matters to us.

To succeed in our relationships, therefore, we must learn to *recognize and deal with the hidden relationship-destroying patterns within us*. Not only must we know how to deal with these patterns in ourselves, but we must also know how to deal with similar patterns in other people as well.

We have already discussed several of these patterns. Take the issue of control, for instance. Much of our relationship stress comes from our conscious and unconscious efforts to change or control other people. We want others to behave in certain ways, and when we can't get them to, we become angry and resentful. The more we try to change them and fail, the more angry, frustrated, and depressed we become.

We are also very critical and judgmental of other people. Internal conversations such as GOOD/BAD, RIGHT/WRONG, CAUSE/ EFFECT, AND PERFECTIONISM commonly contribute to our interpersonal problems.

▶ NOTE: Many of our relationship-destroying patterns, such as GOOD/BAD, RIGHT/WRONG, PERFECTIONISM, and CON-TROL, have positive benefits in our lives as well. As a physician, for instance, I must often distinguish good from bad and right from wrong. I need to have a reasonable amount of perfectionism in caring for others. And I often need to take control in difficult or life-threatening situations. When I go home, however, and try to assert these same successful patterns with my family, friends, or other individuals, conflicts can occur.

Other Key Relationship-Destroying Patterns

In addition to the conversations and action patterns noted above, there are four key patterns that are very destructive to our relationships. If you learn to recognize and deal with these four patterns, you will be able to prevent or eliminate much of the relationship stress you experience.

> THE
> BLAME
> GAME

Of all the relationship-destroying patterns that affect both men and women, the most damaging is our tendency to blame someone or something other than ourselves when relationship difficulties arise. This pattern is hard to resist, since we can usually find many irritating habits or behaviors in others that seem to be the cause of our problems.

There are two good reasons you should refuse to play this game. The first is that it keeps you from relating to your relationship problems as "feedback." As we have already seen, there are many advantages to adopting this feedback perspective, and you lose these advantages when you blame things outside of yourself—even when some degree of blame may seem justified.

The second reason you should refuse to play the blame game is that it is based upon a false understanding of the nature of human relationships. Relationships are not "things" that can be good or bad, right or wrong, or satisfying or unsatisfying in and of themselves. They are *processes* that evolve over time and whose outcomes are determined by the behavior of their components. Any qualities such as "good" or "bad" that we attribute to our relationships, therefore, are not fixed or immutable characteristics—they are *temporary states* that are always subject to change.

When we blame either our partner or our relationship as the source of our dissatisfaction, we not only fail to acknowledge how we may have contributed to our problems, but we also fail to see that we often have the power to successfully resolve them.

EXAMPLE: Jean complained that her husband never talked to her anymore, that he had little intimate contact with her, and that he immersed himself in his work to hide from her. She repeatedly maintained that her marriage had gone sour, that there was no joy or satisfaction to be derived from it, and that the only possible solution was to seek a divorce. By blaming both her husband and her relationship for being the source of her dissatisfaction, Jean placed herself in the weakest possible position for dealing with her problems successfully. Had she related to her husband's behavior as feedback, and had she assumed that the poor quality of her relationship was in part a by-product of her own unconscious attitudes and behaviors, she could have explored many other options. She could have tried new and creative ways of interacting with her husband that might have made him more willing to recognize and address some of the problems she knew existed.

The same could be said for Jean's husband as well. Surely he was aware of the loss of affection and communication in the relationship, and he could have taken the initiative to restore these ingredients too. Instead, he was busy playing the blame game himself—secretly criticizing and punishing his wife for the relationship's demise.

The blame game also causes problems in our relationships with our children. Parents often are frustrated and perplexed by behavioral or emotional problems in their kids. They may even take one of their children to a therapist because they believe the child is primarily to blame for such problems. For therapy with children to be successful, however, parents must often be helped to stop playing the blame game and adopt a feedback perspective. This can enable them to identify their own role in causing their children's problems to occur or persist. By learning to modify their own behavior as parents the behavior of their children will often improve as well.

> KICKING
> YOUR
> SEEING-EYE DOG

Another relationship-destroying pattern I see in many couples is KICKING YOUR SEEING-EYE DOG. This pattern is based upon the principle that opposites attract. Most of us become attracted to other people not because they are similar to us, but because they possess certain talents, skills, and qualities we lack. This is why outgoing individuals often hook up with shy, introverted partners. It is also why intellectually-oriented people tend to marry emotion-oriented individuals, and why impatient people often end up with slower, leisurely-paced mates.

If you think about your own romantic relationships, past and present, you will probably notice that you and your spouse or lover differ in many ways.

For example, my wife, Christina, and I differ from each other in the following ways:

-One of us is more intellectually oriented, the other is more sensation-emotion oriented.
-One is talkative and outgoing, the other quiet and reserved.
-One likes sports, the other hates sports.
-One likes camping, the other hates camping.
-One spends money very easily, the other is a frugal saver.
-One likes to watch TV, the other rarely watches TV.
-One likes to go to parties, the other finds excuses to avoid them.
-One likes the kitchen to be clean and neat, the other leaves it messy.
-One likes Apple computers, the other IBM.
-Etc.

When we fall in love with someone, we often hope that their strengths and talents will become available to us, and that we can contribute our strengths and abilities in return. If I am an undisciplined spender, for example, it may be good for me to associate with someone who saves (and vice versa). If I tend to be intellectually-inclined, it might be good for me to have a partner who can remind me of the emotional side of life (and vice versa).

Like a person who knows he or she is blind, we often hook up with others who can function as "seeing-eye dogs" for us in life. When we find someone who can fill this valuable role, we tend to marry them to keep them around.

But then a very curious pattern emerges. This is the pattern I call KICKING YOUR SEEING-EYE DOG. Often, it begins very slowly, but eventually it becomes full-blown and threatens the survival of the relationship.

KICKING YOUR SEEING-EYE DOG is the pattern whereby you try to change or mold your partner into someone who thinks, feels, and acts *just like you*. Instead of respecting and appreciating your partner's differences, you begin to judge them negatively for being the way they are. Instead of keeping yourself open to what their differences have to offer you, you embark upon a foolish and futile project to change them to be like you.

This very common pattern makes no sense at all. Indeed, if we were aware of it, we would stop it very quickly. It's as though one day we recognize we are "blind," so we go out and find a seeing-eye dog to be our partner. Then, we bring the dog home and every time it tries to pull us in a certain direction, we kick it for disturbing us. This is exactly what we do to our spouses and other loved ones. No wonder they resent us and claim, quite correctly, that we don't respect or appreciate them.

INVALIDATING
OTHERS'
OPINIONS AND
POINTS OF VIEW

Another relationship-destroying pattern is INVALIDATING OTHERS' OPINIONS AND POINTS OF VIEW. Most people who fail to deal with this pattern have trouble maintaining successful interpersonal relationships.

This pattern stems from our basic tendency to *want to be right* most of the time. We want to be right about our thoughts and ideas. We want to be right about our feelings, opinions, and ways of acting in life. We want to be right about our theories, values, and moral standards. In short, we want to be right about almost everything, and when we actively pursue this goal, we can destroy our relationships in the process.

You see, in order for you to be right, you must view other people's thoughts, feelings, and opinions as wrong or invalid, especially when they differ from yours. While proving yourself right may allow you to feel temporarily satisfied, your partner often ends up feeling hurt and resentful. These small hurts are not easily forgotten. They often come back to you in subtle—and not so subtle—ways.

The secret to dealing with this hidden cause of stress is to: a) recognize when this pattern has been triggered within you; b) resist the temptation to act upon it; c) do the exact opposite—i.e. consider that other people are "right" rather than "wrong" as much as possible. While this may appear like a foolish thing to do, most people benefit from creating this context.

▶ NOTE: Choosing to view someone else as right does not mean you must view yourself as wrong or invalidate your own opinions and points of view. The purpose of this strategy is simply to compensate for your automatic tendency to invalidate other people. As I pointed out earlier, most people—including yourself—are right about their point of view in one way or another. By consciously creating the context WHEN I THINK SOMEONE IS WRONG, THAT PERSON MAY BE RIGHT, you can compensate for your tendency to overlook this possibility.

```
FAILING TO BE
A BEGINNER
```

Most people assume they know what it takes to succeed in interpersonal relationships. They think that if they just find the right partner, or if they feel strongly in love with another person, their relationship will succeed and they will live happily ever after. This common fallacy is another hidden cause of stress.

FAILING TO BE A BEGINNER is a pattern whereby we fail to admit that we don't really know how to succeed in a particular area of life. Instead of finding out what it really takes to succeed, we act like we already know and there is no further need for us to study the matter. Love and marriage are two big areas where this hidden pattern repeatedly gets us into trouble.

For example, most people don't really know what it takes to have a successful marriage (divorce statistics attest to this fact). Many people assume that love is all they need to succeed. Aaron Beck, one of the original pioneers of cognitive therapy, argues against this popular belief in his 1988 book titled *Love Is Never Enough*:

> Although love is a powerful impetus for husbands and wives to help and support each other, to make each other happy, and to create a family, it does not in itself create the substance of the relationship—the personal qualities and skills that are crucial to sustain it and make it grow. Special personal qualities are crucial for a happy relationship: commitment, sensitivity, generosity, consideration, loyalty, responsibility, trustworthiness. Mates need to cooperate, compromise, and follow through with joint decisions. They have to be resilient, accepting, and forgiving. They need to be tolerant of each other's flaws, mistakes, and peculiarities. As these 'virtues' are cultivated over a period of time, the marriage develops and matures. (p. 4)

Beck also points out that we are rarely taught how to establish these personal qualities and skills. In addition, many of the ideas we have about them are also mistaken. Thus, no matter how many times our relationships fail, we rarely question our own fundamental understandings.

It is possible to learn how to create successful relationships. But in order to obtain this wisdom, you must first admit *you don't have it*. Then, you must seek out other people who can teach you to succeed. Many excellent relationship coaches exist who could help you do this. They are not hard to find, if you actively search for them. For example, I suggest you read Beck's *Love Is Never Enough* (see Suggestions For Further Reading). I also suggest that you study the next part of this chapter very carefully. You will also find several other helpful references in the Suggestions For Further Reading section.

Four Key Patterns That Cause Much
Of Our Relationship Stress

- THE BLAME GAME
- KICKING YOUR SEEING-EYE DOG
- INVALIDATING OTHERS' OPINIONS
  AND POINTS OF VIEW
- FAILING TO BE A BEGINNER

What Does It Take To Have Happy, Successful Relationships?

Misunderstanding what is needed to create successful, long-term relationships is another hidden cause of our stress. In the remainder of this chapter, I will briefly discuss ten important ingredients for successful relationships of all types.

PURPOSE

All human beings are purposeful beings. Our purposes in life, both conscious and unconscious, guide our choices and behaviors, especially in our relationships.

We all have a purpose, or purposes, for each interpersonal relationship we enter. These purposes may be either consciously or unconsciously adopted. Some of them are relationship-enhancing. Others, however, can be relationship-destroying.

Most of our automatic—that is unconsciously adopted—purposes tend to be *self-centered*. These cause us to enter into relationships primarily to get things from others—love, sex, happiness, pleasure, security, prestige, or children—instead of making our relationships about pleasing and supporting the other person. This is especially true for marriage.*

The best purpose for marriage, or for any other long-term relationship, is to forget about what you might get in return—although this is still the ultimate motivation—and focus on what you can *give* to the other person. Hans Selye described this as the "philosophy of

---

* Other self-centered purposes for getting married include getting away from your parents, doing what society expects you to do, avoiding the pain of loneliness, having someone to take care of you, etc.

gratitude." According to Selye, the best purpose you can adopt is to be of *service* to others, so much so that they are genuinely filled with gratitude for having you in their life:

> . . . to incite gratitude in others is perhaps the most natural basis for a long-range aim of man. It can be hoarded throughout life and accumulated into a tremendous wealth, which more reliably than any other assures our security and peace of mind in this world. . . . It can be pursued through whatever talents one may have. . . It can be accumulated as long as you live, and even your offspring will benefit by it. . . And—best of all—this is one type of selfishness for which you certainly need not dread censure: no one will blame you for hoarding avariciously the gratitude of your fellow men. . . I know of no other philosophy which necessarily transforms all our egotistic impulses into altruism without curtailing any of their self-protecting values. (*The Stress Of Life*, p. 290.)

I can personally vouch for the wisdom of this philosophy. Whenever I enter into a relationship for the purpose of obtaining things from others, the relationship quickly deteriorates. On the other hand, every time my aim is to ensure the success, happiness, and well-being of other people, the quality of their lives improves and so does mine. Our relationships remains fresh, exciting, and mutually rewarding. This holds true for relationships with spouses, friends, children, parents, colleagues, co-workers, and even total strangers.

▶ NOTE: Most relationship-enhancing purposes are not natural for human beings. We are not "programmed" to adopt them, and we must therefore create them through repeated conscious effort. Frequently I find myself slipping back into my old, self-centered purposes. But the moment I catch myself doing this, I immediately choose to become other-directed.

COMMITMENT

The dreaded "C"-word today is commitment. For many people, commitment means loss of freedom, obligatory suffering, fear of making the wrong decision, fear of financial ruin, and many other negative outcomes. While most people make (and break) commitments all the time, few of us know what it means to live committedly.

In order to have happy, successful relationships with other people, you must understand the nature of human commitment. For example, you must know that commitment has little to do with your thoughts, feelings, desires, or opinions. It is not a mysterious force or ability, such as "will power" or "self-discipline," which some people possess and other people lack.

True commitment is a *context we create* to keep our promises REGARDLESS OF OUR CIRCUMSTANCES. It is an unconditional pledge to ourselves and to others to live our lives consistent with our word. It is a decision—*in advance*—to always rise above our fleeting thoughts, feelings, moods, and situations and to deal with any problem or conflict in a way that enhances, rather than diminishes, the quality of our relationships.

When problems occur during the course of our relationships, each of us is triggered to respond in automatic ways. A key issue for all of us is:

> ARE WE GOING TO ACT FROM OUR AUTOMATIC PATTERNS, OR ARE WE GOING TO ACT FROM OUR PURPOSES AND COMMITMENTS?

Are we going to act on the basis of our triggered thoughts, feelings, moods, or beliefs, or are we going to act in a manner that is consistent with our word? This one ingredient often determines whether our relationships succeed or fail.

Unfortunately, when most people commit themselves to other people, they do so *conditionally.* What they really mean is: "I'll remain true to my commitment as long as you remain true to yours, or as long as I feel good about my promises, or as long as nothing better comes along, or as long as we don't have any major conflicts or difficulties." They know that if certain events occur, or if their thoughts or feelings change—which they frequently do—they can go back on their word.

The reason why commitment is so important for human beings is because that's all there is, in essence, to our relationships. A relationship is a process that flows from the promises—and only the promises—of each individual. It does not flow from our thoughts, feelings, needs, or desires, even though these are obviously important.

For example, two people can interact over time, but if they have no implicit or explicit commitments to each other, they do not have a relationship. Also, when the commitment of one or both members dies, the relationship dies along with it, even if the people remain together. This often occurs in marriages, when one or both spouses struggle to preserve the outward semblances of togetherness even though the heart of the relationship is no longer present.*

As long as we make intelligent, sincere promises to other people, and as long as we endeavor to honor these promises—NO MATTER WHAT HAPPENS—our relationships usually flourish. When we make foolish, naive, or insincere promises, however, or when we violate either the letter or the spirit of our commitments, our relationships tend to die because we destroy the very ground that gives them life. Unfortunately, our society supports and condones such destructive behavior. It exonerates people for breaking their word, especially if they have any reasonable excuse for making such a decision. In truth, most of these excuses are not really justified, except in extreme situations such as repeated physical abuse, verbal abuse, or other serious offenses.

Thus, to have happy, successful, long-term relationships, you must conduct yourself in a manner that supports both you and other people. This includes, but is not limited to, the following types of promises:

Commitments That Support
Successful Interpersonal Relationships

- To promote the health, well-being, personal growth, and success of your partner.

- To communicate openly and honestly.

- To let your partner know if something important is bothering you.

- To deal with any problems or conflicts in a way that both you and your partner feel satisfied.

- To always keep your word or immediately atone for any slips you make.

---

* Sometimes the relationship can be revived!

- To do whatever it takes to preserve the quality and integrity of the relationship, regardless of whether this is comfortable or easy for you to do.

For example, people who avoid dealing with the "little" hurts, disappointments, and minor broken promises in their relationships often suffer as time goes on. Not dealing with such "little" problems is equivalent to intentionally ignoring the early signs of cancer. Your interpersonal problems will continue to multiply, until one day you notice that your relationship is "terminal."

People who make and keep the promises listed above often have a minimum of stress and dissatisfaction in their interpersonal relationships. On the other hand, people who are reluctant to make such commitments, or who try to get around living up to them, often find that their relationships fall apart.

ACCEPTANCE

Another component for successful relationships is accepting other people exactly as they are and exactly as they are not. When we form a relationship with another individual, we should honor and respect that person exactly as they are, including all their faults and weaknesses. Since each person is a composite of positive and negative features, we must accept all of our partner's attributes, even the ones we don't like.

True acceptance of this kind is not a passive act. It is a positive gift that you give to other people. In fact, you could say that love, which we normally assume to be a feeling or emotion, is the natural consequence of such generous acts of acceptance. When you accept other people exactly as they are, they feel love both *from you* and *for you*. Because you grant them the freedom to be the way they are, they feel nurtured and secure whenever they are in your presence.

EXAMPLE: When Christina and I married in 1984, we composed our own vows for our wedding ceremony. Notice how the first of these vows embodies this principle of acceptance:

WEDDING VOWS—MORT ORMAN AND CHRISTINA CHAMBREAU, JUNE 10, 1984:

-I promise to love you just the way you are.
-I pledge to share my life with you, to honor and trust you, and to always be faithful to you.

-I know that the experience of loving you can be mine whenever I choose.

-And I will not hold you responsible for my own happiness and contentment.

-I will cherish you, love you, and be truthful to you through all the changes and miracles in our lives.

When you don't accept people exactly as they are—when you set out to change them, improve them, criticize them, or make them into someone different—they stop feeling loved and appreciated by you.

► NOTE: Most of us have trouble accepting others as they are because we mistakenly believe that our happiness and success are dependent upon others. If you are highly dependent upon someone for your happiness and success, you will strive to change or control that person as much as possible. This will eventually produce feelings of hostility and resentment in the other person, not to mention feelings of frustration, disappointment, and resentment within you.

TRUST

Trust, like commitment, is another essential ingredient for successful interpersonal relationships. Since our relationships are products of our promises and commitments, it is mandatory that our partners trust our basic integrity. It is also essential that we conduct ourselves in a trustworthy manner, and that we demand the same from anyone who wants to have a relationship with us.

LITTLE WHITE LIES AND OTHER MINOR TRANSGRESSIONS ARE MAJOR SOURCES OF DISTRUST IN OUR RELATIONSHIPS.

Many people believe that they can get away with minor transgressions, as long as the immediate consequences are not terribly serious. Trust, however, can easily be destroyed by such minor transgressions.

Since I am dependent upon you to keep the major promises of our relationship, I am going to have doubts that you will come through when times are tough. If you break your word to me on some minor point, why shouldn't I assume you might do the same on more important issues? You may think no harm results from breaking little promises, but my trust in you—not to mention your own trust in yourself—will always be diminished.

Similarly, the way you can rebuild trust in a relationship, once you have damaged that trust, is to demonstrate that you can be counted on to keep your word—NO MATTER WHAT! Never make a promise you know you aren't going to keep, and keep every promise you make or promptly acknowledge when you fail to do so.* This will tell the other person that you are sincere about having integrity and will go a long way toward restoring their faith and trust in you.

► NOTE: Some people assume that trust should be granted to them, regardless of their past behavior. This may be reasonable at the beginning of a relationship, but once you have damaged that trust, only a fool would give it back to you. You must work to earn back the other person's trust by demonstrating that you are now, and intend to remain, a trustworthy individual. Prior to establishing this, you don't really deserve to be trusted.

COMMUNICATION

Everyone knows that successful relationships require good communication. What most people don't know, however, is what separates good communication from poor communication or from verbal or non-verbal interactions that are either inconsequential or destructive.

Good communication is not merely the sharing of experiences, thoughts, or feelings. To create successful, long-term relationships you need to communicate in a way that is *purposeful, powerful,* and *meaningful* to other people.

By *purposeful,* I mean your communications should always be consistent with the purposes and promises of your relationship. If you say that your purpose is to please and empower your partner, both your communications and your actions should attest to this fact. If you say you will love, honor, and cherish your partner exactly as they are and exactly as they are not, your communications and interactions should reflect this commitment.

---

* It is also important to communicate to others *as soon as you discover* you might not be able to keep a promise you made.

By *powerful*, I mean your communications and interactions should be effective. This means they should regularly produce your desired result. If you are angry with your partner, or if you encounter any type of problem that detracts from your sense of love and admiration, you should be determined to communicate until that problem is resolved. Whatever type of interaction might be required, you must not rest until the result has been produced. This is the type of purposeful, powerful communication that is needed to succeed in long-term relationships.

And last, to be effective your communications must be *meaningful* to the other person. It doesn't really matter what you think or how you feel about the things you say or do. The only thing that matters is how others are affected by them.

Two people rarely experience the same event or reality in exactly the same way. Each has his or her own "internal reality" about whatever may have happened, and these internal realities must always be taken into account.

THE SECRET TO GOOD COMMUNICATION IS TO HONOR THE INTERNAL "REALITIES" OF OTHERS.

Remember, the realities you perceive or think you have communicated will often have very little correspondence to the "realities" that appear within others.

NEGOTIATION

Marriage and other relationships are ongoing series of negotiations. Obviously, many minor differences and conflicts must be worked out. Requests must frequently be made of each other, and the option to decline or renegotiate certain requests must occasionally be exercised.

The following rules and guidelines for negotiating often contribute to successful interpersonal relationships:

Guidelines For Successful Negotiations

- Each person should be free to request what they want or need from the other person.

- Each person should be free to decline any request that they can't responsibly honor.

- Any conflicts or differences of opinions should be resolved in a win-win manner (no one should be forced to capitulate to any agreement).

- Each person should be committed to what works for the relationship (as opposed to what works for them, what they personally want, or what would make them happy or comfortable).

SURRENDER

Another key ingredient for successful interpersonal relationships is surrender. This is not the type of surrender where you are forced to do something someone else wants. It is a *voluntary* type of surrender whereby you willfully give up control to someone other than yourself.

One form of surrender is choosing to go along with the thoughts, ideas, and opinions of your partner. This involves voluntarily giving up two of your most cherished desires:

a) Your desire to be right;

b) Your desire to be in control (to have things your way).

Another form of voluntary surrender is allowing others to function as seeing-eye dogs for you. Each of us has gaps in our knowledge, skills, and abilities in life. When we recognize such blind spots, the wisest thing we can do is surrender ourselves to the guidance of another. Let your partner (or a coach) be your guide in these areas. Let them do the seeing for you, since you may get yourself into trouble if you try to do it yourself.

Remember, one of the major benefits of forming intimate relationships with other people comes from sharing your weaknesses and blind spots with them. This is one way you can compensate for some of the limitations and drawbacks of your ingrained, automatic tendencies.

Another type of voluntary surrender involves the promises and purposes of your relationships. Once you make these promises—provided they are well-designed—forget about ever going back on them. Close any door that might provide you with an escape. In other words, voluntarily surrender to your own promises and commitments, and then live as though your life depended on them. It might!

Also, when you create an equal partnership with another person, you must give up certain "rights" to do things as you please. You can no longer function as a separate, unattached individual since your choices and actions will affect the other person. Therefore, in order to succeed in your relationships, you must give up wanting to be right, wanting to have your own way, wanting your partner to think and feel exactly as you do, and many other desires.

> YOU SHOULD SURRENDER THESE RIGHTS, NOT BECAUSE THEY ARE BAD OR IMMORAL, BUT BECAUSE THEY SIMPLY DON'T WORK IF YOU WANT A SUCCESSFUL RELATIONSHIP.

FORGIVENESS

We discussed the nature of forgiveness in the preceding chapter. With regard to our long-term, interpersonal relationships, forgiveness takes on an even larger role. Not only must we forgive our friends, lovers, and partners for what they may have done in the past, but we must also forgive them—in advance—for the fact that they will probably do similar things again in the future.

Biolinguistic organisms (human beings) cannot easily change or control their automatic programming. When you form a long-term relationship with another person, it's important to remember this. Even though the other person may truly want to change or improve certain behaviors, the chances are good that he or she will continue to respond automatically. Thus, you will need to be forgiving and understanding when such slips occur.

RESPONSIBILITY

Responsibility is also a major cornerstone of successful, long-term relationships. As we have already seen, true responsibility means neither credit, nor blame. It is a choice we make to personally take charge of our lives and to always acknowledge the role we—as well as others—play in the problems and conflicts we experience.

One of the central problems in all of our relationships is how we respond when things don't go as we want. Do we blame other people, outside influences, or our relationship itself whenever we experience a lack of satisfaction? Or do we view such problems as feedback signals that we need to learn and grow ourselves? Are we going to try to change or control our partner in order to be happy, or are we going to recognize that our own happiness comes primarily from the contexts and commitments we generate—or fail to generate—within ourselves?

Unfortunately, many forces in society encourage us to adopt a victim's role. These forces tell us that we are not responsible for our problems and that we do not have the power to generate our own satisfaction and happiness. This widespread trend toward "victimization" in our society is another prominent myth that produces much unnecessary stress and suffering.

SUPPORT

The last ingredient to be considered is support. This is related to Selye's "philosophy of gratitude." If you make your relationships about supporting other people, you will find this strategy reaps dividends beyond your wildest imagination. If you are committed to helping others achieve their personal goals and ambitions, they will feel indebted to you and will often repay you in kind. Even if they don't, you can still get pleasure from contributing to their well-being, while finding the support and encouragement you need elsewhere.

One problem with this strategy is that some people are good at giving love, support, acknowledgement, etc., while others are inclined to be "takers." Such givers and takers often end up together. This is because for a giver to give—and feel personally fulfilled—he or she must find someone who takes, and vice versa. Stress can result, however, when givers make the mistake of expecting their giving to be reciprocated. Instead of enjoying the pleasure of supporting their partners, they become angry and resentful when little is given to them in return. It is not so much the inequity that causes them to be resentful, but rather it is their unconscious expectation that the other person should return their generosity in kind, even though they are not programmed to function in this way.

In addition, most of us—whether we are givers or takers—are often reluctant to accept support from others. This is another unrecognized cause of stress which must be overcome if we want to be successful in our interpersonal relationships.

TEN KEY INGREDIENTS FOR
SUCCESSFUL RELATIONSHIPS (OF ALL TYPES)

1) Purpose
2) Commitment
3) Acceptance
4) Trust
5) Communication
6) Negotiation
7) Surrender
8) Forgiveness
9) Responsibility
10) Support

How To Deal With Anger Or Criticism Directed At You By Others

In addition to the issues already discussed, I will briefly address three other topics that have a bearing on stress in our relationships. The first of these is how to deal with anger or criticism when it is directed at you by others.

The secret to dealing with this common situation is to use the technique of Flipping To The Opposite Reality (see Chapter 6 and Appendix B). The best way to deal with anger or criticism from others is to:

TRY TO AGREE WITH THE ACCUSATIONS
OTHER PEOPLE MAKE ABOUT YOU.

Instead of defending yourself or counter-attacking, assume there may be something you can agree with regarding the accusations or criticisms of others.

▶ TIP: I am not suggesting that you should ALWAYS agree with the accusations of others—especially if such accusations are totally incorrect—nor am I suggesting that you VERBALLY agree out loud with the other person. What I am suggesting is that you INTERNALLY take the point of view that the other person may indeed be "right" rather than "wrong" in one way or another.*

The rationale for using this technique is explained in Appendix B (Flipping To The Opposite Reality). In short, no matter how things initially appear to you in terms of right and wrong, you can "flip" to the opposite reality and assume it is true as well. In other words, there must be something you said or did (or didn't say or didn't do) that irritated the other person. People rarely accuse you or criticize you without provocation. Even if you didn't do what you were accused of doing, the fact that someone chose to verbally assault you often means they are angry with you about something else. Thus, even if you are certain that you didn't do anything wrong, it is worth considering that the opposite may be true.

▶ NOTE: If you have trouble following this argument, or if it appears to you that I am encouraging you to tell a lie or agree with something that isn't really true, come back to this section after you have studied Appendix B.

Benjamin Franklin once said "the sting of any criticism comes from the truth it contains." It may be difficult for us to appreciate these truths, however, because of the harsh, critical manner in which they are usually communicated. We are all guilty of sins and omissions that escape our conscious detection. We can be mean, insensitive, inconsiderate, arrogant, insulting, demeaning, unforgiving, or inhospitable in many ways that we aren't consciously aware of. But these behaviors are often very obvious to others, especially when they are hurt or offended by our words or deeds. This is why we should always assume that others are "right" rather than "wrong" when they criticize or accuse us. By agreeing with their accusations, WE PLACE OURSELVES IN THE BEST POSSIBLE POSITION TO RECOGNIZE THE TRUTHS THEY CONTAIN.

Another benefit of this approach is that other people's anger toward you will quickly disappear the moment you stop defending yourself and agree with their accusations. People will feel you have listened

---

* The validity of other people's criticisms and accusations may not be apparent at first glance. If you look at their accusations honestly, however, you will often discover that they do have some merit.

to them, heard them, and that you acknowledge the validity of their observations and points of view. They will respect you for admitting that you may have been wrong—even if you weren't—and they will be grateful you didn't respond defensively. Thus, even when you can't understand how another person's accusations may be true, it is usually a good idea to make this assumption.

Several points are worth noting about this advice:

1. Everyone likes to criticize. It's our way of trying to make the world a better place to live. So don't be shocked or offended when someone decides to criticize you. While it may feel like they are trying to hurt you, they may actually be operating with good intentions.

2. Don't take criticism personally. When someone criticizes you or is angry with you, try to focus on what you did or didn't do and ignore any generalizations or personality attacks that also come along. People can sometimes be very vicious and insensitive when they are angry. If you put their viciousness aside, you can still benefit greatly from the feedback they are providing you.

3. If you don't understand the legitimacy of the other person's anger or criticism, ask them to help you better understand their point of view. As long as you are interested in what you can learn from other people's negative comments (instead of arguing against them), you can usually get them to explain things in more detail.

How To Deal With Distrust In Your Relationships

Earlier, I talked about the importance of being trustworthy. But what should you do when other people break their word to you and your trust in them is diminished? My first piece of advice is try to prevent this problem from occurring whenever you can. When I form a relationship with someone who is important to me, I will often let that person know that my word is very important to me and that I expect them to honor their's as well. When people know you'll be watching them very carefully, they often think twice about breaking their word.

My second piece of advice is whenever such a problem does occur, *don't let it go by.* I will generally confront an individual the first time—and any other time—a major or minor promise is broken. I don't let such violations go by, even though they may be minor and even though it may be uncomfortable for me to address them. The consequences of ignoring such minor transgressions, especially with regard to trust in your relationships, can often be enormous.

Similarly, when people repeatedly fail to keep their word with me or are reluctant to acknowledge such failures as a problem, I either don't get into relationships with them, or I will terminate one if it is already in progress. Would you board an airplane if you saw it only had one wing? Would you try to drive a car, if you noticed it had a defective tire? Why then would you try to have a relationship with someone if you knew he or she lacked the intention to keep their promises? Relationships depend upon trust in the same way airplanes depend upon wings and automobiles depend upon tires. Stress is an inevitable outcome whenever you try to conduct a meaningful relationship when this essential ingredient is missing.

▶ NOTE: This is one good example of where you WOULDN'T want to use the technique of Flipping To The Opposite Reality. If you know someone is dishonest or untrustworthy, don't switch to the opposite reality and assume you can count upon this individual. Remember, Flipping To The Opposite Reality is merely a technique you can use to "see" certain options or alternative interpretations that are not immediately apparent to you. Sometimes you can benefit from these opposite "realities," while at other times you may recognize that it would be imprudent to follow them.

It is important to understand that human beings operate on the basis of two very different types of promises—explicit and implicit ones. People will not only hold you accountable for the promises you verbally make (explicit promises), but they will also hold you to promises they assume you have made or they expect from you (implicit promises). Most of us understand that when we violate our explicit promises distrust will be created. But when we violate an implicit promise, *whether or not we agreed to abide by it*, our trustworthiness will also be reduced in the eyes of other people. Often, you may not know or suspect that you have violated such implicit promises.

This is why FAILING TO CLARIFY YOUR AGREEMENTS AND EXPECTATIONS is a stress-producing pattern. It's important to recognize your own and others' unspoken expectations and get them out on the table. Only then can you be responsible for accepting or rejecting them and knowing the types of standards your behavior will be judged upon.

Teaming With Your Partner To Defeat Your Own (And Their) Relationship-Destroying Patterns

Defeating your relationship-destroying patterns is best accomplished as a team. While both parties in the relationship have their own stress-producing patterns, each can team up with the other to prevent their own internal patterns from becoming destructive. In fact, when you and your partner know and accept each other's relationship-destroying tendencies, these patterns can even become a great source of fun and satisfaction in the relationship. Since you can't change them or elim-inate them anyway, you might as well accept them, have fun with them, and include them as part of your relationship.* Share them openly with your friends, associates, lovers, and other companions. Find out what their secret relationship-destroying patterns are, and ask them to support you in dealing with your own. You can also offer to do the same for them in return. Once you make such a pact, you can then play a game to see who can give up their destructive behavior patterns first. Whenever a problem or conflict arises, the one who "gets free" first can then support the other.

When a friend, lover, or associate agrees to play this game with you, you will have an invaluable ally in your fight against your own relationship-destroying patterns. When both people in a relationship share this basic commitment, the relationship can be strengthened, not pulled apart, by any difficulties that arise.

Where To Go From Here

We have briefly examined some of the hidden patterns and issues that contribute to stress in our relationships. If you agree that these issues are important, I encourage you to continue exploring them on your own (see Suggestions For Further Reading).

Remember, whenever you are faced with a difficult relationship problem, you can return to this chapter and review its contents. Refreshing your memory may be all you need to get yourself focused in a more useful direction.

If you can't seem to resolve a difficult relationship problem by following the step-by-step method outlined in this book, consider getting coaching. This may help you to identify other hidden causes or other potential solutions that may not be apparent to you.

* I am not talking about "acceptance" in the pessimistic sense, such as hopelessness or resignation, but rather as a necessary first step in learning how to deal with such patterns more effectively.

DAY 10: EXERCISES

1. *Think of a time when you were either angry or frustrated. Which of the following contexts might have been helpful to you in that situation?:*

☐ Negative conversations about myself are rarely true.
☐ Negative conversations about life are rarely true.
☐ Negative conversations about other people are rarely true.

2. *What is your understanding of the following context: "The best way to get love is to give love"?:*

_____

_____

_____

_____

3. *What is your understanding of the following statement: "A relationship is what happens between two people who are waiting for something better to come along"?:*

_____

_____

_____

_____

4. *To what extent do the following patterns occur for you in your relationships with others?*

	Almost Never	Occasionally	More Than I'd Like To Admit
A. BLAMING OTHERS	_____	_____	_____
B. KICKING YOUR SEEING-EYE DOG	_____	_____	_____
C. INVALIDATING OTHERS' OPINIONS & POINTS OF VIEW	_____	_____	_____
D. FAILING TO BE A BEGINNER	_____	_____	_____

5. *List four ways in which the issue of CONTROL causes problems in your relationships?*

A _____

B _____

C _____

D _____

DAY 11

STRESS AT WORK

Work-related problems are another major source of "stress." If you work for a living, you probably experience some degree of stress from time to time. If you don't work or are laid off, you probably also experience stress, although of a different kind.

Here is a list of common work-related problems: (Check those that apply to you.)

Work-Related Problems

☐ Too little time
☐ Too many responsibilities
☐ Multiple interruptions
☐ Excessive work loads
☐ Lack of support
☐ Emotional distress (anger/frustration/worry/fear/etc.)
☐ Conflicts with other people
☐ Uncertainty (not knowing what to do)
☐ Poor management
☐ Discrimination
☐ Lack of appreciation/acknowledgment
☐ Lack of advancement opportunities

In addition, every occupation has its own set of unique pressures, problems, and demands.

How To Deal With Work-Related Stress

The best way to deal with any work-related problem is to use the six-step method described in Chapter 4. Most of our work-related stress comes from conversations and action patterns within us, not from pressures, demands, or other external aspects of our jobs. Even when external factors do play a role, hidden patterns within us also contribute to our difficulties.

EXAMPLE #1: EXCESSIVE WORK LOADS

People who end up with burdensome work loads often—but not always—bring this problem upon themselves. This is certainly true for "workaholics," who have been programmed to believe it is "good" or "right" to be excessively overloaded. Others end up with this problem because they: a) refuse to delegate important tasks; b) fail to empower the people they work with; c) refuse to decline requests from others; or d) take on jobs that exceed their talents, skills, or temperament.

EXAMPLE #2: TIME PRESSURES

Deadlines, lack of time, and other time-related issues are believed to be major causes of work-related stress. Actually, deadlines and time constraints are not inherently stressful. They only become sources of stress when we approach them in certain ways—e.g., when we try to accomplish impossible tasks or when we fail to use our time productively.

Therefore, you should never blame time—or the lack thereof—as the primary cause of any stress you experience. Instead, you should always look for hidden conversations and action patterns within you that might also be contributing to such problems. Some of these patterns include:

-Letting things go until the last moment;
-Failing to decline requests from others;
-Failing to prioritize;
-Failing to work efficiently;
-Failing to ask for help.

EXAMPLE #3: CONFLICTS WITH OTHER PEOPLE

Conflicts with other people—customers, suppliers, distributors, office personnel, co-workers, employees, bosses, managers, etc.—

are common sources of job-related stress. As we learned in previous chapters, most of these conflicts come from our own hidden conversations and action patterns. For example, when we don't understand or communicate well with others, we frequently experience stress as a consequence. While such internal causes may be difficult to recognize, much of our interpersonal stress arises from them.

EXAMPLE #4: ANGER, FRUSTRATION, WORRY, GUILT, FEAR, AND OTHER NEGATIVE MOODS AND EMOTIONS

As we previously discussed, all of our negative moods and emotions, including those we experience at work, result from specific conversations and action patterns that become triggered within us. People who know how to apply the principles discussed in Chapter 9 (Negative Moods And Emotions) find that they have much less emotional stress and tension at work. Remember, no matter what type of job you have or what conditions you work in, you always have the power to make your negative moods or emotions quickly disappear.

EXAMPLE #5: LACK OF CONTROL

Another source of stress in the workplace is lack of control. Most people assume they have little personal control over the everyday problems and conflicts they experience in their jobs.

As long as you subscribe to this theory, you probably will experience a great deal of stress. In truth, however, you usually have much more power and control than you give yourself credit for. Unhealthy work environments, for example, can be changed if enough committed individuals make such changes a priority. Overly demanding work schedules can also be revised. Even uncaring, insensitive bosses can be motivated to modify their problematic behaviors.*

Even when your work situation can't be changed or improved, you still have control over how much stress you experience. You can, for example, create stress-relieving contexts that can transform any type of job into a satisfying, nurturing experience. As we saw in Chapter 7, these winning contexts are always available to you, regardless of your circumstances.

* While some people do unfortunately work for unreasonable bosses, and while economic factors may force them to continue doing so, they still have far more control over their fate than they give themselves credit for. It may be risky, at times, to exercise this control, but sometimes taking such risks is far better than remaining in an unhappy or unhealthy work environment.

You can also look within yourself to recognize and deal with your own stress-producing patterns. This can often enable you to decrease your work-related stress without needing to change or control your external situation.

EXAMPLE: In an important study on physician stress published in the September, 1989 issue of the *Archives Of Internal Medicine*, nineteen physicians were interviewed about their experience of practicing medicine in today's social, political, and economic climate. Twelve of the nineteen physicians reported that they were either ambivalent (3) or dissatisfied (9) with their professional activities. Most of these doctors blamed external circumstances and events as the source of their discontent.

Seven physicians, however, were highly satisfied despite having to deal with similar external conditions. What distinguished these doctors from the others was their refusal to blame external situations and events. According to the authors of this study, the doctors who remained highly satisfied "recognized there were problems facing them in the practice of medicine, but they defined these problems as internal ones and adjusted primarily through psychological means." In the words of one physician who was interviewed in the study:

> I've tried to control stress by controlling the situation. If I feel stressed, the problem is in *me* (emphasis added). Even though life can deal you a lot of hard knocks, ultimately you are responsible for your own happiness, and no one else is; and the more you think someone else is, the more angry and resentful you are going to be because it just isn't the case. So I usually come around to saying, 'If something is bugging me, let's look at it. I've got to change or something's got to change, but generally speaking, the world around me isn't going to change.'

Other Hidden Causes Of Work-Related Stress

Here are some of the conversations and action patterns within us that contribute to our work-related stress:

Conversations:

-"I shouldn't have done what I did"
-"I should have known better"
-"Other people shouldn't have done what they did."
-"Don't take risks"
-"Nothing is working"

Action Patterns:

-Failing To Make Requests Or Demands Of Others
-Failing To Clarify Agreements & Expectations
-Failing To Assess Commitment Of Others
-Failing To Prioritize
-Failing To Do Homework Or Research

In addition, other hidden causes contribute to our work-related stress. Here are some of the major ones that we frequently overlook:

▶ NOTE: The major purpose of this chapter is to draw your attention to these often-unrecognized, hidden patterns. In my experience, once people are able to recognize these patterns, they can usually find ways to deal with them successfully.

MORE IS BETTER/BIGGER IS BETTER

This pattern is insidious because it is part of our achievement-oriented society. The conversations and action patterns that make up this pattern include but are not limited to:

-"If a certain level of success is good for me, then more must be better."
-"If I can handle a certain amount of work fairly easily, then I should push myself to handle even more."
-"The more I accomplish, or the bigger my business gets, the more money I will make and the more freedom, success, and happiness I will achieve."

The problem with this pattern is that it can cause people to do stupid things. I have seen it cause people to leave good jobs in favor of new ones that turned out to be much less satisfying and rewarding. I have also seen it cause people to expand their businesses to a point where they grow too large for their owners to manage them competently.

Sometimes this pattern can trick you into accepting a new job or position with greater financial rewards, but with significantly increased responsibilities, pressures, worries, and other problems. Instead of evaluating the wisdom of such a move, you can unconsciously become seduced by the lure of something bigger, though not necessarily better. This is usually not a problem if you have made a reasoned choice. But sometimes, it may be your MORE IS BETTER /BIGGER IS BETTER pattern that makes the decision for you.

► EXAMPLE: Many of my patients advanced in their careers to a point where their stress levels became unbearable. When I asked why they left jobs they previously enjoyed and were good at, many of them said, "I don't know, it just seemed like the thing to do at the time."

Be on the lookout for this hidden cause of stress. Make sure it is *you*, not this pattern, that is making the important decisions in your life. There is nothing wrong with staying where you are if you currently have a job that is satisfying and rewarding. As long as your work is meaningful, both to you and to others, it makes little difference whether you do it on a large or small scale.

Also, don't let the lure of money entice you into something you probably won't be happy with. Remember, *bigger is not always better* in the business or professional world. Sometimes you may take home more pay, but end up with more headaches and less enjoyment.

MY VALUE AS A PERSON IS DEPENDENT UPON...

This hidden pattern causes a great deal of unnecessary stress and suffering. It is based upon the fallacy that your self-worth and self-esteem are primarily determined by factors *outside* of you. Variations of this pattern include:

"My value as a person is dependent upon how much money I earn."
"My value as a person is dependent upon how much power and prestige I have."
"My value as a person is dependent upon the car I drive."
"My value as a person is dependent upon what others think of me."
"My value as a person is dependent upon my relationships with people who are important to me."
Etc.

This pattern also includes internal factors that we want externally validated by others:

"My value as a person is dependent upon how smart I am."
"My value as a person is dependent upon how nice I am."
"My value as a person is dependent upon how young, sexy or athletic I am."
"My value as a person is dependent upon how much I do for others."
Etc.

While all of these factors can contribute to self-esteem, none of them is essential to it. TRUE SELF-ESTEEM IS MOSTLY INTERNALLY, NOT EXTERNALLY, GENERATED. It is a product of our own values and standards which we are free to select, as long as they are not detrimental to ourselves or to others.

When you incorrectly believe that your self-worth is tied to anything outside of you, you will be insecure. When things are going well, your self-esteem will be high. But when things go bad, or when the external factors you depend upon are diminished or removed, your self-esteem will plummet. Since many external factors do change over time, you will have a constant, low-grade fear that your self-esteem might suddenly vanish.

Living with this fear is a common but unrecognized cause of job-related stress. It can make you a prisoner of your job and keep you from standing up for what you deserve or what you think is right. Instead of knowing that you are a valuable person and that your career is secure as long as you have something worthwhile to contribute to others, you may cling to a particular job as if your livelihood, happiness, identity, and self-worth were totally dependent upon it.

EXAMPLE: Research has shown that MY VALUE AS A PERSON IS DEPENDENT UPON . . . is one of the major causes of what has been called Type A behavior. Type A individuals are hard-driving and competitive. They do not consciously choose to be this way. Rather they are compelled to live high-pressured lives because one of the unconscious conversations ingrained in their bodies is that their worth as a person is dependent upon their performance. The more productive they are, the better they feel about themselves, regardless of the cost to their health and well-being. This is why many Type A individuals find it difficult to relax. The moment they become unproductive, their self-esteem drops. In order to ward off such feelings of unworthiness, they keep themselves functioning at a non-stop pace.

Be on the lookout for this hidden pattern, even if you are not a Type A individual. It is very prevalent in our society, and it is frequently at the bottom of much of our stress.

COMPROMISING YOUR OWN OR OTHERS' INTEGRITY

It is easy in the business world to succeed by being dishonest. You can lie about your intentions, misrepresent the value of your products, falsify documents, or authorize fictitious or unwarranted services. Large amounts of money can be made dishonestly. Many opportunities also exist to profit at other people's expense; witness the cocaine industry that has flourished in our country.

EVERY TIME YOU COMPROMISE YOUR OWN OR OTHERS' INTEGRITY, YOU PAY A PRICE IN RETURN.

This price may not be apparent to you, but it is extracted nonetheless.

EXAMPLE #1: A salaried employee of a large corporation called in sick one day even though he was perfectly well. He stayed home to work on his house, which was in need of minor repairs. While working on his roof that day, he fell and broke his neck.

EXAMPLE #2: A patient of mine, a high-level manager, asked one of his employees to falsify a minor report. The employee complied, but neither party felt good about the deception afterward. The employee worried that he would get caught and lose his job. The manager worried that the employee might confess someday and cause him problems. Both suffered a loss of respect for each other. In addition, each wondered privately what other breaches of integrity might be going on behind their backs.

EXAMPLE #3: A salesman who came to see me did well financially by misrepresenting certain features of his product. The majority of his customers were one-time buyers, which made it easier for him to justify his actions. After a while, however, he found it difficult to get to sleep. This problem didn't go away until he confronted his lack of integrity and cleaned up his sales presentation. He made less money once he did this, but he felt much better about himself and his career in general.

When most people search for the causes of their stress, they rarely look at their own personal integrity. I suggest you consider this, since most of us occasionally indulge in immoral or unethical behaviors that may be costing us in the long-run.

In addition to a lack of personal integrity, a lack of corporate integrity can also contribute to our stress. If your company or corporation engages in practices you know are wrong or deceitful, you can personally suffer as a result.

Jerry Harvey, a management consultant, wrote about this problem in a book titled *The Abilene Paradox*. Harvey describes how large corporations foster alienation, distrust, and fear among their workers. He called this phenomenon the "Abilene Paradox" because it reminded him of a personal experience he had one day while he and his wife were visiting his wife's parents in Coleman, Texas. According to Harvey, it was a hot summer day, with the temperature rising to 104 degrees, when his father-in-law suggested that the four of them pile into his unairconditioned 1958 Buick and drive to Abilene for dinner. None of the other three wanted to go, but they didn't speak up for fear of upsetting the old man. The trip turned out to be a disaster, as they knew it would. But it was only after they returned home that they openly discussed their feelings. To everyone's surprise, the father-in-law revealed that *he really didn't want to go to Abilene either!* He just made the suggestion because he thought everyone was getting bored from sitting around the house all day. Since nobody objected, he assumed everyone wanted to go.

Harvey asserts that organizations often function in this way. People seem to know when their companies make bad decisions, but nobody says anything for fear of alienating their superiors or possibly losing their jobs. They allow their own integrity to be compromised, and they lose respect for other members of the organization who are doing the same. This breeds an atmosphere of anxiety and distrust, which further compromises people's ability to stand up for what they believe is right.

FAILING TO DEAL WITH "LITTLE" PROBLEMS

Another hidden pattern that causes a great deal of work-related stress is FAILING TO DEAL WITH "LITTLE" PROBLEMS. When people are very busy, they tend to let "little" problems go by. They justify this action by thinking "I don't have time to deal with this right now," or "I've got other more important things to do."

The problem with this behavior is twofold. First, when problems first surface, they are usually small and easy to handle. Second, the longer they go unattended, the bigger they become and the more they lead to other problems. Thus, by failing to address problems when they first appear, you may have to spend much more time (and money) to resolve them at a later date.

It's almost always to your advantage, therefore, to handle minor problems as soon as you become aware of them. The amount of time required is often negligible. And even if it does take some time, the amount of stress and additional problems you can prevent is significant.

Our bodies are programmed, however, to do just the opposite. They tell us "take care of it later, you don't really have the time." In order to overcome this hidden cause of stress, you must learn to go against this "normal" human tendency.

FAILING TO EMPOWER OTHERS

Another hidden cause of work-related stress is our failure to empower other people. Work is fundamentally a team event. It requires dedication, competence, and a high degree of commitment and cooperation from everyone involved. If we are reluctant to involve other people, or if we don't know how to mobilize their committed participation, we can end up experiencing stress as a consequence. We can even experience stress when we do involve other people, if we fail to provide them with the tools, resources, or support they need to get their job done.

Lack of empowerment in the workplace is very common. People are often ordered or instructed to perform certain tasks without any concern for their personal feelings or desires. Most organizations are structured in a hierarchical fashion, with the bulk of the power and control located at the top. The lower people on the organizational chart usually are not given much opportunity to contribute to important decisions. Thus, the creativity and commitment of lower-ranking employees is rarely nurtured or appreciated. This robs most companies of one of their most valuable resources.

The failure to empower occurs in other ways as well. Individuals are sometimes not given the proper training, resources, or support they need to get their jobs done. Bosses, managers, and other company leaders often fail to back up employees when they take a stand for something they consider important. And employees and co-workers often disempower each other and their bosses by failing to function as a team or by being more concerned with their own individual performance and advancement instead of focusing on what is best for the company and everyone involved.

THE MYTH OF CORPORATE LOYALTY

In the business world, most employers say that they care about their employees. After all, people are their most important resource, so they'd better take care of them or they may lose them in the long run.

As an employee, you may feel comforted by such public expressions of loyalty and concern. You might even assume that your corporate leaders really do have your best interests at heart.

While Japanese companies are very loyal to their employees (and vice versa), business decisions in the United States are primarily motivated by money. For many U.S. companies, dollars are far more important than people. When the chips are down, money will be conserved and people will be sacrificed. It really doesn't matter how much you may have contributed in the past or what your family's needs are or even that you are only a few short years away from qualifying for your pension. When times get tough, you can be out the door in an instant. And if you're "lucky" enough to stick around, your work load will often be increased without the slightest regard for your health or well-being.

The reason why money is more important to these companies than you are is because you can be replaced. If you burn out, have a heart attack, or otherwise become disabled, someone else will take your place. The leaders of many companies know this, so there is no real incentive for them to be concerned about your welfare. In fact, it will cost them money to care about your well-being, and most companies are not willing to foot the bill, especially during times when they are fighting for their survival.

I don't mean to imply that every company or all corporate leaders are insincere about their commitment to their employees' well-being. Sometimes you will find a company or a boss who is truly committed to you and your welfare. If you are lucky enough to find such an individual or company to work for, you should appreciate how rare this is in the business world today.

> THE PROBLEM WITH THE MYTH OF CORPORATE
> LOYALTY IS THAT IT PRODUCES A GREAT DEAL OF
> STRESS WHEN IT TURNS OUT TO BE BOGUS.

The lack of corporate loyalty itself is not the major culprit. Rather it is our unconscious conversations and expectations that produce most of our stress and suffering. For example, if you've been a loyal and dedicated employee for many years, you probably assume that your loyalty will be returned. If this expectation doesn't come true, feelings of anger and betrayal can be enormous.

Remember, just because you *assume* that a company is committed to your welfare doesn't mean that company really is. As long as you understand this, you won't be shocked or surprised by any decisions the leaders of that company make. You will also be able to prepare yourself—both psychologically and financially—for anything bad that might happen to you.

THE MYTH OF JOB SECURITY

The myth of job security goes hand-in-hand with the myth of corporate loyalty. Just because you've worked for a company for many years, or just because you are a trustworthy and dedicated employee, doesn't mean your job is secure. In fact, *few things in life are totally secure*—not your job, your health, your marriage, your house, your car, your bank account, or your investments. Any day, you can wake up and discover that some or all of these are gone.

Thinking that your job is secure *when it really isn't* is another hidden cause of work-related stress. At an unconscious level, you know your assumption of security is false, yet you continue to behave as if it were true. This can make you chronically anxious, since you know you are walking around with a false sense of security and you are not really prepared for the possible loss of your job.

The best way to deal with this hidden cause of stress is to assume just the opposite. Consider that your job—and many other things in your life—are not truly secure. Then do what you can to make sure you retain them. At the same time, you can spend small amounts of time preparing yourself, both psychologically and otherwise, for the possible loss of these important parts of your life. Even if such losses never occur, you will have greatly reduced some of the anxiety that comes from not being prepared for them. And if something "terrible" does occur, your sense of panic and loss will not be so great.

▶ NOTE: There is no need to become overly preoccupied about such remote possibilities. But even though the chances are remote, such events can be devastating, especially if you have given no thought at all to how you might cope with them successfully.

IGNORING YOURSELF / IGNORING YOUR BODY

In our society, there is a pervasive attitude that it's O.K. or even heroic to sacrifice your health for the good of your occupation. Taking care of business or taking care of others is often considered much more important than taking care of yourself. This attitude is prevalent, for example, in professional and collegiate sports, where human bodies are frequently sacrificed for the good of the team or institution.

The truth about most occupations, however, is that you've got to take care of yourself and your body if you want to be successful. In the long run, you can ignore your own needs for only so long. Sooner or later, you will pay a price in terms of job dissatisfaction, decreased health, and reduced productivity.

In order to neutralize this stress-producing pattern, you may have to buck the established "norms" of our achievement-oriented society. You will have to create both the time and the desire to care for yourself properly. And since other people—e.g., your boss, co-workers, and clients, among others—might be encouraging you to do just the opposite, you will need to find ways to cope with their demands and expectations, in addition to your own internal patterns which keep pushing you to do more and more.

MOANING, GROANING, AND COMPLAINING

It is commonplace for workers to moan and groan about the problems they encounter. In fact, if you don't participate in this daily office ritual, you run the risk of being socially ostracized.

Several problems arise from these common behaviors. The first is that MOANING, GROANING, AND COMPLAINING rarely accomplish anything of value. The second is that they reinforce the notion that people are passive victims of their surroundings.

> MOANING, GROANING, AND COMPLAINING SHOULD
> BE VIEWED AS A SIGN THAT PEOPLE ARE NOT
> BEING RESPONSIBLE FOR THE POWER THEY POSSESS.

When you engage in these behaviors, you are denying your ability to create happiness and satisfaction in your life. On the other hand, people who understand that they do have the power to determine their own happiness and satisfaction rarely engage in activities such as MOANING, GROANING, and COMPLAINING. They are busy taking charge of their lives and dealing creatively with any problems they encounter.

▶ NOTE: Happiness and satisfaction cannot be created by merely "wishing" or "wanting." You need specific inner skills and abilities such as creating winning contexts. We all possess these inner skills and abilities, even though we sometimes fail to utilize them.

FAILING TO DEAL WITH PROBLEMS CREATIVELY

FAILING TO DEAL WITH PROBLEMS CREATIVELY is one of the underlying causes of MOANING, GROANING, AND COMPLAINING.

The fundamental issue underlying most types of work-related stress is: do we have the power to solve most of the problems we encounter? The answer is usually "yes," but we often have to be creative in order to do so. Whatever problems are bothering you—bad management, low morale, unnecessary hassles, excessive work loads, personality conflicts—they can all be reduced or solved through creative intervention. The only things that can stop you are your own internal conversations and action patterns which argue to the contrary.

Things You Can Do To Decrease Your Stress And Dissatisfaction At Work

Most of the "solutions" promoted for stress in the workplace never address the true causes of worker dissatisfaction. Time management programs, diet and exercise programs, relaxation techniques, and other stress management skills are fine for what they do, but they only scratch the surface of the problem. In order to deal with most types of work-related stress effectively, you must learn to identify and deal with the internal causes of your suffering.

Here are some of the specific things you can do:

1) *Create Contexts That Can Help You Prevent Or Eliminate Work-Related Stress*

Each of the contexts listed below can help you reduce your work-related stress. These very same contexts can also be used to create happiness and satisfaction in your job, regardless of your circumstances.

▶ NOTE: Remember, for a context to be stress-relieving, you must use it as a stepping stone for viewing life differently and for adopting new conversations and behavior patterns that nullify your automatic tendencies.

Contexts For Reducing Stress At Work:

-EVERYTHING IN LIFE IS ALWAYS WORKING—whenever it looks like "things aren't working," they probably are. They are working exactly the way life is supposed to work when people think and behave in ineffective ways.

-WHATEVER HAPPENS IN LIFE CAN BE USED TO MY ADVANTAGE—when bad things—i.e. things people consider to be "bad"—happen, look to see how you could turn these into advantages or opportunities. Creativity is often required here.

-THERE IS NO SUCH THING AS A STRESSFUL OCCUPATION—it's not your job or your profession that is causing you to experience stress. It's the way you are consciously or unconsciously approaching your job or profession that is causing all the trouble. Once you accept this self-empowering principle, you can set out to discover—and do something about—the many subtle, inapparent ways you contribute to your problems.

-IF I'M FEELING STRESSED BY MY WORK, I MUST BE SOMEHOW CREATING MY PROBLEMS—this is the general principle of "feedback" discussed in previous chapters. Instead of blaming your job, your working conditions, management, or the behavior of others for your stress, consider that you may be its primary cause. By consciously adopting this point of view, you can empower yourself to discover the many ways in which it is true.

▶ NOTE: Remember, if you experience even more stress from adopting this perspective, you should consider this as "feedback" as well—i.e. as a helpful warning sign that you are probably doing something wrong!

-SUCCESSFUL PEOPLE FREQUENTLY ASK FOR HELP—forget about being a hero or doing it all yourself. You're not a wimp for asking for, or receiving, help from others. Seek support and guidance from other people as often as you can. If you are having problems and you aren't actively using this strategy, this may be one hidden cause of stress you can rectify.

-PEOPLE NATURALLY WANT TO CONTRIBUTE TO OTHER PEOPLE—this context is important to remember when somebody does something you think is wrong or offensive. Most people are trying to contribute to others in the best way they know how. If you reflect upon their actions in this light, you will often understand their motives more accurately.

-LIFE CAN BE A WIN-WIN PROPOSITION—despite our cultural tendency toward win/lose thinking and competitive behavior, you can decide to make your life about win-win interactions. Win-win is often a more satisfying and rewarding game to play than either win-lose or lose-win.* You can choose to make win-win the goal of all of your interactions with clients, co-workers, your boss, your spouse, your children, your friends, etc. Adopting a win-win philosophy not only enhances the quality of your life, but it can also lead to financial gains and many other satisfying rewards as well.

▶ NOTE: For an excellent discussion of win-win thinking see Stephen Covey's *The Seven Habits Of Highly Effective People*, which is listed in the Suggestions For Further Reading section.

2) *Create Purposes And Goals That Make Your Work More Satisfying And Rewarding*

In addition to adopting a win-win philosophy, you can also create the following purposes and goals to make your job more satisfying and rewarding:

* "Lose-win" means allowing others to take advantage of you or profit at your expense.

a) Define your own criteria for your self-worth as an individual (these do not have to be the same as society or any group endorses);

b) Define your own criteria for "doing your job well" (as long as fulfilling these criteria enables you to accomplish the job you are being paid to do);

c) Create purposes and goals for yourself that are *other-directed* rather than self-directed. These might include:

-Taking care of the people you work with;
-Taking care of your boss;
-Helping others achieve their goals;
-Having your company be the best in its field;
-Having your company be a fun place to work.

The important thing to notice about each of these purposes is that they are not dependent on the nature of your circumstances. In other words, you can always adopt them regardless of what is happening around you.

3) *Keep Your Promises And Follow Through On Your Commitments*

Even though other people may not keep their promises, you will be amazed at how much stress you can eliminate when you keep your own word. Not only will your stress at work greatly diminish, but stress in all other areas of your life will go down as well.

4) *Don't Make Promises You May Not Be Able To Keep*

This will support you in keeping your word. It also prevents many of the problems that occur when you let other people down. When you make promises to other people, they often make promises based on what they expect you to do. And the people they make promises to make additional promises, and so on and so on. When you fail to honor your promises, therefore, whole networks of commitments may suddenly collapse. This can create huge logistical and emotional problems for many individuals. If everyone were careful not to make promises they knew they might not be able to keep, a great deal of stress could be avoided.

5) *Clean Up Breaches Of Integrity*

Whenever you do break a promise or fail to keep your word, acknowledge this fact to others as quickly as you can. Clean up other lapses of integrity whenever they come to your attention—e.g. neglecting to pay a bill, forgetting to do something for someone, or saying something cruel to someone. This may require you to apologize to others, refund their money, or otherwise offer to make amends. But by diligently cleaning up your breaches of integrity, you will reduce the number of them you commit in the future. After all, if you know you will have to clean up such breaches, you will be much less likely to let them occur.

6) *Be A Team Player*

Another good way to reduce your stress at work and make your job more rewarding is to be a team player. In addition to getting your own job done, make it your business to support other people who work with you. Instead of adopting the attitude "that's not my job" or "I'm not paid to do that," you can choose to adopt more team-oriented perspectives, such as:

-"Everything is my job."
-"If something needs to be done, you can count on me to help do it."
-"If one of us loses, all of us lose in the long run."

While it may appear that taking on such responsibilities, in addition to your own job, would increase your levels of stress and tension, just the opposite usually happens. The more you help others out, the more they may be inclined to help you in return. In addition, by making things easier for your co-workers and colleagues, you will be helping to create a more supportive and nurturing environment to work in, which will often make your job easier and more pleasant.

7) *Clarify Agreements And Expectations*

This basic strategy, which was discussed in earlier chapters, can help you eliminate many types of work-related stress.

8) *Don't Ignore "Little" Problems*

This important strategy, which was discussed earlier in this chapter, is also useful for preventing many types of stress.

9) *Seek Help, Advice, And Coaching From Others*

Coaching is very useful for dealing with stress in any area of life. It is particularly useful in business, finance, management, and other work-related areas.

10) *Learn To Empower Others*

The more you learn to empower other people, especially those who work for you and with you, the less stress and tension you will experience in your job. Most people are not "programmed" to empower others effectively. Thus, you should make it your business to find out how to do so. There are many books, seminars, and other helpful resources available on this subject. Once you recognize the need for improving this important skill, you will find many opportunities to learn more about it.

11) *Take Care Of Yourself/Take Care Of Your Body*

You may need to literally fight for the time to take care of yourself and your body. Even if it costs you some money or a promotion to do so, you may want to consider the advantages of such a trade.

Here are some of my personal recommendations:*

a) Try to set aside 1-2 hours in your work schedule every day (or at least 3 days a week) for "self-time." This can include lunch-time, as long as you have it to yourself and are not conducting business. Even if you have to come to work an hour earlier or stay an hour later, it is often worth it to have a relaxing break in your day. Some people are even willing to reduce their pay, work part-time, or take a demotion in order to create this type of arrangement.

b) Use your self-time to do whatever pleases you or relaxes you. Forget about whatever work is undone, since it will ultimately get accomplished in whatever time you have. In fact, if you take time out for yourself every day, you will probably be much more refreshed, energetic, and productive overall.

c) If you fail to get a good night's sleep, don't let this happen two nights in a row. Most people can tolerate an occasional night with little sleep. When several sleepless nights occur in succession, stress can greatly increase.

d) Do some type of physical exercise for at least 30-60 minutes 3-4 days each week. The type of exercise you do is not terribly

---

* Few people will be able to follow all of these recommendations. They are presented merely as guidelines to expand your coping options.

important as long as you do it *regularly* and as long as you make it *enjoyable*. Don't get caught up in pushing your body too hard or expecting it to do more and more. Just let your body relax, and make sure you always have fun with whatever type of exercise you choose.

e) Try to follow a sensible diet. While I am not a big proponent of diet and exercise as *primary* strategies for coping with stress, both can be helpful to some degree. If you consume large amounts of caffeine or junk foods, for example, try to cut down on these. If you feel tired and sleepy after lunch every day, experiment with different foods (such as eliminating sugar and carbohydrates) or with the amount of food you eat for lunch to see if such changes make a difference. And instead of eating to deal with any stress you experience, learn how to make your problems disappear naturally by applying the strategies and tools described in this book.

f) Don't put work ahead of other major priorities in your life. If you have a spouse or a family, *don't neglect them*. Their happiness and well-being is part of your job as well. When you take care of your family you are also taking care of yourself, since if their needs are neglected, yours will be too!

g) Listen to your body. Don't ignore the symptoms that occur in it. Sometimes these symptoms can alert you to the need to slow down, make changes in your thinking or behavior, or go to a doctor. Remember, work is never more important than taking care of your body, for if your body is not healthy, your work will invariably suffer.

12) *Create Supportive Relationships*

Make sure you have several individuals, both at home and at work, with whom you can share your positive and negative experiences. Sometimes organized support groups are good for this purpose. But you can create your own network of friends and associates, whom you can meet with and talk with on a regular basis.

Learn To Deal With The Non-Obvious Causes Of Job-Related Stress

The main point of this chapter was to show you that non-obvious causes—in addition to the causes you easily see—are often responsible for your job-related stress. Once you are able to pinpoint these hidden causes, you can usually figure out how to deal with them successfully.

DAY 11: EXERCISES

1. *List at least one way you could benefit from viewing each of the following work-related problems as feedback—i.e. from the point of view that you may be the cause of whatever "stress" you experience from them:*

Example:

A. Multiple schedule interruptions:

   Response: "I could put a DO NOT DISTURB sign on my door and train my co-workers and employees to honor it.

B. Poor management: _____

   _____

C. Lack of appreciation for the work you do:_____

   _____

D. Uncertainty (not knowing what to do): _____

   _____

2. *List at least one way each of the following internal conversations contributes to your "stress" at work:*

A. GOOD/BAD:_____

   _____

B. RIGHT/WRONG: _____

   _____

C. CREDIT/BLAME: _____

   _____

D. PERFECTIONISM: _____

   _____

E. I'VE GOT TO DO IT MYSELF: _____

   _____

3. *List at least one way each of the following internal action patterns contributes to your ''stress'' at work:*

   A. FAILING TO MAKE REQUESTS/DEMANDS OF OTHERS:

   _____

   _____

   B. FAILING TO DECLINE REQUESTS/DEMANDS FROM

       OTHERS: _____

   _____

   C. FAILING TO ASSESS THE COMMITMENT OF OTHERS:

   _____

   _____

   D. FAILING TO KEEP YOUR PROMISES: _____

   _____

   E. FAILING TO DEAL WITH PROBLEMS CREATIVELY:

   _____

   _____

4. *If you could design your own criteria for ''doing your job well,'' what would these be?:*

1. _____

   _____

2. _____

   _____

3. _____

   _____

4. _____

   _____

DAY 12

STRESS-RELATED PHYSICAL PROBLEMS

The relationship between "stress" and physical illness is quite complex. Many physical problems such as high blood pressure, headaches, stomach ulcers, and heart disease are either caused by, or aggravated by, high degrees of stress. Many other illnesses such as diabetes, certain auto-immune disorders, and possibly even some forms of cancer are probably caused by stress to some degree, even though we lack the evidence to prove this convincingly.

Illness itself is a major source of stress in our lives. When we are sick, we can become angry, irritable, depressed, or even hostile. We also may have contact with doctors, hospitals, needles, tests, and other stressful aspects of the health care system. Feelings of helplessness, hopelessness, guilt, and humiliation are also very common, as are concerns about finances, pain, recovery, abandonment, loneliness, and death.

Even when we are healthy and well, the fear of getting sick can cause us to experience stress. Will I get AIDS? Will I develop cancer? Am I eating the right foods? Is my blood pressure O.K? Is my cholesterol too high? These and many other health-related concerns are in the background of our thinking every day.

We also have concerns about the health and well-being of our friends and loved ones. What if my husband has a heart attack? What if my wife becomes ill? What if my child becomes a drug addict? Will my friend make it through surgery?

Thus, the relationship between "stress" and physical illness includes at least three different types of health-related problems:

Figure 12-1

Major Types Of Health-Related Problems

PHYSICAL ILLNESSES OR SYMPTOMS IN YOUR BODY	PHYSICAL ILLNESSES OR SYMPTOMS IN OTHER PEOPLE'S BODIES	OTHER HEALTH-RELATED PROBLEMS AND CONCERNS

The best way to deal with each of these types of problems is to use the six-step method outlined in Chapter 4.

Feedback

The secret to winning against any type of "stress" is to adopt a feedback perspective. This is especially true for health-related problems. Unfortunately, most of us have been trained to do just the opposite. We have been taught to believe that the physical symptoms and illnesses we develop have little to do with us or with our choices, decisions, and habits in life. Instead, we believe that our physical symptoms and illnesses largely occur because of heredity, old age, dietary factors, toxic agents, viruses, bacteria, or other external factors beyond our control. Because of these widespread beliefs, we seriously underestimate—or fail to consider at all—the role *we often play* in bringing our physical problems about.

In order to reduce our physical and other health-related problems naturally, we must learn to deal with our own internal conversations and action patterns that contribute to them. This is true for our own physical problems, the "stress" we experience when others become ill, and other associated health-related problems such as anger, frustration, worry, guilt, fear, and financial difficulties.

Stress-Related Physical Symptoms And Illnesses (In Your Own Body)

The following physical symptoms are commonly—but not always—associated with "stress": (Check those that apply to you.)

Figure 12-2

Physical Symptoms Commonly Associated With "Stress"

☐ Headaches
☐ Indigestion
☐ Heartburn
☐ Muscle tension
☐ Fatigue
☐ Irritability
☐ Palpitations
☐ Shortness of breath
☐ Chest pains
☐ Excessive sweating
☐ Muscle twitches
☐ Diarrhea
☐ Abdominal pain
☐ Inability to concentrate

☐ Lightheadedness
☐ Dizziness
☐ Teeth grinding
☐ Loss of sexual desire
☐ Cold hands/cold feet
☐ Neck pains
☐ Back pains
☐ Skin rashes
☐ Menstrual irregularities
☐ Urinary difficulties
☐ Increased appetite
☐ Decreased appetite
☐ Generalized nervousness
☐ Difficulty sleeping

The following illnesses are also highly associated with "stress":

Figure 12-3

Physical Illnesses Commonly Associated With "Stress"

Migraine headaches
High blood pressure
Heart disease
Strokes
Stomach ulcers
Esophageal problems
Asthma

Colitis
Thyroid disorders
Prostatitis
High cholesterol
Alcoholism
Drug addiction
Sudden death

You can use the method outlined in Chapter 4—along with other traditional and non-traditional treatment approaches—to deal with these problems more effectively.

▶ **WARNING**: Any advice I give in this chapter should only be followed after you have been professionally evaluated. If you are concerned about your health, if you do not feel well, or if you have any of the symptoms or illnesses listed above, *first consult with your doctor or other health care provider.* While the method discussed in this book can be used to deal with physical problems such as headaches, fatigue, chest pains, palpitations, and indigestion, these symptoms can also be signs of *serious medical conditions* that may require prompt professional evaluation and treatment.

STEP 1: DEFINE YOUR PROBLEM(S) SPECIFICALLY

It is important to define your physical problems specifically. For example, people can suffer from many different types of headaches. There are migraine headaches, tension headaches, mixtures of migraine and tension headaches, sinus headaches, etc. In addition, headaches vary in frequency, severity, time of onset, duration, and precipitating factors.

The more specific you can be about a headache problem, the easier it will be for you to identify its underlying causes. For example, sinus-type headaches that only occur during the ragweed pollen season probably have nothing at all to do with "stress." On the other hand, headaches that occur only at work or only after an argument with your spouse are very suggestive of underlying conflicts.

STEP 2: RELATE TO YOUR PROBLEM(S) AS "FEEDBACK"

As I have already mentioned, the best way to deal with any type of health-related physical problem is to adopt a "feedback" perspective. This means assuming that you may be a cause of such problems, even if you can't possibly imagine how this could be true.

Unfortunately, when most of us become sick or disabled, we tend to adopt the opposite perspective. We tend to assume that:

a) external factors have caused us to become ill;
b) illness is a sign that something is "going wrong" with our bodies;
c) there are no "positive" benefits to be gained from becoming ill;
d) the best way to deal with our physical problems is to make them go away by directly attacking them, i.e. by using medications, diet, exercise, biofeedback, relaxation techniques, etc.

In order to adopt a "feedback" perspective, we must consciously adopt a different set of assumptions:

a) internal factors—i.e. conversations and action patterns within us— may have something to do with our physical symptoms and illnesses;
b) illness can sometimes be a sign that things are "going right" with our bodies;*
c) there are many positive benefits to be gained from becoming ill;
d) the best way to deal with physical problems and symptoms is to make them go away naturally—by recognizing and dealing with their underlying causes.

Figure 12-4

Relating To Physical Symptoms And Illnesses As "Feedback"

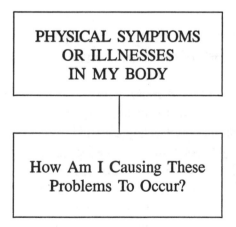

▶ NOTE: Adopting this perspective does not preclude you from attacking your symptoms directly. It also does not preclude you from using any other treatment or coping strategy. The "feedback" approach described in this book can be used either in lieu of, or to complement, any other treatment method you choose.

---

* Instead of viewing your physical problems as "malfunctions" of your body, you can view them as useful warning "messages" as well. For example, pain can be viewed as something "going wrong" within your body. It can also be viewed as something "going right" in the sense that pain often can alert you to other hidden problems that need to be identified and dealt with effectively.

Remember, you don't always need to use this approach, especially if you are suffering from a minor physical problem or ailment. But if you develop a serious problem, or if a minor ailment becomes worse or recurrent, you should consider adopting this feedback approach, in conjunction with a visit to your doctor or other health care provider.

Why Should You Adopt A "Feedback" Perspective?

There are several good reasons to adopt a feedback perspective:

1. *Many of our physical problems and illnesses do in fact result from our own thoughts, beliefs, attitudes, and behaviors.* Many illnesses, for example, are caused, at least in part, by lifestyle factors such as smoking, drinking, lack of exercise, dietary habits, and chronic overwork. Physical problems can also result from many other thoughts and behaviors of which we are usually unaware.

EXAMPLE A: Several years ago, I developed an annoying "ringing" sensation in both of my ears. I consulted an ear specialist who was unable to determine a cause. When the problem continued, I decided to adopt a feedback perspective. I asked myself, "How could I be causing this problem to occur?" Several minutes later, I realized something that had completely escaped my attention. About three weeks before my symptoms began, I had purchased a Walkman radio (with earphones) to use when I went jogging. I had been playing music very loudly through the earphones, but I had totally neglected this as a possible cause of my problem. Once I stopped using the earphones, the ringing sensation in my ears quickly disappeared.

EXAMPLE B: A 45-year-old businessman came to see me for recurrent bouts of pericarditis.* He had been treated for several years by a prominent cardiologist, who refused to believe that his problem was stress-related. After several months of counselling, however, during which this man identified and dealt with a number of important conflicts in his life, his episodes of pericarditis completely subsided.

---

* An inflammation of the membrane that surrounds the heart.

2. *Many of our physical symptoms and illnesses also result in part from underlying problems such as unresolved emotions, interpersonal conflicts, and work-related issues.*

Figure 12-5

Physical Problems Can Be Caused By Underlying Conflicts

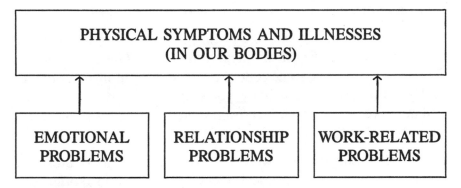

As we have seen in previous chapters, each of these types of causes are themselves caused by hidden conversations and action patterns that occur within us.

Tension headaches, for example, can result from suppressed emotions, relationship conflicts, or work-related difficulties. Sleep disturbances, palpitations, indigestion, nervousness, fatigue, muscle aches, and many other physical symptoms can also result from similar underlying causes. The same is true for many stress-related illnesses and diseases, such as high blood pressure, heart disease, strokes, and stomach ulcers. Thus, by adopting a "feedback" perspective, you can learn to identify and deal with some of these underlying causes of your physical problems.

3. *Even when a health-related problem is believed to be caused primarily by external agents, internal causes may also be playing a role.* By choosing to adopt a "feedback" perspective, you may be able to identify and deal with these internal causes.

EXAMPLE: Colds, sore throats, and other respiratory tract infections are believed to be caused by infectious agents. While this may be true to a large degree, some people can identify other contributing causes. Some people notice, for example, that their colds or respiratory infections frequently occur after certain stressful incidents or events. People who suffer a sudden, unexpected loss of something valued in their lives often come down with a cold or respiratory tract infection one or two days later. Some people with asthma notice that their acute attacks are often precipitated by emotional upsets or by other types of "stress." Thus, by looking within yourself to identify these internal causes, you may be able to gain some control over the frequency, severity, and duration of any illnesses they produce.

4. *Even when you play no role at all in the cause of a particular illness, adopting a "feedback" perspective can still be advantageous.* By assuming you have some control over a symptom, illness, or other biological process in your body, you may adopt certain habits that end up having a positive effect (even though there may be no scientific proof that this is possible).

EXAMPLE: Suppose you were told you had multiple sclerosis. If the diagnosis is correct, medical science has very little to offer you. The best you can do in such situations is to assume that you may have played a role in causing your multiple sclerosis to occur—whether this is true or not—and that you may also be able to make it go away, or at least retard its progress. This will give you the best possible chance of exerting whatever influence and control you do truly have.

5. *The final advantage of a "feedback" perspective is that it allows you to use any symptom or illness as an opportunity to enhance the quality of your life, regardless of whether your physical problem improves or disappears.* By relating to your illness as a "feedback" signal—similar to a warning light on the dashboard of your car—you can search for other underlying problems in your life and make an effort to deal with these more effectively. Sometimes this will help your physical condition, but even if it doesn't, you may prevent other physical problems from occurring and improve the quality of your life as well.

► NOTE: For some people, developing a serious illness, such as a stroke, heart attack, ulcer, or even cancer, has turned out to be a major "positive" turning point in their lives. On rare occasions, it has even led to significant medical breakthroughs, such as the healing power of humor described by Norman Cousins in his book *The Anatomy Of An Illness.*

Why Are So Many People Opposed To This "Feedback" Perspective?

If a "feedback" perspective has so many benefits, why are we so reluctant to adopt it? The major obstacle, I believe, is the tremendous amount of confusion and misunderstanding that exists today about the true causes of our physical symptoms and illnesses. Much of this confusion comes from mistaken beliefs about the causative role of genetic, dietary, and environmental factors.

Even when genetic, dietary, or environmental factors do play a role in causing our physical problems to occur, *they are rarely the entire story.* Conversations and action patterns within us and within our society also play a role. So do unresolved emotions, relationship conflicts, and work-related issues. This is why cancer specialists such as Carl and Stephanie Simonton and Bernie Siegel encourage people to assume they may have played a role in causing their illness to occur. They don't do this to make people feel guilty or depressed. They do it because *it can enable people to harness their own internal healing capabilities,* whatever these might be.

STEP 3: IDENTIFY THE SPECIFIC CONVERSATIONS AND ACTION PATTERNS (WITHIN YOU) THAT ARE CAUSING YOUR PROBLEM(S) TO OCCUR OR PERSIST

Once you identify specific conversations and action patterns within you that may be contributing to your physical or other health-related problems, you can then take action to deal with these causes directly. If you are successful, your physical symptoms or problems will often improve or even disappear.

▶ NOTE: Some physical problems may be so far advanced by the time you apply this approach that you may not be able to reverse them. Some evidence exists, however, that even severely-blocked arteries and some forms of cancer can be reversed in certain cases. Even if a problem can't be reduced or cured, how you choose to relate to it may have a bearing on the rate at which it progresses.

The following tips and suggestions may help you identify some of the not-so-obvious causes of your health-related problems:

● *Certain stress-related symptoms and illnesses are associated with particular underlying problems.*

The following associations frequently hold true:

Figure 12-6

Physical Symptom/Illness	*Common Underlying Problems*
Teeth grinding/jaw pain	Unresolved anger Chronic resentment
Headache	Perfectionism Excessive need for control
Stomach ulcer	Anger at a loved one
Situational diarrhea	Acute anxiety Worry
Insomnia	Chronic anxiety Acute anxiety Worry Insecurity
Decreased appetite	Depression
Increased appetite	Anxiety Frustration Anger Sadness Low self-esteem Depression
High blood pressure	Impatience Anger/resentment Hostility
Decreased sexuality	Relationship conflicts Poor communication Worry Anxiety

► NOTE: Many of these physical symptoms and illnesses have other causes as well. But if you are aware of these associations, they can sometimes provide you with clues to the types of underlying problems that may be affecting you.

• *Know which hidden conversations and action patterns are likely to be involved*

Most of the time, the hidden conversations and action patterns that are contributing to your physical problems will not be obvious to you. It helps, therefore, to know what types of hidden causes are likely to be involved.

For example, the following internal (and societal) conversations are responsible for many of our physical problems:

Conversations:

-GOOD/BAD
-RIGHT/WRONG
-CAUSE/EFFECT
-CREDIT/BLAME
-PERFECTIONISM
-CONTROL

In addition, the following action patterns frequently contribute to our health-related problems:

Action Patterns:

-FAILING TO RELATE TO PHYSICAL PROBLEMS AS
   "FEEDBACK"
-NOT TAKING CARE OF YOUR BODY
-FAILING TO DEAL WITH "LITTLE" PROBLEMS
-FAILING TO ASK FOR HELP
-COMPROMISING YOUR OWN OR OTHERS' INTEGRITY
-DEPENDING UPON DRUGS, ALCOHOL, CIGARETTES,
   TRANQUILIZERS

We have already talked about each of these action patterns. COM-PROMISING YOUR OWN AND OTHERS' INTEGRITY, for example, is a common source of physical "stress" since we are quite capable of punishing ourselves—often unconsciously—for any real or imaginary crimes we believe we have committed.

The pattern of NOT TAKING CARE OF YOUR BODY is also very important. When you don't give your body enough rest, sleep, or relaxation, you lower its resistance to many disease-producing factors. If you are not physically active, if you eat a poor or unbalanced diet, or if you ingest too much caffeine or other chemical substances, you can also cause certain physical problems to emerge.

DEPENDING UPON DRUGS, ALCOHOL, CIGARETTES, TRANQUILIZERS and other chemical coping methods, including FOOD, is another common behavior pattern that contributes to physical deterioration. As I mentioned in the Introduction, the main drawback of these band-aid coping methods is that they work very well. While they temporarily relieve much of our physical and emotional distress, they can produce serious health-related problems when used too frequently. In addition, they keep us from learning how to deal with our problems more naturally. Thus, the more you depend upon such chemical coping "solutions," the more you guarantee that your problems will persist.

▶ **WARNING**: Never stop or change any prescription medicine without first consulting with your health care provider. While learning to use the method described in this book may eventually reduce your need for medication, it may take time before you can safely cut back. And for certain types of physical problems, you may need to stay on medication indefinitely.

• *Be aware that some physical reactions are not necessarily "abnormal" or "inappropriate"*

Many situations in life can cause our bodies to react. The following situations and life transitions, for instance, often cause powerful physical and emotional reactions:

Figure 12-7

Common Situations And Life Transitions That Produce Strong Physical/Emotional Reactions In Our Bodies

Situation	*Life Transition*
1. Death of a loved one	1. Getting married
2. Losing your job	2. Having a baby
3. Being rejected by a lover	3. Starting a new business
4. Winning the lottery	4. Moving to a new community
5. Witnessing a disaster	5. Transferring to a new school
6. Going to the dentist	6. Becoming disabled

Having strong emotional or physical reactions to such events is not abnormal. For example, when people get married, get promoted, have a baby, or move to a new community, their bodies go into a state of physical and emotional turmoil for a while. Similar reactions occur when someone close to you dies, the stock market crashes, your business fails, or an important relationship suddenly ends. When these events occur, it is normal to feel temporarily "out of sorts." As long as these reactions are not severe or excessively prolonged, they will usually go away as you successfully adjust over time.

Remembering this point may keep you from judging yourself harshly when such physical or emotional reactions occur. At times, you may get trapped in conversations such as "I shouldn't be feeling this way," "something serious must be wrong with me," or "maybe I'm having a nervous breakdown," when all that's happening is your body is responding, quite appropriately, to some painful, challenging, or disturbing turn of events.

• *Use the feedback approach to deal with anger, frustration, worry, guilt, relationship conflicts and other types of "stress" that result from physical problems in your own or other people's bodies*

For example, the following conversations are responsible for much of the emotional distress we experience when our own body becomes physically ill:

Conversations:

-"This is very bad." (GOOD/BAD)
-"I shouldn't be feeling this way."
-"Being sick is a sign of weakness." (STRONG/WEAK)
-"There's nothing that can be done about my problem anyway."
  (RESIGNATION)

When someone close to you becomes sick or disabled, the following conversations and action patterns may become triggered within you:

Conversations:

-"What happened to this person was terrible." (GOOD/BAD)
-"If I worry hard enough, maybe I can help them get well.
  (CAUSE/EFFECT; UNREALISTIC EXPECTATION)

-"I should be able to make them feel better."
 (CAUSE/EFFECT; UNREALISTIC EXPECTATION)
-"Their life is going to be ruined." (NEGATIVE THINKING)

Action Patterns:

-TRYING TO SOLVE OTHER PEOPLE'S PROBLEMS
-TRYING TO CONTROL THE WRONG THINGS
-FAILING TO EMPOWER OTHERS
-BLAMING YOURSELF OR OTHERS

Thus, the best way to deal with any type of health-related problem is to look for internal conversations and action patterns that may be causing it to occur.

STEP 4: REMIND YOURSELF: THESE HIDDEN CAUSES ARE IN YOUR BODY, NOT YOUR MIND

This will remind you that you can't simply get rid of your underlying conversations and action patterns once you become aware of them. You also can't stop them from becoming triggered over and over again, so don't judge yourself negatively whenever this occurs.

STEP 5: TAKE ACTION TO NEUTRALIZE YOUR HIDDEN, INTERNAL CAUSES

As we have seen, there are two basic ways to complete this step:

a) You can challenge your stress-producing conversations;
b) You can disrupt your stress-producing action patterns.

EXAMPLE: If you believe a physical problem you are experiencing is primarily caused by genetic or environmental factors, try challenging this assumption by looking for other hidden causes, such as unresolved emotions or relationship conflicts, that might also be playing a role. Or, if you have an urge to use cigarettes, alcohol, food, or other chemical coping methods to deal with your "stress," try to ignore these urges and learn how to cope with your problems in more natural and effective ways.

Stress-Relieving Contexts

In addition to challenging your hidden conversations and disrupting your hidden action patterns, you can also create certain contexts that can help you deal with your health-related problems and concerns. Some of these contexts include:

-EVERYTHING IN LIFE—INCLUDING MY BODY—IS
  ALWAYS WORKING
-WHATEVER HAPPENS IN LIFE—INCLUDING THINGS
  THAT HAPPEN IN MY BODY—CAN BE USED TO MY
  ADVANTAGE
-HOWEVER I AM FEELING IS EXACTLY HOW I SHOULD
  BE FEELING
-IF I'M FEELING PHYSICALLY "STRESSED" IN ANY
  WAY, I MUST BE SOMEHOW CREATING MY
  PROBLEMS
-SUCCESSFUL PEOPLE FREQUENTLY ASK FOR HELP
-THE STATE OF MY BODY HAS MUCH TO DO WITH
  THE WAY I AM LIVING LIFE

STEP 6: IF YOUR PHYSICAL PROBLEMS OR SYMPTOMS DON'T IMPROVE OR DISAPPEAR, REPEAT STEPS 1-5 AND/OR GET COACHING

If you are unable to make your physical problems or symptoms disappear, repeat each step in the method, looking for errors or omissions you may have made. If this doesn't work, consider getting coaching.

Remember, some physical problems may be irreversible by the time they come to your attention. Thus, they may never completely disappear, no matter what approach you use.

Summary And Conclusions

Instead of trying to manage your physical symptoms of stress, you should pay more attention to what may be causing them to occur. The best way to do this is to adopt a "feedback" perspective. The more you train yourself to use this approach, the easier it will become for you to make your stress-related physical problems and concerns disappear naturally, without using drugs, relaxation exercises, or stress management techniques.

DAY 12: EXERCISES

1. *When you say that you have a physical problem or illness that is "caused by stress," which of the following are you actually saying:*

☐ A. You have a physical problem that is caused by external pressures and demands in your life.

☐ B. You have a physical problem that is caused by marital, family, or other interpersonal conflicts.

☐ C. You have a physical problem that is caused by unresolved emotions.

☐ D. You have a physical problem that is caused by your failure to deal with problems and conflicts—both internal and external—in your life effectively.

☐ E. Any or all of the above.

2. *During the ten year period between 1979-1988, the state of California had a 700% increase in disability claims attributed to "mental stress," whereas disability claims for all other causes increased by only 18%. What percentage of these claims do you think could have been avoided if people were more aware of the principles and strategies described in this book:*

☐ A. 100%?
☐ B. 75%?
☐ C. 50%?
☐ D. 25%?
☐ E. 0%?

3. *How might the feedback approach described in this book help you better understand your own role in causing each of the following physical problems to occur:*

EXAMPLE: *A sore throat*
     Response: not getting enough rest; not communicating about something that is bothering me.

A. A stomach ulcer: _____

B. Hemorrhoids: _____

_____

C. Venereal disease: _____

_____

4. *How might the feedback approach described in this book help you better understand your own role in causing each of the following health-related problems:*

EXAMPLE: *Fear of cancer*
> *Response:* not understanding the warning signs of cancer correctly; exaggerating concerns about cancer based on newspaper stories or the experiences of others.

A. Anger about being sick: _____

_____

B. Worrying about the health of a loved one: _____

_____

C. Fear of having surgery:

_____

DAY 13

OTHER TYPES OF STRESS

In addition to the areas already discussed—emotional distress, relationship conflicts, work-related stress, and physical problems—you can use the step-by-step approach outlined in this book to cope with many other problems, including:

- Financial stress
- Economic recessions
- The stress of raising children
- The stress of public speaking
- Unexpected crises and changes
- Death
- Disasters
- Retirement
- Legal conflicts (including the stress of being sued)
- Community problems
- Societal and global problems
- Bureaucratic inefficiency

FINANCIAL STRESS

The best way to deal with financial stress is to adopt a feedback perspective. This means assuming you are the cause of any financial problems you experience:

-If your business is failing, the chances are good that you may be one of the causes. Even if your competition is stiff, markets are

depressed, or other external factors are involved, how well you anticipate and deal with these factors often determines whether you succeed or fail.

-If you don't have enough money to live on, you are probably spending too much, managing your finances poorly, or not taking advantage of opportunities to increase your income.

-If financial problems are causing you to worry or feel depressed,
your own internal conversations and action patterns—not your financial situation—are probably causing you to feel bad.

Thus, while you can always blame bad luck, a sluggish economy,
or other outside influences for your financial woes, you are much
better off when you look within yourself.

Here are some specific conversations and action patterns that commonly contribute to financial stress:

Internal Patterns	*Examples*
POSITIVE THINKING	You overestimate your market or underestimate your needs or financial resources.
UNREALISTIC EXPECTATIONS	You set impossible goals for yourself or try to meet unrealistic production schedules.
HOPE	You expect things will go well when there is no foundation for such optimism.
I SHOULDN'T HAVE DONE WHAT I DID	You "beat yourself up" whenever your financial decisions don't work out.
FEELINGS=TRUTH	You assume that your "gut" feelings about a particular financial decision are accurate when they are not.
THOUGHTS=TRUTH	You assume that your conscious beliefs or hunches about a par-

ticular financial decision are accurate when they are not.

FAILING TO DO YOUR HOMEWORK/RESEARCH	You don't check things out carefully before moving ahead with a big financial decision (e.g. buying a house, buying a car, etc.).
FAILING TO CLARIFY AGREEMENTS AND EXPECTATIONS	You fail to clarify contract terms precisely; you don't make sure your employees are aware of, or accountable for, their job responsibilities.
FAILING TO ASSESS COMMITMENT OF OTHERS	You don't pay attention to the degree of sincerity and commitment behind other people's promises.
FAILING TO ACKNOWLEDGE YOUR WEAKNESSES	You are reluctant to acknowledge the financial areas you don't handle well (e.g. cash flow, record keeping, marketing, sales, etc.).
FAILING TO ANTICIPATE BREAKDOWNS AND DELAYS	You don't have contingency plans to avoid financial disaster when unplanned problems or interruptions occur.
FAILING TO ASK FOR HELP	You refuse to ask for, or accept, help or criticism from others.

In addition, there are many other internally-generated causes of financial stress.

EXAMPLE: Jacques Rebibo, a financial counsellor in McLean, Virginia, claims that most people are unclear about the differences between:

1) Investing
2) Pioneering
3) Gambling.

Investing is giving money to someone who has a proven track record of success in a particular business area. Pioneering is giving money to someone who has been successful in the past, but who is now taking on a new type of business or financial venture. And gambling is *giving or loaning money to anyone else with the intention of getting it back.*

According to Rebibo, thinking you are "investing" when in fact you are pioneering or gambling can cause you to lose your money. It can also produce feelings of anger, guilt, and other types of "stress" when your hard-earned savings suddenly disappear.*

ECONOMIC RECESSIONS

Economic booms and recessions have a well-known cyclical history. When times are good and jobs are plentiful, our careers are more secure and our mood is one of hope and prosperity. When the economy falters, however, workers get laid off, careers come to an end, and the mood of the populace becomes somber and fearful.

Even when a recession does occur, you don't have to end up feeling "stressed" because of it. After all, there are far worse things that could happen to you and your family. In addition, there are always hidden opportunities in every type of economy, and if you use your natural creativity and resourcefulness, you can often find ways to capitalize on these opportunities.

Failing to prepare for economic low-periods (FAILING TO ANTICIPATE BREAKDOWNS AND DELAYS) is another hidden cause of "stress" when a recessionary cycle comes around. Everyone should have funds in reserve to cover such eventualities. Regardless of whether you are a teenager working at your first job or a career executive with a six-figure income, you should strive to put enough money away so that you and your family can live for *at least a year* with no other source of income. Instead of spending money on nonessential items when things are going well, you should make it a priority to build up your financial reserve first. When you lack this type of financial reserve, your anxiety will be heightened and you will be easily upset by anything that threatens your income.

* Gambling and pioneering are not necessarily bad, as long as you know when you are doing them and are aware of the risks involved.

There are many other ways by which we add to, or create, the stress we experience during economic recessions. If you work with the tools provided in this book, including the lists of conversations and action patterns located in Appendix A, you should be better able to recognize and deal with these hidden causes.

THE STRESS OF RAISING CHILDREN

Many people believe that raising children is invariably stressful: "The little brats never do what we tell them to do, they constantly get into trouble, and when they get older, they break our hearts and give us ulcers." While this may be an exaggeration, it's not far off from many parents' experiences.

The truth about raising children, however, is that it need not be stressful. Much of the stress we experience as parents is self-created. For example, we often feel frustrated and "stressed" when our children repeatedly misbehave. While we easily recognize *their* problematic behavior, we often fail to notice how *our own* negative judgements (BAD, WRONG, STUPID) and our own desires for CONTROL may be playing a role. Parents are also frequently guilty of TRYING TO CONTROL THE WRONG THINGS. Instead of struggling to control their children's behavior directly, they may need to work on controlling their own emotional and verbal responses or applying appropriate and consistent consequences that induce their children to behave.

Also, when we try to SOLVE OUR CHILDREN'S PROBLEMS FOR THEM or SHIELD THEM FROM THE CONSEQUENCES OF THEIR BEHAVIOR, we rob them of opportunities to become responsible for themselves. These behavior patterns place all of the responsibility for solving such problems on us, which can be stressful. Other parents, however, shift some of these responsibilities to their children at very early ages. They carefully monitor their children's choices and decisions, but they only step in and take control when this is truly needed.

In addition, all of the conversations and action patterns discussed in Chapter 10 (Stress In Relationships) also apply to our relationships with our children. Patterns such as the following are frequently at the bottom of our parent-child conflicts:

-PERFECTIONISM
-UNREALISTIC EXPECTATIONS
-NEEDING TO BE RIGHT
-FAILING TO CLARIFY AGREEMENTS AND EXPECTATIONS
-INVALIDATING OTHERS' OPINIONS AND POINTS OF
  VIEW
-FAILING TO BE A BEGINNER (especially with regard to
  knowing how to deal with children)

So is the pattern of KICKING YOUR SEEING-EYE DOG. Children are often remarkably perceptive of their parents' "blind-spots" and self-destructive tendencies. Because we view ourselves as "parents" rather than "people," however, we may be reluctant to consider that our children can help us grow and mature ourselves.

Also, we can get ourselves into trouble by having the desire to shape our children's personalities and interests. Instead of allowing them to develop their own individual talents and abilities, we often try to force them to follow a plan we have in mind. This often leads to unnecessary power struggles, as well as frequent hurt feelings on both sides.

Thus, instead of blaming your kids for any "stress" you are experiencing, you should always adopt a feedback perspective. Use the strategies and tools provided in this book to discover how you may be contributing to your child-rearing problems. Once you can see exactly how you are doing this, you can then use some of the other strategies and tools in this book to deal with your internal stress-producing patterns more effectively.

THE STRESS OF PUBLIC SPEAKING

One of the major causes of the stress of public speaking is our unconscious need for approval. Wanting other people to think well of us activates our patterns of PERFECTIONISM and CONTROL. It also makes us fearful of being ourselves, since any imperfections that became revealed might cause others to judge us negatively.

Public speaking, itself, is not highly stressful. Sometimes it can even be fun if you're not taking it, or yourself, too seriously. Instead of trying to please every listener, realize that some people will be critical no matter what you say or do. As long as you please the majority of your listeners, consider your talk a success no matter what others might think.

Also, the best way to prepare for a talk is to focus on: 1) the three or four major points you want to get across; and 2) your purpose for speaking to your audience. Usually, your purpose will be to contribute something useful to other people. But sometimes, it may be to convey unpopular information, to motivate others to take action, or to explain something that is complex or potentially confusing. By all means, never think your purpose is to *get something* from your audience. If you're not in the "giving" mode, there's a very good chance your talk will be stressful.

Whenever you experience any type of stress with public speaking, you should assume that you, not the task itself, are the primary cause. You should then try to identify the specific ways in which you are making public speaking into a stressful activity. Once you become aware of these hidden causes, you can learn to overcome them and speak in a more confident, relaxed, and "unstressed" manner.

UNEXPECTED CRISES AND CHANGES (INCLUDING DEATH AND DISASTERS)

Unexpected crises and changes can trigger considerable stress and tension for any of us. Losing your job, losing a loved one, or suffering through the trauma of a major natural disaster are always going to be upsetting, and there's no way to get around a certain amount of pain.

It's important to remember, however, that much of the stress we experience when such events occur is generated within us. Internal conversations and action patterns can make events such as deaths and disasters much more stressful than they need to be. Many people, for example, live through the death of loved ones or the loss of their jobs with a minimum of personal stress and suffering. This is because they don't get caught up in stress-producing conversations such as:

- "Look how bad or wrong it was for this to happen."
- "I can't be happy or feel good because of this."
  "My value as a person is dependent upon what I have lost."

Such individuals are quick to challenge these and other stress-producing conversations when they become triggered in their bodies. They approach major crises and changes in their lives with acceptance and optimism, and they refuse to believe they are helpless victims of their circumstances. While they recognize the seriousness of many things that happen—either to themselves or to others—they refuse to become overly distraught about them, especially once they have already occurred. This attitude is particularly useful for dealing with the many minor crises, disruptions, and changes we all experience every day.

RETIREMENT

Retirement is another type of change that can be stressful. Whether you are single or married, rich or poor, have children or don't have children (or grandchildren), sudden changes in your lifestyle can cause many new problems to occur.

One source of retirement stress is the many habits and routines that have become ingrained in your body over the years. When you retire, you are stuck with these automatic tendencies, even though they may no longer be appropriate for your situation.

EXAMPLE: The issue of motivation is a good example. When you are working at a job or profession, your life is mostly determined by the challenges, duties, and responsibilities of your occupation. These external factors provide the meaning and purpose for your life. Once you retire, however, this external source of motivation disappears. The burden is upon you to wake up every day and create your life for yourself. Your body, however, is not accustomed to "creating" much of anything. This sudden disappearance of external motivation can produce a tremendous amount of stress, especially if you keep looking for something other than yourself to give your life meaning.

In addition, the extra time you now have to spend at home can disrupt many of the patterns and routines your family members have established. This can lead to conflicts and tensions that also must be dealt with creatively.

Financial concerns also tend to change upon retirement. Many of these concerns were absent when you were working. Upon retiring, however, you may need to budget more carefully, reduce certain expenditures, and otherwise modify your previous financial habits. These changes can also be upsetting, especially if you are not accepting of them.

Reduced activity levels after retirement, coupled with advancing age, can also lead to an increase in health-related problems and concerns.

Thus, there are many hidden causes—both internal and external— that contribute to the stress of retirement. Each of the causes, however, can be identified and dealt with successfully.

LEGAL CONFLICTS (INCLUDING THE STRESS OF BEING SUED)

If you've ever been in an extended legal battle, you know how stressful a lawsuit can be. In addition to the time and expense required, the emotional wear-and-tear can be devastating.

It is important to remember, however, that much of the stress we experience in such situations comes from us. Both our legal conflicts and the stress that often accompanies them are primarily produced by our own internal conversations and action patterns.

For instance, many legal battles result from failures in our interpersonal and business relationships. These failures could have been prevented, had we followed some of the principles discussed in Chapter 10 (Stress In Relationships).

And once our relationships do turn sour, our automatic patterns tend to make matters worse. Rather than peacefully working out our differences with the parties involved, internal conversations such as WIN/LOSE, RIGHT/WRONG, CREDIT/BLAME, and FORGIVE/PUNISH lead us to make angry accusations, unreasonable or punitive demands, and engage in other vindictive behaviors that are usually returned in kind.

In addition, behavior patterns such as FAILING TO KEEP YOUR PROMISES, FAILING TO ADMIT YOU ARE WRONG, FAILING TO DEAL WITH PROBLEMS CREATIVELY, and TAKING THINGS PERSONALLY almost always aggravate an already tense situation.

The behavior patterns of lawyers can also contribute to your stress. In most legal battles, you've got to "roll with the punches" the other lawyer throws at you. While you can't control his or her behavior, you can control your own emotional and behavioral responses, and you can also control the responses your attorney is authorized to make on your behalf. While you shouldn't allow an opposing attorney to walk all over you, you don't always need to respond in kind.

Of course the best way to settle any legal dispute is to work things out with the principals involved. If you review some of the strategies discussed in Chapter 10, you may discover ways to bring such successful resolutions about.

The stress of being sued can also be reduced by recognizing the internal conversations and action patterns that get triggered within you by such an event.

When people sue you, they usually believe you have done something very wrong (unless they are using the threat of a lawsuit as a ruse to take advantage of you). If you look at their accusations honestly, you will probably discover that you have indeed hurt, disappointed, or damaged them in some way.

The fact that they may have hurt, disappointed, or damaged you as well is not of interest to them. Thus, instead of trying to defend your actions or get other people to admit they were wrong too, see if you can relate to their lawsuit as feedback. Is there anything you need to apologize for? Have you defaulted on your promises, and if so, are you refusing to make amends? Do you owe people money or services which they have a legitimate right to expect? If you handle these issues honestly and responsibly, you may be able to work things out with only a minimum of stress and inconvenience.

▶ NOTE: While it is also possible to *increase* your legal problems by attempting such negotiations, many people would prefer to settle their legal disputes with you, provided you approach them in a non-threatening, non-accusatory fashion.

COMMUNITY, SOCIETAL, AND GLOBAL PROBLEMS

The step-by-step method outlined in this book can also be used to deal with community, societal, and other social problems. Take the problems of increased crime (both locally and nationally), drunk driving, drug abuse, and world hunger, for example. How you think about these problems and how you relate to them—consciously and unconsciously—often determines how much "stress" they produce for you (assuming they don't affect you directly).

In addition, you can easily become "stressed" by attempting to improve or solve some of these large-scale problems. While millions of people are actively working on these problems, most "average" citizens are resigned or apathetic about them. They have many negative conversations and action patterns that overpower their commitment to do something constructive about these issues.

As long as you understand the type of hidden patterns—both within yourself and within others—that you are up against, you can work on such large-scale problems without feeling angry, frustrated, or hopeless. Even though we have a long way to go before we eliminate any of these problems, you can make a difference as an individual if you know how to: a) empower other people, b) put them back in touch with their visions and true commitments, and c) enlist their committed partnership and support.

BUREAUCRATIC INEFFICIENCY

This is another social problem that causes a great deal of "stress" for many of us today. Again, the best way to deal with bureaucratic inefficiency is to use the step-by-step coping method outlined in this book.

Bureaucracies are made up of people who are supposed to perform certain tasks. These tasks are not always performed in a timely or competent manner. When we interact with bureaucracies, therefore, we must accept a certain level of imperfection. While it is always possible to reduce such imperfections, many will still exist at any point in time. Not accepting this fact—expecting things to be different than the way they are—is a major source of unnecessary stress and suffering for many individuals.

Another source of stress in dealing with bureaucracies is the way we automatically treat other people. When we are nasty, impatient, demanding, or insensitive to bureaucratic officials, we often won't be treated well in return. People are still people and, regardless of how they do their jobs, they are much more likely to do things for us when we treat them with kindness, understanding, appreciation, and respect.

When we don't expect too much from bureaucracies, when we plan for frequent breakdowns and delays, and when we are prepared to deal with any problems we encounter creatively and non-judgmentally, we often experience much less stress than do other individuals.

Summary and Conclusions

It doesn't matter what type of "stress" you are experiencing— once you know how to apply the step-by-step coping method described in this book, you should be able to deal with it more effectively. If you are not initially successful with this approach, consider getting coaching. This will further improve your chances for success.

DAY 13: EXERCISES

1. *Which of the following problems CANNOT be addressed by using the step-by-step approach outlined in this book?:*

☐ Your children complain that you don't spend enough time with them.
☐ Your spouse becomes unhappy or depressed.
☐ You are unexpectedly fired from your job.
☐ A friend criticizes you for something you did wrong.
☐ Your bank claims to have no record of your last deposit.
☐ You are left off the invitation list for an important family affair.

2. *How could the context "WHATEVER HAPPENS IN LIFE CAN BE USED TO MY ADVANTAGE" help you to deal with each of the following problems:*

A stock market crash: _____

_____

Making a mistake while speaking to a group: _____

_____

Having a salesperson hound you: _____

_____

Discovering your child has lied to you: _____

_____

DAY 14

THE ROAD TO SUCCESS

In 1978, M. Scott Peck, M.D., wrote a book called *The Road Less Traveled*. In this book, he invited people to take a bold, courageous path to greater happiness and success. He encouraged readers to acknowledge their problems, take responsibility for the role they played in causing them, and free themselves from many of the lies, myths, and other misconceptions they were told—or told themselves—in the past. Peck called this "the road less traveled" because most people do the opposite. They tend to deny their problems, blame someone or something other than themselves for their misery, and uncritically accept the popular "wisdom" of their times.

In *The 14 Day Stress Cure*, I have invited you to take a similar "road less traveled." I have invited you to abandon the path that most people take in dealing with their stress—stress management—and adopt a different method entirely. I have invited you to stop looking *outside* of yourself to understand why your "stress" is occurring and look *within* yourself instead. I have also given you strategies and tools for conducting such an internal inquiry, and I have shown you several ways to deal with your conversations and action patterns once you become aware of them.

You Win Twice Every Time You Choose This Road

Every time you choose this road you become a *double winner* in your fight against stress. In addition to eliminating the immediate "stress" you are experiencing, you gain valuable insights about yourself and about life that will be useful to you in future situations. This knowledge can help you prevent certain types of problems from recurring, or at the very least it can enable you to deal with these problems more effectively.

The Choice Is Yours

From reading this book, you now know that every time you feel "upset," "worried," "nervous," or "stressed," *you always have a choice* between three different ways of coping: a) the band-aid approach (using drugs, alcohol, cigarettes, food, etc.); b) the stress management approach (using exercise, relaxation techniques, stress avoidance techniques, etc.); or c:) the "feedback" approach, which is the path "less traveled."

If you want to avoid chemical or pharmaceutical methods, you are left with a choice between the stress management (SM) approach and the "feedback" approach. Each of these methods is based upon an underlying "mentality" which is usually not recognized:

The SM Mentality	*The "Feedback" Mentality*
1. Stress is inevitable.	1. Stress is not inevitable—it all depends on how well we understand and deal with its causes.
2. Stress exists and can be coped with directly.	2. Stress does not exist—it is just a word that we use to stand for hundreds of specific problems and conflicts both inside and outside our bodies.
3. Stress is largely caused by external factors.	3. Stress is largely caused by internal factors—i.e. by conversations and action patterns that have been "programmed" into our bodies.
4. Human stress is a mind-body phenomenon.	4. Human stress is a Biolinguistic phenomenon. While it may appear that our "minds" play a role, it is language, not our "minds," that causes most of our stress to occur.

5. Stress means something is. "going wrong" within our bodies.

5. Stress can also mean things are "going right" within our bodies—i.e. that our bodies are signaling us to look within ourselves to recognize specific conversations or action patterns that may be getting us into trouble.

6. Some degree of stress is "good" or "healthy" for us.

6. Since "sress" is a word that stands for problems and conflicts, there are no such things as "good" or "healthy" stress.

7. The best way to deal with stress is to:
a) avoid it;
b) manage it.

7. The best way to deal with stress is to make it disappear naturally (without drugs, relaxation exercises, or other stress management techniques) by learning to recognize and deal with its underlying causes. (This can be done either in lieu of stress management or in conjunction with it.)

Parting Suggestions

While the title of this book is *The 14 Day Stress Cure*, it may take you more than fourteen days to master all of the strategies and tools it contains. Your *understanding* of human stress, however, may have already been changed forever. This type of permanent change has happened for me, and it also has happened for people who read earlier drafts of this book.

As you continue to explore this road to success, I offer you the following tips and parting suggestions:

1) *Learn to enjoy being wrong!*—There's no point in adopting a "feedback" perspective if you aren't willing to acknowledge that your own internal conversations and action patterns may be wrong or inappropriate much of the time. There should be no shame or humiliation in admitting this fact since we have all been programmed to misunderstand life in many important ways. Instead of feeling dumb, stupid, weak, or incompetent in response to discovering you

are wrong, you could also focus on the potential benefits that come from such recognitions. The willingness to be wrong has helped me enormously in my own life. It has helped me with my moods and emotions, my relationships with others, my work as a physician, and in many other areas. It has helped me so much that *I now actually look forward to finding out that I am wrong!* I am usually thankful and appreciative whenever this occurs.

I am not talking here about trivial types of being wrong, such as adding or subtracting a series of numbers incorrectly, making a wrong turn, or sending a letter to a wrong address. I am talking about another type of being wrong that is not readily apparent to ourselves or other people. I am talking about being wrong about your deepest, most cherished theories and beliefs. I am talking about the willingness to admit you may be wrong about many things that you feel very strongly about. This may include things your mother and father may have taught you, things your friends and family members currently believe in, or even things that the vast majority of human beings assume to be true.

I am talking about two very deep-seated internal conversations that produce much of the stress we normally experience:

My **Thoughts=Truth**	**My** **Feelings=Truth**

Since the beginning of human civilization, these two conversations have contributed to more sickness, disease, death, wars, atrocities, and human misery than any other causes. They can almost always be found at the bottom of any type of stress we are experiencing, and the only way to become free of them is to welcome the idea that—whether you know it or not—you possibly could be wrong!

2) ***Don't be a loner when it comes to dealing with "stress"***—don't make the mistake of thinking it's always best to cope with stress on your own. Unfortunately, we live in a society that glorifies individual achievement. The truth is, however, that we are much better able to deal with our stress when we involve other people. Without such help from others, we can remain hopelessly stuck in our own limited perspectives and inaccurate "realities."

3) *Learn to master the invisible*—while most other people are busy trying to deal with their stress by controlling what is obvious (and usually external) to them, you can be working on becoming a master of the invisible. As human beings, we actually have much more power and control over the invisible processes within us—i.e. our conversations and action patterns—than we do over that which is visible or external to us. While you may not have much direct personal control over events and situations that occur in your life, you do have control over how you choose to relate to such events. These invisible choices—including many of the coping strategies described in this book—are always available to you regardless of your circumstances.

4) *Don't believe everything you see, hear, or read*—just because some expert tells you something about stress, don't assume he or she is necessarily correct. Remember, most of what people are being told about stress today is not really true. There is an enormous amount of false or misleading information that people receive from radio and t.v. talk shows, newspaper and magazine articles, and other authoritative sources.

Therefore, you should adopt a cautious attitude toward everything you see, hear, or read about stress. You should even do the same for everything I have said in this book. Please don't accept my ideas as gospel, and keep yourself open to the possibility that new and even better coping methods may some day be developed.

5) *Become a perpetual student of life and human nature*—the last thing I want to point out is that no matter how smart you are, how wise you may have become, or how much knowledge or experience you currently possess, there are still many things about life and about human beings that you probably don't know or understand very well. We are all more or less beginners when it comes to understanding ourselves and other people, so always be on the lookout for opportunities to expand your insights and horizons. Whatever you do, keep challenging your internal conversations and action patterns, because the more you do this, the less stress and tension you will generate for yourself and for others.

In closing, I hope that whenever you hear the word "stress" from now on you will remember the step-by-step approach you learned from this book:

"STRESS"

1. BE SPECIFIC

2. RELATE TO YOUR PROBLEMS AS "FEEDBACK"

3. IDENTIFY YOUR HIDDEN CONVERSATIONS AND ACTION PATTERNS

4. REMEMBER, THESE ARE IN YOUR BODY, NOT YOUR MIND

5. TAKE STEPS TO NEUTRALIZE THESE INTERNAL CAUSES

6. REPEAT THE ABOVE AND/OR GET COACHING.

DAY 14: EXERCISES

1. *Take the day off! (You deserve it).*

Appendix A

Stress-Producing Conversations And Action Patterns

This appendix contains master lists of the most common internal conversations and action patterns that produce stress for human beings. For additional information about using these two lists, consult Chapter 5.

Stress-Producing Conversations

Good/Bad	Right/Wrong	Cause/Effect	Credit/Blame	Win/Lose
Perfectionism	Control	Unrealistic Expectations	Negative Thinking	Positive Thinking
Resignation	Hope	Strong/Weak	Stupid/Smart	Forgive/Punish
"Feelings=Truth"	"Thoughts=Truth"	"Thoughts & Feelings Cause People To Behave"	"My Value As A Person Is Dependent Upon ..."	"People Can/Can't Be Trusted"
"I've Got To Do It Myself"	"Things Aren't Going My Way"	"Nothing Is Working"	"That's Just The Way I Am"	"I'm Not Good Enough"
"I Shouldn't Be Feeling This Way"	"I Shouldn't Have Done What I Did"	"I Should Have Known Better"	"Don't Take Risks"	"Don't Make Mistakes"

Stress-Producing Action Patterns

Failing To Challenge Internal "Realities"	Failing To Relate To Stress As Feedback	Failing To Make Requests Or Demands Of Others	Failing To Decline Requests From Others	Failing To Clarify Agreements & Expectations
Failing To Assess Commitment Of Others	Failing To Keep Your Promises	Failing To Do Homework Or Research	Failing To Be A Beginner	Failing To Admit You May Be Wrong
Failing To Prioritize	Failing To Delegate	Failing To Empower Others	Failing To Anticipate Breakdowns & Delays	Failing To Deal With "Little" Problems
Failing To Ask For Help	Failing To Acknowledge Your Strengths & Abilities	Failing To Acknowledge Your Weaknesses	Trying To Control The Wrong Things	Trying To To Solve Other People's Problems
Trying To Change Yourself	Trying To Change Others	Needing To Be Right	Blaming Yourself Or Others	Invalidating Others' Opinions & Points Of View
Moaning Groaning & Complaining	Kicking Your Seeing-Eye Dog	Shielding Others From The Consequences Of Their Behavior	Compromising Your Own Or Others' Integrity	Depending Upon Drugs, Alcohol, Cigarettes, Tranquilizers
Failing To Deal With Problems Creatively	Taking Things Personally	Taking Things Too Seriously	Not Taking Care Of Your Body	Overeating To Deal With Stress

Appendix B

Flipping To The Opposite Reality

Whenever an internal *conversation* is contributing to your stress, consider Flipping To The Opposite Reality as one way to challenge it.

EXAMPLE: If something happens that you believe is "bad" or "wrong," try flipping to the point of view that whatever happened may have been in some way "good" or "right"—and see what you notice when you look from this perspective.

Obviously certain events—such as the death of a loved one or the occurrence of a natural disaster—may never be seen as "good" no matter what techniques you use. But more often than not, Flipping To The Opposite Reality will reveal aspects of a problem or situation that were not immediately apparent to you.

You can also use this strategy with your stress-producing *action patterns*. Whenever you notice an automatic behavior pattern that is causing you to suffer, imagine the opposite behavior and see if you might benefit by acting in this way (provided you avoid any actions that might be harmful or dangerous).

EXAMPLE: If someone accuses you of doing something wrong, try agreeing with all or part of this accusation instead of defending yourself as you might normally do.

If someone accuses you of being a liar, a cheat, or a scoundrel, for instance, see if you can agree with *any part* of such accusations. Perhaps you did tell a lie or did do something underhanded that your accuser has correctly recognized. Thus, by choosing to "flip" to the opposite "reality," you will often find that the other person does really have a legitimate gripe.

Understandably, most people are skeptical about using this approach: "Why should I adopt a belief or behavior that is completely opposite to what I think or feel is true? If something looks or feels wrong to me, why should I consider that it might be right? Or if something appears very bad to me, why should I switch to the point of view that it might in some way be good?"

There is a very good reason why you should frequently—but not always—use this coping strategy. Unfortunately, most people don't understand this reason. Consequently, they believe (incorrectly) that Flipping To The Opposite Reality is a foolish, naive, or even dangerous thing to do.

Why Does Flipping To The Opposite Reality Work?

The best way to understand the rationale for this technique is to consider the following demonstration, which I use in most of my seminars and workshops. This demonstration focuses on our CAUSE/EFFECT pattern of thinking, which is one of several "either/or" patterns that contribute to our stress.

To conduct such a demonstration, I set up a small table in front of a room full of people. On this table, I arrange the following objects as shown below: a wooden ramp, six white rubber balls (which I bunch together at the low end of the ramp), and a red rubber ball (which I hold in my hand near the top of the ramp):

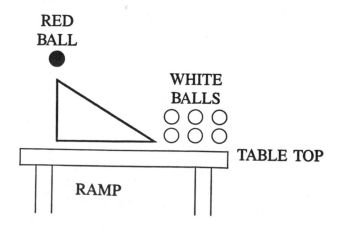

RED
BALL

WHITE
BALLS

TABLE TOP

RAMP

After warning the group that I am about to perform a simple experiment, I release the red ball from my hand. Predictably, it rolls down the ramp and crashes into the white balls, causing several of them to fall onto the floor. (These balls are usually retrieved by people sitting in the front row.)

I then draw a diagram of this experiment on a blackboard and ask members of the group to tell me what they observed in terms of causes and effects. Usually someone starts off by saying the red ball was the cause of the crash, and the movement of the white balls was its effect. I note this on the diagram by placing the word "cause" beneath the red ball and the word "effect" beneath the white balls:

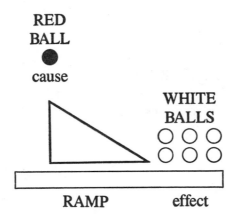

Someone else usually points out, however, that the ramp was really the cause, and the movements of the red ball and white balls were both its effects. I add this to the diagram by placing the word "cause" beneath the ramp and by adding the word "effect" beneath the word "cause," which I had previously placed under the red ball:

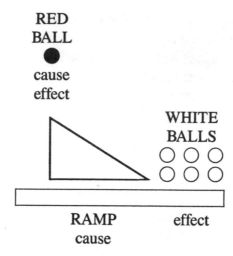

RED
BALL

cause
effect

WHITE
BALLS

RAMP   effect
cause

Someone else in the group usually points out, however, that gravity was really the cause of what happened, and everything else, including the influence of the ramp and the movements of the balls were its effects. Once again, I change the diagram (adding gravity as a "cause" and the word "effect" beneath the ramp) to include this observation:

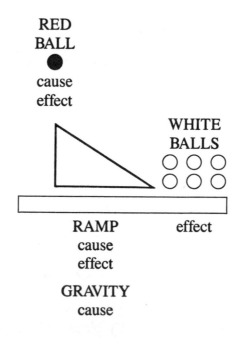

RED
BALL

cause
effect

WHITE
BALLS

RAMP   effect
cause
effect

GRAVITY
cause

At this point, I usually turn to the group and say, "Is this the whole story or does anyone see something else?" Eventually, another participant says, "Well, you set this demonstration up and you released the red ball from your hand, so you were really the cause and everything else (gravity, the ramp, the movement of the balls, etc.) were effects of you." I acknowledge this is true by adding a figure representing myself (as a cause) and by adding the word "effect" beneath the designation for gravity:

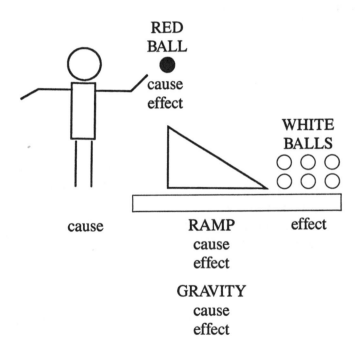

As soon as I do this, however, someone else usually comments, "Yes, but we caused you to set up this demonstration by coming to the workshop, so we were really the cause, and your behavior, including setting up the table, positioning the ramp, etc., was the effect of our being here." Since this is also true, I note this on the diagram by adding the word "effect" beneath the figure of myself.

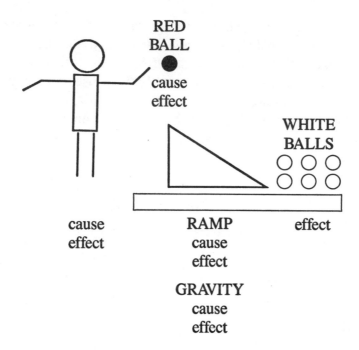

► NOTE: This line of reasoning could be extended even further, since someone else had the idea of doing this workshop in the first place. Also, had my parents not given birth to me, none of this would have happened, so my parents could also be viewed as a cause, and everything else could be seen as their effects.

After exhausting this line of reasoning, which could be carried even further, I turn the group's attention to the white balls and say, "Well, at least we know this part of the experiment is purely an effect." But as soon as I do this, someone else says, "Wait a minute, the white balls rolled off the table and caused several people to pick them up, so the white balls were also a cause as well." Again, I acknowledge this is true and add this feature to the diagram.

When all is said and done, our CAUSE/EFFECT analysis looks like this:

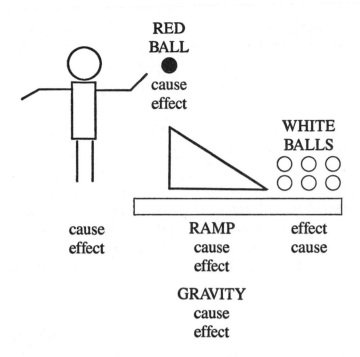

Notice what this demonstration reveals! Depending upon how you look at what happened, you can view any part of this demonstration as either a "cause" or an "effect," AND NO MATTER WHICH "REALITY" YOU CHOOSE, YOU WILL NOT BE TELLING A LIE!!! In other words, no matter how things originally appeared to you in terms of causes and effects, you could "flip" to the opposite reality and IT WOULD BE TRUE AS WELL! Even if you had no idea of the truthfulness of this opposite reality, or even if you strongly disliked it or completely disagreed with it, *it would still be true nonetheless.*

This is why Flipping To The Opposite Reality is such a powerful coping technique. It can help you compensate for some of the "blind-ness" your internal conversations and action patterns automatically produce. In the case of this demonstration, your internal CAUSE/EFFECT pattern thinking (and perceiving) made you blind to the fact that life doesn't really occur in linear sequences of causes and effects. Life is considerably more complex, and everything that happens usually has multidimensional patterns of causation, as the demonstration above clearly shows.

Our bodies, however, are not equipped to perceive such multidimensional phenomena. We are conditioned to view life "as if" things occur by way of linear sequences of causes and effects, even though this gives us a misleading view of the way things really happen.

EXAMPLE: Our belief that high blood cholesterol causes heart disease to occur in a linear cause-effect relationship is another example of this problem. Cholesterol is only *one of many* factors that contribute to the development of heart disease. At least ten other factors have also been identified, and there are probably others we don't yet understand. In addition, some people with very high cholesterol levels live into their 80s and 90s (without developing heart disease), while some people with normal cholesterol levels die of heart attacks in their 30s and 40s.

One way "either/or" patterns of thinking such as GOOD/BAD, RIGHT/WRONG, and CAUSE/EFFECT contribute to our stress is by making us "blind" to certain truths about life. By using the technique of Flipping To The Opposite Reality, you can help yourself compensate for such common types of "blindness." Obviously, you wouldn't want to use this technique in every situation, but most people can usually distinguish when it would be harmful or dangerous for them to do so.

"Flipping" The Hidden Causes Of Your Negative Moods And Emotions

Flipping To The Opposite Reality can be used to deal with many types of stress. When used in conjunction with the Index Card Technique, it is especially useful for dealing with your negative moods and emotions.

Take the emotions of anger and guilt for example. As we saw in chapter 3, these two emotions have similar internal causes. Both share the conversations:

"Somebody did something they shouldn't have done."
"Somebody was hurt, harmed, etc. by what was done."

Frequently, one or both of these conversations will be untrue. One way to discover this fact is by "flipping" each conversation to its opposite "reality."

EXAMPLE: Suppose someone was late for an important meeting with you. If you felt angry about this, or if the other person felt guilty, both of you must have assumed that being late "shouldn't have happened." While this is sometimes true, it is not always the case. What if you "flipped" to the opposite reality and assumed that being late was exactly what "should have happened?" In each of the following scenarios, this opposite reality could be true:

- Suppose an urgent problem or crisis had occurred for the person who was late—a problem that couldn't be put off without significant consequences.

- Suppose the person who arrived late was angry with you for something you did to them earlier, and arriving late was this person's way of consciously or unconsciously punishing you.

- Suppose this person always runs late, and you knew this from previous experiences. And suppose you ignored this knowledge and hoped, quite unrealistically, that the person would arrive on time.

"Flipping" can also be used to deal with the second conversation that produces anger and guilt in human beings—"Someone was hurt, harmed, etc. by what was done":

- Is it really a big deal that someone arrived late?
- Were you really hurt or harmed?
- Could you make up for lost time by working more diligently in the remaining time you have?

Anger and guilt are also dependent upon an underlying assumption of unilateral responsibility or "blame." (This is another example of either/or, cause/effect thinking). When we are angry, we assume someone did something to harm us—i.e. they were the cause and we were an innocent victim. When we feel guilty, our internal conversation of unilateral "blame" is reversed—i.e. we caused something bad to happen and someone else was innocently victimized.

As we have just seen, however, all such linear cause/effect theories are misleading. At best they are only half-truths; at worst they may be completely inaccurate. Whenever you find yourself feeling angry or guilty, therefore, you should always consider "flipping" your automatic assessments of "innocence" and "blame."

AUTOMATIC ASSESSMENTS OF BLAME		FLIPPING TO THE OPPOSITE REALITY
ANGER	"Someone else was to blame."	"I may somehow have been responsible for what happened.'
GUILT	"I was totally to blame."	"Someone or something else may have played a role."

It is important to note that this is *not* the same as shifting blame from one person to another. Many people are reluctant to use this technique because they misunderstand this crucial point. Flipping To The Opposite Reality does not mean—in the case of anger—that you should consider yourself to blame and the other person to be completely innocent. As we saw in the cause/effect demonstration above, "flipping" is merely an *artificial device*—a useful fiction—that you can use to recognize certain things you don't normally see. When you are angry, for instance, you might easily recognize what other people did, or didn't do. You might not notice, however, what you may have done to contribute to their behavior. Choosing to adopt the opposite viewpoint—that you may have partly "caused" such problems to occur—doesn't deny the role other people may have played. It just broadens your view of what really happened.

The same applies when you unilaterally blame yourself for something and end up feeling guilty. Often, other people or factors may also have played a role. Acknowledging these other causes in no way denies the role you may have played. Usually all parties involved in a particular problem have some cause in the matter, so it is almost always a mistake to point the finger of blame in only one direction, especially at yourself.

"Flipping" The Hidden Causes Of Other Types Of Stress

"Flipping" can also be used to deal with the hidden causes of other types of stress, including relationship stress, work-related stress, health-related problems, and many others. For example, choosing to do the opposite of the following behavior patterns can prevent or eliminate much of your relationship stress:

AUTOMATIC BEHAVIOR PATTERN	CONSCIOUSLY-CHOSEN OPPOSITE BEHAVIOR
Failing to make requests or demands of others.	Choosing to make requests or demands of others.
Failing to decline requests from others.	Learning to responsibly say "no" to others.
Failing to clarify agreements and expectations.	Openly discussing mutual promises and expectations.
Failing to assess commitment of others.	Paying attention to the sincerity and commitment behind people's promises.
Failing to keep your promises.	Consciously choosing to keep your promises or renegotiate them.
Failing to admit you may be wrong.	Being willing to admit you may frequently be wrong.
Failing to acknowledge your weaknesses.	Being willing to acknowledge your weaknesses (to yourself and to others).

The Double Role Of Language In Human Stress

Coping techniques such as Flipping To The Opposite Reality are unique to human beings. Dogs, cats, chimpanzees, and other animals cannot make use of them. Neither can computers, although they can be programmed to simulate this behavior.

We can utilize such powerful coping techniques because, unlike animals, we live our lives in language. This means that language plays a double role in most of the problems we encounter. On one hand, language—speaking, listening, internal conversations and action patterns, etc.—is responsible for much of the blindness and stress we experience. On the other hand, language provides us with powerful self-correcting capabilities that are always available to us. Thus, while we may not be able to change the way we've been programmed, there is much we can do to compensate for our blind spots and other language-mediated deficiencies.

Flipping To The Opposite Reality is just one example of how language can be used as a stress-reducing device.

Appendix C

Arguments For And Against The Mind-Body Viewpoint

For thousands of years, we have pondered the question "what makes us different from other living species or from non-living matter?" For the most part, our answers have had something to do with "mind," "soul," or "spirit":

> The difference between a rock and a man is, according to many philosophers, to be found in the fact that in man there is a mind which is absent in the rock. This mind, they argue, controls that part of the individual which is not mind. The not-mind is called matter. (S.E. Frost, Jr., *Basic Teachings Of The Great Philosophers*, p. 227.)

This mind/matter duality has its roots in our past. As early as 430 B.C., the Greek philosopher Anaxagoras defined the mind as "a substance which entered into the body and made it alive." Later Greek thinkers such as Plato and Aristotle believed that our bodies were inhabited by a soul or spirit which they called "psyche." Jewish and Christian religions taught that our soul or spirit was divinely created, whereas Eastern religions held that our spirit was part of a "cosmic consciousness" shared by all living species. Descartes embraced the Greek and Western religious views, but he postulated that the mind and body were two entirely different types of substances. Each affected the other, but the mind was purely subjective in nature, whereas the body obeyed the laws of physical nature.

Thus, for the past 2,500 years, we have struggled with the problem of how two such fundamentally different parts of ourselves—our minds and our bodies—co-exist. Proponents of mind-body dualism argue that we must believe in the existence of the mind because:

a) It is the only way to explain how we differ from other living species;

b) It is the only way to explain our subjective, personal experiences, including the "I" that thinks and reasons;

c) Without the mind, there would be no beauty, truth, values, or morals;

d) The existence of mental illnesses and the wealth of scientific data about the mind prove its existence beyond any doubt.

Despite these compelling arguments, the mind-body viewpoint has been challenged in recent years. One of the first to do so was the philosopher Baruch Spinoza (1632-1677), a contemporary of Descartes, who argued that mind and matter were not two different substances but rather two manifestations of the same universal substance. Friedrich Nietzsche (1844-1900) also spoke out against the mind-body-spirit division:

> Through the long succession of millennia, man has not known himself physiologically; he does not know himself even today. To know, for example, that one has a nervous system but no 'soul' is still the privilege of the best informed. (From Nietzsche, *The Will To Power*, Section 229, p. 132, 1967 Random House edition, Walter Kaufmann, Ed.)

Numerous twentieth century thinkers have also criticized the mind-body view:

1. Gilbert Ryle

One of the first people to suggest that the mind does not exist was the British philosopher Gilbert Ryle (1900-1976). In a book titled *The Concept Of Mind* (1949), Ryle strongly objected to Descartes' mind-body hypothesis, stating that it was tantamount to believing that our mechanistic bodies are somehow inhabited by a non-biologic "ghost" which we call a "mind." Ryle's "ghost in the machine" analogy launched a flurry of criticism against the mind-body view.

2. John Searle

John Searle, Professor of Philosophy at the University of California at Berkeley, is another outspoken critic of the mind-body view. In his 1984 book *Minds, Brains, And Science,* he states:

> Mental states are biologic phenomena...[They are] part of our bio-
> logic life history, along with growth, reproduction, the secretion of
> bile, and digestion. (p. 41.)

Searle points out that neither Descartes nor anyone else has successfully bridged the gap in our knowledge about how the mind and
the body interact. According to Searle, all such gap-filling efforts
have failed for a very simple reason:

> I am going to claim that all the gap-filling efforts fail because there
> isn't any gap to fill. (p. 42.)

3. Gerald Edelman

This Nobel-prize winning neuroscientist also urges us to abandon
our mind-body views. In his 1987 book *Neural Darwinism: The Theory Of Neuronal Group Selection,* Edelman outlines a totally new
theory of human learning based entirely upon structural changes
occurring in the brain and other parts of the nervous system. His
theory of neuronal group selection rejects the widespread notion that
we learn as a result of information processing or other "cognitive"
processes which take place in our "minds." He argues that in order
to properly understand the true nature of learning and behavior—
including perception, emotion, and human cognition—we need "a
new theory, one that has widespread consequences for neuroscience
as well as for our understanding of our own place in nature."

What These Critics Are NOT Saying

It's important to understand what these and other critics of the mind-
body viewpoint are *not* saying:

- They are not saying that mental-appearing phenomena (such as
  thoughts, beliefs, values, reasoning, etc.) do not exist;
- They are not saying that personal or subjective experiences do not
  exist;
- They are not saying that personal or subjective experiences are
  less real or less important than objective existence;
- They are not saying that the term "mind" is just another way of
  talking about the brain—i.e. that when we say "mind-body" we
  are really referring to brain-body processes within us.

What they are saying is that *the mind is an explanatory principle.* It is not something that actually exists, but rather it is a historical misunderstanding about what really goes on inside human beings.

Explanatory Principles

Gregory Bateson, noted anthropologist, biologist, psychotherapist, and a keen observer of animals and human beings, clearly understood the dangers of explanatory principles. While Bateson was not the first person to comment upon this phenomenon, he did much to promote our awareness of it.

According to Bateson, an explanatory principle is a word or phrase that is offered as an explanatory theory for why something happens in life. The principle itself need not be true or accurate, as long as it satisfies our need for an explanation. In the following excerpt from one of his essays, titled "Metalogue: What Is An Instinct?," we can get the flavor of Bateson's understanding of this point. In this metalogue, a father (F) is having a discussion with his inquiring daughter (D):

D: Daddy, what is an instinct?
F: An instinct, my dear, is an explanatory principle.
D: But what does it explain?
F: Anything—almost anything at all. Anything you want it to explain.
D: Don't be silly. It doesn't explain gravity.
F: No. But that is because nobody wants "instinct" to explain gravity. If they did, it would explain it. We could simply say that the moon has an instinct whose strength varies inversely as the square of the distance. . . .
D: But that's nonsense, Daddy.
F: Yes, surely. But it was you who mentioned "instinct," not I.
D: All right—but then what does explain gravity?
F: Nothing, my dear, because gravity is an explanatory principle.
D: Oh.

(From Bateson, *Steps To An Ecology Of Mind,* p. 38.)

According to Bateson, explanatory principles are concepts that are invented by human beings—through language—to explain things we really don't understand. In other words, they originate as temporary fill-ins for explanations we desire but which are not currently available to us.

For example, Isaac Newton was clear that the word "gravity" was a temporary concept he chose to use until a more accurate understanding of the relationships he had observed appeared. In his writings, he states that objects in space and time behave "as if" they are attracted to each other by a force that varies with their mass and is inversely proportional to the square of their distance from each other. He also states that this "force" might not truly exist, but it is a good concept to use until a better understanding is found.

Other explanatory principles, such "Id, Ego, Superego," "will power," and the "mind," also came into being when theorists, attempting to understand some complex natural process, proposed them as "causes" for events they observed. These explanations give us the appearance of true understandings *when no such understandings exist.* Other people, however, latch on to explanatory principles and "reify" them—assume they are real things that actually exist—thereby causing them to become integrated as "facts" of accepted "knowledge." Further inquiry into the true nature of a phenomenon is suspended, as most people assume that the correct answer has been found.

Again, turning to Bateson's metalogue about "instinct," we find the following passage:

D: Daddy, is an explanatory principle the same thing as a hypothesis?
F: Nearly, but not quite. You see, an hypothesis tries to explain some particular something, but an explanatory principle— like "gravity" or "instinct"—really explains nothing. It's a sort of conventional agreement between scientists to stop trying to explain things at a certain point.

(From Bateson, *Steps To An Ecology Of Mind,* p. 39)

Bateson maintains that the problem with explanatory principles is that they are very seductive in their appeal. They relieve the uncertainty that stimulated our original inquiry, and they make us forget that they aren't true explanations at all. The gradual acceptance of explanatory principles leads to what Bateson calls a widespread "conceptual fog" that impedes, rather than stimulates, further scientific and intellectual progress.

For the most part, we are unaware of the influence such pseudo-explanations have in our lives. The "conceptual fog" Bateson refers to goes way beyond the fields of science—it penetrates into every aspect of our lives, including our "common sense" understanding of ourselves as human beings. Freud's "Id, Ego, and Superego," for instance, have never been proven to exist, and many respected scholars, such as French psychoanalyst Jacques Lacan, have cogently argued that there are no such things inside human beings. (Freud, like Newton, was well aware of this fact.)

This is why many contemporary scholars now agree that the human "mind" does not exist. They are clear that "mental" phenomena are not really caused by an independent, subjective "mind," but rather they are by-products of our biologic capacities for language. Just as Einstein's general theory of relativity proved that Newton's concept of "gravity" was incorrect—there is no "attractive force" operating between objects in the universe—the concept of "mind" can now be replaced by a new and more accurate Biolinguistic explanation.

In his best-selling book, *The Dancing Wu-Li Masters,* physicist Gary Zukav notes:

> One of the most profound by-products of the general theory of relativity is the discovery that gravitational "force," which we had so long taken to be a real and independently existing thing, is actually our. . .creation. There is no such thing in the real world. (pp. 186-187).

It is important to understand that when a physicist makes such a statement, he is not saying that the *phenomena* we observe and attribute to "gravity" don't exist. That would be nonsense. Things do fall "down" and not "up." The presence of the moon does affect the ebb and flow of the tides on earth. Weightlessness in space is something we have all observed for ourselves on television from time to time.

It is not the existence of such phenomena that is being challenged, but rather it is the false or misleading *causal* theories that have been offered to expain them. Thus, when modern scholars assert that the "mind does not exist," they are merely challenging the *theory of mental causation*, which has never been satisfactorily explained by any mind-body theory. In other words, they are saying that SOMETHING VERY DIFFERENT IS GOING ON INSIDE HUMAN BEINGS—something that may look like it is being produced by an independent, subjective "mind" but which is actually being produced by a completely different set of causes. These causative processes are not independent of the body, nor are they non-biological (i.e. subjective) in nature. They are products of human language, a biologic capacity that really does exist and that can account for all of the phenomena we have previously attributed to the "mind," "soul," or "spirit."

Thus, as Nietzsche wrote more than 100 years ago:

> 'I am body and soul'—so speaks the child. . . But the awakened, the enlightened man says: 'I am body entirely, and nothing besides; and soul is only a word for something in the body.' (From Nietzsche, *Thus Spoke Zarathustra*, Penguin Books, 1969, p. 61., originally published in 1883.)

Language—unlike "mind," "soul," and "spirit"—is not an explanatory principle. Language clearly does exist. No leaps of faith are required to understand the influential role it plays in our lives. Thus, we no longer need to invoke mythical, ghost-like entities to explain what makes us different from rocks, machines, or other living creatures.

Not The Same As The Eastern, Holistic View

The Biolinguistic model I have described in this book is not the same as Eastern, holistic views. By arguing against the mind-body viewpoint, I am not suggesting that we are all part of a cosmic "mind" or "consciousness." Such viewpoints are also, in my opinion, examples of mistaken explanatory principles. While it is indeed true that we are a part of nature and not separate or distinct from it, our nature is to have a highly developed form of language that no other organisms possess. Through language, we also experience a shared existence with other human beings, both living and dead. This is not the same, however, as assuming that the "cause" of this relatedness is an extra-corporal mind or cosmic consciousness. While no one can disprove such theories, we have no good reason to accept them when a theory based upon language—which everyone agrees exists—can explain things equally well.

Not The Same As The Biochemical Theory Of Mental Illness

I also want to be clear that in arguing against the mind-body viewpoint, I am not arguing *for* the biochemical theory of mental illness. In recent years, there have been trends—both popular and scientific—to view many forms of mental illness, such as schizophrenia and major depression, as being caused by "biochemical imbalances." While biochemical abnormalities can often be found in the brains of such individuals, we must be careful about prematurely ascribing a *primary causal role* to them. These biochemical abnormalities could just as well be *secondary* to other causative factors.

For example, a person who was sexually abused as a child, who has low self-esteem, who is afraid of being assertive, and who constantly thinks in a negative manner may become depressed. If a scientist steps onto the scene and measures certain chemicals in this person's brain, abnormalities will probably be detected. The moment someone proclaims, however, that such biochemical changes are *primary or fundamental* causes of depression, that person is committing an error in logical reasoning. As I have already pointed out, all such linear cause-effect theories are fraught with inaccuracies. Also, the fact that depression or schizophrenia can be successfully treated with drugs that alter biochemical processes in our brains does not prove that such illnesses *arise from* biochemical causes primarily. Most of the time, multiple causal factors are probably involved.

Not The Same As Brain-Body Thinking

Finally, I want to emphasize that the Biolinguistic model described in this book is not the same as brain-body thinking. While brain-body theories have been an improvement over mind-body dualism, they are also inaccurate. Clearly, our brains play a role in many of the phenomena—including language—which we have previously attributed to the workings of the "mind." Most of these phenomena, however, are not *exclusively* produced by the brain. Other parts of our bodies also play a role.

Candice Pert, a leading researcher on emotion-producing chemicals in the brain, including brain cell receptors (structures on the surface of a cell membrane where other molecules attach) for endorphins, opiates, PCP, and other mind-altering substances, summarized the effect recent advances in this field have had on her previous brain-body assumptions:

> In the beginning of my work, I matter-of-factly presumed that emotions were in the head or the brain. Now I would say they are really in the body as well. They are expressed in the body and are part of the body. I can no longer make a strong distinction between the brain and the body. (From *The Healing Brain,* pp. 152-153.)

Dr. Pert changed her opinion because of new discoveries such as the following:

- Receptors for endorphins, PCP, and other mind-altering substances are not just found in the brain—they are found in every organ of the body, including the gonads;

- Insulin receptors, which are found throughout the body are also highly concentrated in emotion-centers of the brain;

- Circulating monocytes—white blood cells that constitute part of the body's immune system—also possess receptors for endorphins, PCP, and every known substance thought to participate in human emotions.

Thus, even brain-body models introduce a type of artificial dualism that does not accurately reflect what is really going on inside human beings.

The Belief In The Human "Mind" Is Difficult To Relinquish

While we no longer need to believe in the existence of the "mind," we still find it hard to give up this popular notion. One reason is that the idea is so deeply entrenched in our society that one would be considered foolish for questioning its validity. Another reason was pointed out by historian Thomas Kuhn in his classic book *The Structure Of Scientific Revolutions.* Kuhn documented that every major advance in modern science was initially opposed by the majority of scholastic and scientific leaders. This pattern of resistance—and sometimes even overt hostility—even occurred for such major advances as Copernicus's theory that the planets revolved around the sun, the discovery of oxygen, the discovery of x-rays, and Einstein's theories of relativity. Despite the accuracy, superiority, and utility of these new perspectives, it usually required 50-75 years before they were finally accepted.

A hundred years from now, we will probably look back on our belief in the existence of the human "mind" in much the same way we look back on people who once believed that the world was actually flat. While we like to believe such "flat-earth" thinking has vanished, it has not. It has only taken new forms, which are much more difficult for us to recognize.

The Human Cost Of Mind-Body Thinking

I believe we are currently paying a major price for holding on to our mind-body theories. This cost is primarily being extracted in terms of our health and well-being, as individuals and as a society. In the words of Lewis Thomas, one of our most respected social critics:

> I cannot begin to guess at all the causes of our cultural sadness, not even the most important ones, but I can think of one thing that is wrong with us and eats away at us: we do not know enough about ourselves. We are ignorant about how we work, about where we fit in, and most of all about the enormous, imponderable system of life in which we are embedded as working parts. We do not really understand nature, at all. We have come a long way indeed, but just enough to become conscious of our ignorance.

> ...This is, in a certain sense, a health problem after all. For as long as we are bewildered by the mystery of ourselves, and confused by the strangeness of our uncomfortable connection to all the rest of life, and dumbfounded by the inscrutability of our own minds, we cannot be said to be healthy animals in today's world. (From "Biomedical Science and Human Health: The Long-Range Prospect," Summer, 1977, reprinted by permission of *Daedalus,* Journal of The American Academy of Arts And Sciences.)

As a physician, I look forward to the day when such pervasive myths and misconceptions no longer dominate our thinking.

Appendix D

Index Cards For Six Negative Moods And Emotions

This appendix contains information for constructing your own personal index cards for the following negative moods and emotions:

- Anger
- Frustration
- Sadness
- Guilt
- Fear
- Worry

To construct your own cards, photocopy the next six pages in this appendix. Then, cut out the front and back sides of each card from your photocopies and paste them or tape them to actual index cards.

To obtain a free set of pre-printed cards from Breakthru Publishing, complete and return the coupon below:

Mail to: BREAKTHRU PUBLISHING, P.O. Box 2866, Houston, TX, 77252-2866

FREE INDEX CARD OFFER

Name: _____

Addr: _____

City: _____ State: ____ Zip: _____

How did you hear about
THE 14 DAY STRESS CURE? _____

_____

Please include a self-addressed, stamped envelope
along with this coupon.

ANGER

©Morton C. Orman, M.D.
THE 14 DAY STRESS CURE

CONVERSATIONS:

1) Someone did something they shouldn't have done.
2) Someone was hurt, harmed, humiliated, embarrassed, offended, disappointed, or otherwise inconvenienced by what was done.
3) Some person or persons (other than myself) were unilaterally responsible (to blame) for #1 and #2.
4) The offending person or persons should acknowledge what they did wrong, offer to make amends, and/or be punished.

ANGER

ACTION PATTERNS:

A) Failing to recognize how your own judgments, evaluations and standards might not be valid for other people.
B) Failing to recognize how your own actions, past and present, may have contributed to what happened.
C) Justifying your anger, instead of looking within yourself for its internal causes.
D) Retaliating or seeking revenge, instead of openly and honestly dealing with what happened.

FRUSTRATION

©Morton C. Orman, M.D.
THE 14 DAY STRESS CURE

CONVERSATIONS:

1) I am not succeeding.
2) I should easily be able to succeed in this situation.
3) If I just keep trying harder and harder, I will eventually succeed.
4) If I don't succeed, I must be dumb, stupid, weak, or incompetent.

FRUSTRATION

ACTION PATTERNS:

A) Failing to recognize unrealistic goals and expectations.
B) Failing to challenge your definition of "success."
C) Failing to relate to your "failures" as "feedback."
D) Failing to admit: a) you may not know how to succeed, or b) you might need help from others.

SADNESS

CONVERSATIONS:

1) I have lost something.
2) What I lost is important.
3) I will never be able to replace what I have lost.
4) Without it, I can't be happy or content.

SADNESS

ACTION PATTERNS:

A) Failing to challenge conversations 1-4.
B) Dwelling on the past and what was lost.
C) Withdrawing from your usual activities in life and/or failing to seek out other sources of happiness.
D) Being reluctant to communicate about your loss to others.

GUILT

©Morton C. Orman, M.D.
THE 14 DAY STRESS CURE

CONVERSATIONS:

1) Someone did something they shouldn't have done.
2) Someone was hurt, harmed, humiliated, embarrassed, offended, disappointed, or otherwise inconvenienced by what was done.
3) I am unilaterally responsible (to blame) for #1 and #2.
4) I should suffer (be punished) for what I did wrong.

GUILT

ACTION PATTERNS:

A) Obsessing about what happened in order to heap additional blame and criticism upon yourself.
B) Failing to challenge your assumption that something "bad" or "wrong" actually took place.
C) Failing to recognize other people's responsibility for causing what happened or for any "hurt" or "harm" they experienced.
D) Leaving the situation incomplete—i.e. failing to take action to repair or compensate for any "damage" that was done.

FEAR

©Morton C. Orman, M.D.
THE 14 DAY STRESS CURE

CONVERSATIONS:

1) Something bad might happen.
2) Someone or something (including myself) may be hurt or harmed.
3) I don't have the power (control) to keep #1 or #2 from happening.
4) I should never feel afraid, since fear is a sign of weakness.

FEAR

ACTION PATTERNS:

A) Remaining immobile ("freezing") in response to a fear-producing agent or situation.
B) Fleeing or avoiding the situation.
C) Trying to appear unafraid.
D) Not taking action to deal with the situation effectively.

WORRY

©Morton C. Orman, M.D.
THE 14 DAY STRESS CURE

CONVERSATIONS:

1) Something bad might happen.
2) Someone or something (including myself) may be hurt or harmed.
3) If I worry hard enough (think real hard, feel real bad, focus my attention on a problem, etc.), I can keep #1 and #2 from happening.
4) If I didn't worry, it would mean I don't truly care.

WORRY

ACTION PATTERNS:

A) Trying to magically influence situations or events through internal gyrations—thoughts, feelings, body movements, compulsive ruminating, etc. (the rain dance phenomenon).
B) Indulging in worrying instead of taking effective action to clarify and deal with your problem or situation.
C) Trying to clarify or deal with a problem or situation yourself, when you may lack the necessary skill or experience to do so.
D) Failing to seek help from others who do have the ability to determine if you have a problem and/or help you solve it.

SUGGESTIONS FOR FURTHER READING

The Mind-Body Problem

Minds, Brains And Science
John Searle, Ph.D.
Harvard University Press
Cambridge, Massachusetts, 1984

A short, easy-to-read critique of Descartes' mind-body dualism. Addresses key philosophical issues of our time in an enjoyable and illuminating way.

The Concept Of Mind
Gilbert Ryle
University Of Chicago Press
Chicago, Illinois, 1949

Difficult reading, but Ryle's arguments against the existence of the mind are brilliantly stated and convincingly illustrated.

What Computers Can't Do
Hubert L. Dreyfus
Harper & Row
New York, New York, 1979 (revised)

This book is not about computers! It's about how we function as human beings and how our functioning differs from that of computers. Reviews leading theories of human existence and shows why each is mistaken or incomplete.

Biolinguistics

The Tree Of Knowledge
Humberto Maturana & Francisco Varela
Shambhala
Boston, Massachusetts, 1987

Reads like an eighth-grade biology text (with lots of pictures), but the ideas are all new and the implications are profound. The authors make complex ideas about language and biology simple enough for anyone to understand. A must read for anyone interested in Biolinguistics.

Understanding Computers And Cognition
Terry Winograd & Fernando Flores
Ablex Publishing
Norwood, New Jersey, 1986

Another important book that is more about human beings than computers. The first six chapters focus on the role of language in human life. The last six chapters show how this new understanding of human language has important implications for the design and use of computer technology.

The Language Of The Heart
James J. Lynch, Ph.D.
Basic Books
New York, New York, 1985

Shows how human dialogue—speaking and listening—dramatically affects our cardiovascular systems. Also shows how mind-body concepts are inadequate for understanding what truly happens inside human beings.

Habits Of The Heart
Robert Bellah, Richard Madsen, William Sullivan, Ann Swidler, &
  Steven Tipton
Harper & Row
New York, New York, 1986

An entertaining and well-researched survey of American cultural values and traditions. Shows how the thoughts and ideas of a few specific individuals in the past continue to shape our thoughts, feelings, commitments, and behaviors today.

Contexts

Shifting Contexts: The Generation Of Effective Psychotherapy
Bill O'Hanlon & James Wilk
Guilford Press
New York, New York, 1987

Although written primarily for psychotherapists, this book is excellent for anyone interested in how philosophical and linguistic issues lie at the heart of all modern forms of psychotherapy.

The 7 Habits Of Highly Effective People
Stephen R. Covey
Fireside (Simon & Schuster)
New York, New York, 1990

Covey reviews seven empowering contextual principles that can enhance your effectiveness on an individual, family, or organizational level. Well-written, enjoyable, and very informative.

General

Imaginary Crimes: Why We Punish Ourselves And How To Stop
Lewis Engle, Ph.D. & Tom Ferguson, M.D.
Houghton Mifflin
Boston, Massachusetts, 1990

Reveals how parental messages and other childhood experiences can lead to dysfunction and "stress" in adulthood. Contains a list of more than 60 parental messages that can negatively impact upon people's health and well-being.

How To Stop Worrying And Start Living
Dale Carnegie
Pocket Books
New York, New York, 1985

A classic (first published in 1944) that's still very relevant today. Contains many good ideas and strategies for dealing with worry successfully.

Love Is Never Enough
Aaron T. Beck, M.D.
Harper & Row
New York, New York, 1988

A practical manual, showing how misconceptions, misunderstandings, and faulty communication patterns lead to marital disharmony and stress. Based on the clinical experiences of one of the leading psychotherapists alive today. Highly recommended!

Marital Myths
Arnold A. Lazarus, Ph.D.
Impact Publishers
San Luis Obispo, California, 1985

Arnold Lazarus, another distinguished psychotherapist and marriage counsellor, discusses 24 marital myths, including "husbands and wives should be best friends," "don't have sex when you're angry," and "marriage should be a 50-50 partnership."

The Road Less Traveled
M. Scott Peck, M.D.
Touchstone Books (Simon & Schuster)
New York, New York, 1978

One of the most popular self-help books ever written (on the New York Times best-seller list for more than 400 weeks and still counting!). Contains an excellent review of some of the common myths about love and romance that cause people to suffer and fail in their interpersonal relationships.

False Love
Stan J. Katz & Aimee E. Liu
Ticknor & Fields
New York, New York, 1988

Another superb book on relationships. Shows you what true love really is, how to distinguish it from false love, and how to create it with another person. Highly recommended!

You Just Don't Understand: Women And Men In Conversation
Deborah Tannen, Ph.D.
William Morrow & Company, Inc.
New York, New York, 1990

How women and men fail to appreciate each other's communication styles and needs. Shows how the childhood conditioning of boys and girls leads each to live in different "realities" about life, love, communication, intimacy, etc.

The One Hour Orgasm
Bob Schwartz
Breakthru Publishing
Houston, Texas, 1989

A practical guide to increasing your own and your partner's sexual enjoyment. Based on the work of Dr. W. Victor Baranco, Ph.D. of More University, this book is not just about sex—it's about how to enhance the overall quality of your relationships.

The Power Of Ethical Management
Kenneth Blanchard & Norman Vincent Peale
Fawcett Crest (Ballantine Books)
New York, New York, 1988

Ken Blanchard, co-author of *The One-Minute Manager*, combines with Norman Vincent Peale, author of *The Power Of Positive Thinking*, to produce a superb book on the value (both personal and financial) of ethics and honesty in business and management.

The Richest Man In Babylon
George S. Clason
Bantam Books
New York, New York, 1976

A short, wonderful book on achieving financial success and avoiding financial disasters. Set in the ancient city of Babylon, where Bansir, a poor chariot builder, learns to master the seven basic principles of financial success from Arkad, the richest man in Babylon. Highly recommended!

How To Raise Your Self-Esteem
Nathaniel Branden
Bantam Books
New York, New York, 1988

Nathaniel Branden, an international expert, has written numerous books on self-esteem. This is one of his best. Easy to read and very helpful.

The Good Enough Parent
Bruno Bettelheim
Alfred A. Knops Inc.
New York, New York, 1987

An excellent book on how to deal with common child-rearing problems. Bettelheim shows parents how to better understand the behavior and needs of their children. He also shows parents how to disrupt some of their automatic patterns of thinking and behaving that lead to unnecessary conflicts and power-struggles with their children. Highly recommended!

Rules For Raising Kids
Robert I. Lesowitz, M.D.
Charles C. Thomas
Springfield, Illinois, 1974

Also highly recommended! Lesowitz, a child-psychiatrist, discusses eight basic rules for dealing with kids successfully. He also discusses specific child-rearing problems such as discipline, lying, stealing, school problems, bed-wetting, eating problems, sex and drug education, and many others.

Why Smart People Fail
Carole Hyatt & Linda Gottlieb
Simon & Schuster
New York, New York, 1987

Based on interviews with 200 people (some very famous) who used major "failures" as spring-boards to future happiness and success. Filled with clear, practical, and inspiring coping strategies for dealing with setbacks in your life. Shows that "failure" is a conversation people have that often has little to do with the reality of their situation.

Diets Still Don't Work
Bob Schwartz
Breakthru Publishing
Houston, Texas, 1990

Schwartz, who authored the best-selling *Diets Don't Work* in 1982, comes back with an even better sequel. He shows how the "Diet Mentality" keeps people stuck in a no-win relationship with their weight. Based on observations of naturally thin people, Schwartz has developed a non-dieting approach to weight loss that has worked for many people who have been unsuccessful with diets in the past.

Feel The Fear And Do It Anyway
Susan Jeffers, Ph.D.
Harcourt Brace Janovich
New York, 1987

A book about how to deal with fear when it stops you from having what you want or deserve in life. Shows how to challenge faulty beliefs and disrupt limiting action patterns that keep you "stuck." (Dr. Jeffer's advice also applies to the risks involved in learning how to "win" against stress.)

The Way Of The Physician
Jacob Needleman
Harper & Row
New York, New York, 1985

Addresses the human side of medicine, especially the internal dilemmas and conflicts practicing physicians face. Needleman, a philosopher, talks about both the dreams and the realities of modern medicine. A must read for every physician and medical student.

Off The Pedestal
Michael Greenberg, M.D.
Breakthru Publishing
Houston, Texas, 1990

Greenberg, a dermatologist, has written a book to help physicians (and non-physicians) deal more successfully with the threats of malpractice, greed, and advanced technology in medicine today. Based on his own personal journey from caring-physician, to businessman-physician, back to caring-physician again, Dr. Greenberg presents an interesting and provocative model for transforming the business side of medical practice.

Barrett, William. *The Illusion Of Technique.* New York: Anchor Press (Doubleday), 1979.

Bateson, Gregory. *Steps To An Ecology Of Mind.* New York: Ballantine Books, 1972.

Beck, A. *Love Is Never Enough.* New York: Harper & Row, 1988.

_____. *Cognitive Therapy and the Emotional Disorders.* New York: International Universities Press, 1976.

Bellah, R., Madsen, R., Sullivan, W., Swidler, A., & Tipton, S. *Habits Of The Heart.* New York: Harper & Row, 1986.

Branden, N. *How To Raise Your Self-Esteem.* New York: Bantam Books, 1988.

Capra, Fritjof. *The Turning Point.* New York: Simon & Schuster, 1982.

Carroll, J. (ed.). *Language, Thought, And Reality:* Selected Writings of Benjamin Lee Whorf. Cambridge: M.I.T. Press, 1956.

Covey, S. *The 7 Habits Of Highly Effective People.* New York: Fireside (Simon & Schuster), 1990.

Dreyfus, H.L. *What Computers Can't Do.* Rev. ed. New York: Harper & Row, 1979.

Dyer, Wayne. *You'll See It When You Believe It.* New York: William Morrow & Co., 1989.

Ecker, Richard. T*he Stress Myth.* Downers Grove, Illinois:InterVarsity Press, 1985.

Edelman, Gerald. *Neural Darwinism:* The Theory Of Neuronal Group Selection. New York: Basic Books, 1987.

Engle, L. & Ferguson, T. *Imaginary Crimes:* Why We Punish Ourselves And How To Stop. Boston: Houghton Mifflin, 1990.

Everly, Jr., G.S. *A Clinical Guide To The Treatment Of The Human Stress Response.* New York: Plenum Press, 1989.

Everly, Jr., G.S. & Rosenfeld, R. *The Nature And Treatment of the Stress Response.* New York: Plenum Press, 1981.

Frankl, Vicktor. *Man's Search For Meaning.* New York: Pocket Books (Simon & Schuster), 1963.

Friedman, M. & Rosenman, R. *Type A Behavior And Your Heart.* Greenwich, Connecticut: Fawcett Publications, 1974.

Frost, Jr., S.E. *Basic Teachings Of The Great Philosophers.* New York: Dophin Books (Doubleday), 1962.

Harris, Thomas. *I'm O.K., You're O.K.* New York: Harper & Row, 1969.

Harvey, Jerry. *The Abilene Paradox.* Lexington, Massachusetts: Lexington Books, 1988.

Hayakawa, S.I. *Language In Thought And Action (Fourth Edition).* San Diego: Harcourt Brace Jovanovich, Inc., 1978.

Hellman, C., Budd, M., Borysenko, J., McClelland, D., & Benson, H. A study of the effectiveness of two group behavioral medicine interventions for patients with psychosomatic complaints. *Behavioral Medicine:* Winter 1990.

Hillman, James. *Healing Fiction*. Barrytown, New York: Station Hill Press, 1983.

Knaus, W. & Hendricks, C. *The Illusion Trap*. New York: World Almanac Publications, 1986.

Kuhn, Thomas. *The Structure Of Scientific Revolutions*. Chicago: University of Chicago Press, 1970.

Kushner, Harold. *When Bad Things Happen To Good People*. New York: Avon Books, 1981.

Lacan, Jacques. *The Language of the Self*. Baltimore: Johns Hopkins University Press, 1968.

Lynch, J. *The Language Of The Heart*. New York: Basic Books, 1985.

MacLeod, Robert. *The Persistent Problems of Psychology*. Pittsburgh: Duquesne University Press, 1975.

Maddi, S. & Kobasa, S. *The Hardy Executive*. Chicago: Dorsey Professional Books, 1984.

Maturana, H. & Varela, F. *The Tree Of Knowledge*. Boston: Shambhala, 1987.

Nietzsche, Friedrich. *Thus Spoke Zarathustra*. (R.J. Hollingdale, Ed.). London: Penguin Books, 1969.

———. *The Will To Power* (Walter Kaufmann, Ed.). New York: Random House, 1967.

O'Hanlon, B. & Wilk, J. *Shifting Contexts:* The Generation Of Effective Psychotherapy. New York: Guilford Press, 1987.

Ornstein, R. & Swencionis, C (Eds.). *The Healing Brain*. New York: Guilford Press, 1990.

Osler, William. *The Collected Writings Of Sir William Osler*. Birmingham, Alabama: Classics Of Medicine Library (1985 Vol. 1), 1985.

Peck, M.S. *The Road Less Traveled*. New York: Touchstone Books (Simon & Schuster), 1978.

Price, V.A., *Type A Behavior Pattern: A Model For Research And Practice*. New York: Academic Press (Harcourt Brace Jovanovich), 1982.

Reames, Jr., H. & Dunstone, D. Professional satisfaction of physicians. *Archives Of Internal Medicine:* Vol. 149, September 1989.

Ryle, Gilbert. *The Concept Of Mind*. Chicago: University Of Chicago Press, 1949.

Searle, John. *Minds, Brains And Science*. Cambridge, Massachusetts: Harvard University Press, 1984.

Selye, Hans. *The Stress Of Life*. New York: McGraw-Hill, 1956.

Thomas, Lewis. Biomedical science and human health: the long-range prospect. *Daedalus,* Journal of the American Academy of Arts and Sciences, Summer, 1977, Vol. 106/3.

Winograd, T. & Flores, F. *Understanding Computers And Cognition*. Norwood, New Jersey: Ablex Publishing, 1986.

Zukav, Gary. *The Dancing Wu-Li Masters*. New York: Bantam Books, 1988.

The author wishes to thank the following publishers and copyright holders for permission to reprint the material listed below:

Beacon Press: for excerpts from *Man's Search For Meaning* by Vicktor Frankl, published by Pocket Books, a division of Simon & Schuster, 1963.

Classics Of Medicine Library: for excerpt from *The Collected Writings Of Sir William Osler* by William Osler, 1985.

Daedalus, Journal of the American Academy of Arts and Sciences: for excerpt from "Biomedical science and human health: the long-range prospect" by Lewis Thomas, published in the issue entitled, "Discoveries and Interpretations: Studies in Contemporary Scholarship Volume I," Summer 1977, Vol. 106/3.

Doubleday: for excerpts from *The Illusion Of Technique* by William Barrett, copyright 1979 and from *Basic Teachings Of The Great Philosophers* by S.E. Frost, Jr., copyright 1962.

Guilford Press: for excerpt from "The wisdom of the receptors: neuropeptides, the emotions, and body-mind" by Candace Pert, published in *The Healing Brain*, edited by Robert Ornstein and Charles Swencionis, 1990.

Harcourt Brace Jovanovich, Inc: for excerpt from *Language In Thought And Action (Fourth Edition)* by S.I. Hayakawa, copyright 1978.

HarperCollins, Inc: for excerpt from *Love Is Never Enough* by Aaron Beck, copyright 1988.

Harvard University Press: for excerpts from *Minds, Brains And Science* by John Searle, copyright 1984.

InterVarsity Press: for excerpt from *The Stress Myth* by Richard Ecker, copyright 1985.

James J. Lynch: for permission to reprint illustration from *The Language Of The Heart*, published by Basic Books, 1985.

McGraw-Hill, Inc: for excerpts from *The Stress Of Life* by Hans Selye, copyright 1956.

Mouton de Gruyter: for excerpts from "Metalogue: What Is An Instinct?" by Gregory Bateson, published in *Approaches To Animal Communication*, Thomas Sebeok (Ed.), copyright 1969 and reprinted in *Steps To An Ecology Of Mind*, published by Ballantine Books, 1972.

Penguin Books (London): for excerpt from *Thus Spoke Zarathustra*, copyright by R.J. Hollingdale (Ed.), 1969.

George Quasha: for excerpt from publisher's preface to *Healing Fiction* by James Hillman, copyright by George Quasha, 1983.

ABOUT THE AUTHOR

Morton C. Orman, M.D., is an internist in private practice in Baltimore, Maryland. He is a graduate of Duke University (B.A., 1969) and the University of Maryland Medical School (1973). He completed his residency training at Mercy Hospital in Baltimore (1973-1976), and he was Board Certified in Internal Medicine in 1976.

Dr. Orman completed a two-year post-doctoral training program in Contextual Therapy in 1987-89. He has also studied and worked with several prominent stress experts and psychotherapists. He is the Founder of The Health Resource Network, a non-profit organization for the advancement of humanistic competence in health care, and he was instrumental in forming the Society For Professional Well-Being, a national association for the prevention of stress in physicians and other health care professionals.

Dr. Orman has lectured widely about his unique approach for dealing with stress. He has also conducted seminars and workshops for thousands of individuals. He is the author of *Conversations For Well-Being:* An Experimental Training Manual For Humanistic Competence In Health Care (1985), and his views on physician stress were recently featured in *Missouri Medicine* (January, 1990).

His wife, Christina Chambreau, D.V.M., is a holistic veterinarian.